NOW WRITE!
MYSTERIES

NOW WRITE! MYSTERIES

Suspense, Crime, Thriller, and Other

Mystery Fiction Exercises from

Today's Best Writers and Teachers

Edited by SHERRY ELLIS

and LAURIE LAMSON

JEREMY P. TARCHER/PENGUIN
a member of Penguin Group (USA) Inc.
New York

JEREMY P. TARCHER/PENGUIN

Published by the Penguin Group

Penguin Group (USA) Inc., 375 Hudson Street, New York, New York 10014, USA •
Penguin Group (Canada), 90 Eglinton Avenue East, Suite 700, Toronto, Ontario
M4P 2Y3, Canada (a division of Pearson Penguin Canada Inc.) • Penguin Books Ltd,
80 Strand, London WC2R 0RL, England • Penguin Ireland, 25 St Stephen's Green,
Dublin 2, Ireland (a division of Penguin Books Ltd) • Penguin Group (Australia),
250 Camberwell Road, Camberwell, Victoria 3124, Australia (a division of Pearson
Australia Group Pty Ltd) • Penguin Books India Pvt Ltd, 11 Community Centre,
Panchsheel Park, New Delhi–110 017, India • Penguin Group (NZ), 67 Apollo Drive,
Rosedale, North Shore 0632, New Zealand (a division of Pearson New Zealand Ltd) •
Penguin Books (South Africa) (Pty) Ltd, 24 Sturdee Avenue, Rosebank,
Johannesburg 2196, South Africa

Penguin Books Ltd, Registered Offices: 80 Strand, London WC2R 0RL, England

Most Tarcher/Penguin books are available at special quantity discounts for bulk purchase for sales
promotions, premiums, fund-raising, and educational needs. Special books or book excerpts also can be
created to fit specific needs. For details, write Penguin Group (USA) Inc. Special Markets, 375 Hudson
Street, New York, NY 10014.

ISBN 978-1-585-42903-5

Printed in the United States of America
3 5 7 9 10 8 6 4 2

Book design by Gretchen Achilles

While the authors have made every effort to provide accurate telephone numbers and Internet addresses at
the time of publication, neither the publisher nor the authors assume any responsibility for errors, or for
changes that occur after publication. Further, the publisher does not have any control over and does not
assume any responsibility for author or third-party websites or their content.

Now Write! Mysteries
is dedicated to the inspiring memory of

SHERRY ELLIS

a bright, witty, fun-loving soul,
a caring social worker and writing coach,
an avid reader, committed writer, passionate editor,
and a terrific friend to the whole writing community.

CONTENTS

CONTENTS

CONTENTS

CONTENTS

CONTENTS

A NOTE FROM LAURIE LAMSON

Sherry Ellis, my aunt, got involved in the literary scene in 2002 when she started interviewing fiction authors she admired, including Pulitzer Prize winners, National Book Award winners, and an NEA recipient. Her background as a social worker and her love of literature combined to create deep, dynamic interviews that were published in *The Bloomsbury Review, Glimmer Train, The Kenyon Review, Writer's Chronicle,* and other magazines.

In 2006, Tarcher/Penguin published the first *Now Write!* anthology of eighty-nine writing exercises by fiction authors and teachers—many my aunt had previously interviewed. She then put together *Now Write! Nonfiction*, which was published in 2009, also by Tarcher/Penguin. The same year, Red Hen Press published her book of author interviews, *Illuminating Fiction*.

From the start I cheered her on from the sidelines. When I suggested the next *Now Write!* book could be about screenwriting, she generously invited me to be her coeditor, and *Now Write! Screenwriting* was published in 2011.

My aunt was collecting the exercises for *Now Write! Mysteries* when she was told she needed heart surgery. She requested I take over as editor if she wasn't able to finish this book, and those were hard conversations for me. I never believed it would become necessary. Sadly, she passed away a few days after the surgery.

I want to thank all the contributors from the bottom of my heart for participating in this book, and for all your compassion as I took on such an emotionally challenging task. I couldn't have done it without your support and kindness.

I'm proud of my aunt Sherry for creating a wonderful legacy with her books, one that will surely serve and inspire writers for generations to come.

DETECTIVE WORK

The Art and Science
of Research

STEPHEN JAY SCHWARTZ

Dontcha Just Hate the Research Part?

STEPHEN JAY SCHWARTZ is the bestselling author of *Boulevard* and *Beat*. He spent years as director of development for Wolfgang Petersen, where he helped develop AIR FORCE ONE, OUTBREAK, RED CORNER, BICENTENNIAL MAN, and MIGHTY JOE YOUNG. Stephen has written for the Discovery Channel, and he works as a freelance screenwriter and script doctor. He is currently writing his third novel and is on assignment rewriting a 3-D zombie film. He has personally interviewed half a dozen zombies and he's lucky to have made it out alive.

I might be in the minority here, but I actually love it. With a capital L. I can trace the moment back to college, when I convinced five professors that the research I would do in the Navajo reservation was important enough to excuse me from two weeks of classes, and it would require the rescheduling of my midterm exams.

I can understand why my screenwriting professor went along with this, and maybe even the guy who taught Film as Literature. But how did I convince my American history, astronomy, and sociology professors? Somehow I got them on board, and then I was off on a road trip that took me through California, Utah, and northern Arizona, taking the picaresque journey I was writing for the protagonist in my screenplay.

What the hell was I doing? I had a broken-down Toyota Corolla and a hundred bucks to my name. Was I ducking my responsibilities, intent upon reenacting my own version of Kerouac's *On the Road*?

Yes! And yet it was one hundred percent university-stamped-and-approved, under the dubious title . . . RESEARCH.

But then a funny thing happened. The road trip became a life lesson. I met amazing people—Native Americans and Anglos alike—and, after skating through Mojave Desert flash floods and sucking rainwater from my car's overwhelmed carburetor, I somehow landed at an acquaintance's house in Window Rock, Arizona, on New Year's Eve with a .32 revolver under my pillow. The next day I found myself strapped to a wild beast in a snowy desert plain after saying the words, "Sure, why not?" to the little Navajo kid who asked me, "Wanna ride my daddy's rodeo horse?"

Dangerous? Maybe. Fun? Hell, yes. I ended up near a place called Rough Rock, without electricity, plumbing, or running water, surrounded by hundreds of dogs and thousands of sheep wandering the hills looking for shrubs. I played duets with an ancient Navajo medicine man—his tribal flute to my soprano sax—and he fed me peyote for my ailing back and blessed it with cedar bark and eagle feathers, and soon I saw spirits in the linoleum on his kitchen floor.

And I rode horseback through Canyon de Chelly to view the Anasazi Indian ruins firsthand, and I interviewed Navajo teachers and prophets and politicians and farmers. On my last day, I was driven out to the boonies (it was all the boonies) to the home of a Navajo educator who had promised to drive me back to Gallup. It was late and cold when I arrived and he saw me and said, "It's an old Navajo tradition to sleep in the same bed for warmth, you know," and I realized that I had just met the first gay Navajo I'd ever known and I said, "Thank you, I'll just stay over here in this bed . . ." and when I awoke I found him standing over me peering out the window saying, "Doesn't look good. We'll be snowed in for days . . ." and he was right, the snow had descended on our little world and there I was.

Then at breakfast I met his parents who figured I was one of those hippies who blew through in the sixties, stopping to herd their sheep for weeks on end. They asked if I would herd their sheep and I declined. And during my stay I discovered that the gay Navajo (who was respecting my boundaries, by the way) was an amazing writer who had graduated from St. John's School of Great Books and had, in his youth, danced professional ballet in New York City and had been a good friend to Andy Warhol.

When you call yourself a writer, people talk. People will tell you the

4

most amazing things. Everyone wants to be remembered, and everyone has a story to tell. And if you're willing to listen . . . watch out!

When I start a project, I like to do what I call "wallowing in research." Sometimes I call it drowning, or sponging, or diving off the deep end. It's boots-on-the-ground stuff, and you'll discover things about yourself and your characters you'll never learn from Internet research or books alone. If you're unpublished, you might think you don't have the credentials to ask for an interview. Nonsense. Writers ask questions. Writers need to know. Define yourself as a writer and move forward. The odds are that you know someone who knows someone who knows the thing you need to know. Contact the guy you know and begin the process.

I tend to believe that we're all just three degrees of separation from the person who has all our answers. Still, when I was writing my first novel, *Boulevard*, I was desperate to find a contact at the L. A. Coroner's Office. I called everyone I knew and asked if they could get me in. No one had a lead. I finally broke down and sent an e-mail to the Chief Coroner Investigator. I didn't think I'd get a response, but lo and behold, he wrote back with an invitation to tour the facility and interview him personally. In a half-hour tour I saw over two hundred bodies and six simultaneous autopsies, which, combined, included every variant of death and decay you can imagine. It was strangely serene and the experience reinvented my paradigm for writing about dead bodies. When I returned home I rewrote all the scenes I had placed at the Coroner's Office, because the book research I'd done didn't capture the essence of the world I had just seen.

My second novel, *Beat*, brought *Boulevard*'s protagonist, Hayden Glass, to San Francisco. I spent many days over a period of many months embedded with members of the San Francisco Police Department. I rode with narcotics officers, sergeants, and patrol officers, interviewed captains and city councilmen, went on vice calls and foot patrol in the Tenderloin, interviewed everyone who had an opinion. I've been seen with so many officers in North Beach that I can't convince the locals I'm not an undercover cop.

When I meet them I become them. Through research I've been an astronaut on the International Space Station, a deep-sea submersible pilot, a cosmonaut on Mir, a Nobel Prize–winning physicist, a member of an organization that hides women from human traffickers, a Special Agent for the FBI.

After six months of doing research for *Beat*, I suddenly realized I had only three months left to deliver my novel. What was I thinking? Research. I was thinking research.

EXERCISE

Take at least two subjects from your current work in progress and commit to meeting and interviewing an expert in that field. For example, if you have a character who's a chess champion, research whether there's a grand master in your community, find the person, and offer to take him or her to lunch. If you're writing about crime in your city, commit to meeting and interviewing a police officer or detective. Don't depend on the research done by others—do the boots-on-the-ground research yourself.

Stay in touch with these consultants and e-mail them occasionally with further questions. Ask if they wouldn't mind reading passages of your novel to ensure that you captured their world accurately and with authenticity.

And remember them in the acknowledgments of your book.

ANDREA CAMPBELL

Investigative Techniques

ANDREA CAMPBELL has a degree in criminal justice, is a trained forensic sculptor and artist, and is editor for the *Arkansas Identification News*. She has authored books about criminal justice and forensic science, and her *Legal Ease: A Guide to Criminal Law, Evidence and Procedure* is used as a university textbook. Andrea is also the forensic specialist on a blog featuring professional women in the criminal justice industry (Women In Crime Ink), which has garnered over 200,000 hits and is what *The Wall Street Journal* calls a "must read."

The study of forensic science disciplines and the actual cases of criminal law are stories you can find nowhere else outside of the criminal justice industry. In my book *Legal Ease*, I write: "Laws truly are a mirror, holding up to its face, images of societal change. The events of men and women in desperate situations, entwined by the law in sometimes unbelievable ways, show us a continuing story of how a country deals with population growth, lack of resources and opportunities for all, immigrant expansion, open boarders, and fanatical hate." What could be more exciting than that!

I came into forensics through the back door. I studied graphology—the study of handwriting analysis—with a Catholic priest who used it in his counseling of couples, girls' school students, and inmates in a men's prison. Little did I know that scientists consider graphology a kind of cult, little better than reading newspaper horoscopes. Still, knowledge about it led me to membership in the American College of Forensic Examiners, where I was member 471 in an organization that now has over 15,000 professional associates. This introduction allowed me to research, write about, and study with working law enforcement officers, FBI agents, and scientists, and I began to chronicle these disciplines at a feverish pace—it was such a new, exhilarating world. I earned a Diplomate and Fellowship standing for advancing the field of criminalistics through my writing. And soon I was learning behavioral profiling from FBI agent and famous criminal profiler John Douglas, molding clay with Betty Pat Gatliff, a pioneer in forensic sculpture using skulls, and making eyewitness drawings under the watchful eye of Karen T. Taylor, a renowned forensic artist and frequent guest on *America's Most Wanted!*

If you are going to write about criminal law and forensic science investigation for mysteries, thrillers, and other subgenres, I urge you to get it right. Through research, you can include viable details as you develop and analyze frantic characters in desperate situations doing desperate things. Here are some investigative technique tips to help you out.

Verisimilitude: this is a big word that you should know. It means, the appearance of something that is true or real. The steps in how your mystery or thriller character proceeds, the details of his investigation, and the statements that he makes regarding a criminal case must ring true. There are too many experts out in reader-land, and if you try to fudge or write something that doesn't seem believable, you've lost your credibility as a writer, but just as important, you've probably lost readers. Faux pas in writing are indelible—they are inscribed in ink on paper or as digital text in e-readers, and, unlike a misstep in a conversation that you can apologize for, errors are there for the lifetime of your publication.

You, the writer, should try not to use stereotypes. Stereotypes are hackneyed writing tags that are overused and never seem to change, even though time marches on. Cop clichés are what make those in law enforcement angry when they read a mystery or see a movie.

I wrote an article for *The Writer* and created a popular sidebar, "10 Things Police Wish You Would Omit." In it, I exposed shopworn and often erroneous characterizations, including cops always shown eating doughnuts or portrayed as fighting alcoholism. Today's police officers are just as likely to work out, drink bottled water, or help someone else get off booze. And they are not likely to be found in such phony circumstances as ordering someone to surrender a gun by throwing it, or hiding behind a car door when being shot at—unless they have a death wish.

Now that you know how important it is to get the procedural and descriptive details about police, investigation, and crime scenes right, how do you conduct an investigation? Try the following exercise and fine-tune *your* own procedures.

EXERCISE

You could be the ultimate researcher and ask your local police department if you could ride along during a squad car patrol, but it would probably not transpire because of the liabilities involved and the department's lack of insurance to cover you.

The second-best way to gather details is to befriend a law enforcement official and ask questions. This, you must understand, is most likely a one-time shot, as policemen and policewomen have lives and can spend only a limited amount of time helping writers. You can shorten your interview time by asking cogent questions and working with more than one source.

Failing live sources, the alternative is to exercise your right as an American citizen and attend criminal courtroom cases when court is in session and the public is welcome. The prosecutor will generally call police and forensic scientists to outline their "day in the life," so to speak, and you can hear it in a linear way, since cases generally follow an understandable time line.

Another way to avail yourself of the facts is to read academic or trade books and periodicals. If you have a criminal justice degree or some type of background in criminalistics, you can join a professional organization and subscribe to its periodicals and newsletters and attend its conventions and training conferences. As a trained forensic sculptor and artist, I am a member of the International Association for Identification and have been able to attend annual training workshops that have taught me everything from rolling major case prints, to how to cook meth, and the correct way to collect evidence, among dozens of other disciplines—so much training, in fact, I would never have been able to afford it on my own, even if it were available to the public.

Whatever method you employ to learn investigative techniques, a few things can help. The first is to know that there is no standardization; investigative techniques differ from jurisdiction to jurisdiction. The way detectives collect evidence in Hot Springs, Arkansas, will be different from how local law enforcement does it in Austin, Texas; Santa Barbara, California; or New York, New York. Tasks and methodology vary according to the resources available, time allotment, and the training commitment within a particular department.

Incorporate the methods I've described: interviewing the principals, including police officers, detectives, and prosecutors; forging connections with others in the criminal justice industry; reading trade texts and periodicals; learning a discipline or earning a degree; joining a professional organization and going to conferences; and attending local courtroom cases. If you do so, you'll be well on your way to gathering the information you need to write in the most accurate way possible about police procedures and detective investigations.

HENRY CHANG

Setting and Atmosphere: Writing *from* the Element and Writing *in* the Elements

HENRY CHANG is the author of the acclaimed Chinatown trilogy *Chinatown Beat*, *Year of the Dog*, and *Red Jade*, featuring Chinese-American NYPD detective Jack Yu. He is currently at work on the next book in the Detective Jack Yu series of investigations.

riting from *the element.* It's true that many good writers can create bestselling novels without ever having to get out from behind their desks or laptops.

I'm not one of those.

For me, there's nothing as vivid as being in the moment, where reality spikes the imagination, and creativity is visceral, emotional, rather than intellectual. This is precisely why some writers will ride along with cops on patrol or with firefighters on an alarm run. This is why war correspondents get themselves embedded into combat units, to get an intimate perspective on the hell of war.

This experiential methodology worked for me because I'd grown up in New York's Chinatown (where my crime mysteries are set) around street gangs, gambling houses, bad cops, tong gangsters, dope peddlers, and Chinese organized crime. The Chinatown beat was a natural for me.

I'd already experienced violence on the mean streets of Chinatown, a world of poolrooms, karaoke clubs, and after-hours bars. I was well acquainted with the neighboring precincts, cruising along on predatory road trips through the various ethnic enclaves of Manhattan's Lower East Side. I was living in and knowing this element, even before I found the voice with which to tell and write the stories.

Story-wise, there wasn't much I had to dream up.

My writing style is very organic; I like to feel and experience, as much as possible, the environment I'm setting my characters in. (More on that later.)

Recording the Chinatown underworld in action—the images, the people, the emotions—was another matter. Normally, you'd carry a pocket-size recorder and camera, just to get things right. But when you're cruising the criminal underworld, those tools are forbidden.

Obviously, you can't pull out a pad and start taking notes when you're in a gambling house or drug factory, with tong managers and gang members all around. You need to observe, soak up the environment, and participate in it, unless it's a danger to yourself or others (in which case look for the nearest exit). I've been able to condense an hour's observation into a few sentences and key headers hastily written on my forearm during trips to the restroom. Seems clandestine, undercover, I know. I've jotted down numbers and symbols on my palm when I couldn't find a scrap of paper. I've taken disposable items from the location, like a matchbook or a playing card, if I feel it'll spark a memory, an image, an idea later on.

Basically, you rely on your memory, however splintered it might be after a night of carousing with your questionable companions.

The opportunity for recall came for me, many times, in the wee hours between three and six a.m., after the gambling houses and after-hours bars had closed, when dawn drifted wearily over Chinatown. This was when we gathered together in the all-night Chinatown dives, hungrily ordering up hot Cantonese plates of rice dishes, with the street boyz teasing me about my furious jotting-down of notes onto stacks of paper table napkins.

They'd trusted me by then.

"Telling tales again," they'd snicker.

"Got to," I'd answer, "our stories are too important not to tell."

Nights with my Chinatown brothers, my *hingdaai*, were always spiked with extraordinary urban experiences that were dark and gritty, with sexual visions and violent vignettes. I'd been a victim, and I'd dealt out some retaliation as well, so how I'd been able to channel the fear and anger from those incidents becomes apparent in the rendering of my characters and their actions. You never understand those emotions as clearly until men with bad intentions come at you with knives, until someone points a gun in your face.

Experiential. Empirical.

Again, I don't recommend conducting such dangerous research, but if it comes with the territory that you're writing in and writing about, then try to capture those emotional or physical traumas. Those experiences will help you to understand the human condition and to render the emotional landscape in your settings and characters.

Writing in *the elements.* For the main components of my stories, I prefer to be out on the streets, to feel the wind or rain or sun on my face as the Chinatown New York City milieu unfolds.

Consider the settings in your story. In what season(s) do key events take place? If it's an outdoor setting, consider how it might look and feel if the weather changes.

In New York City we experience the four seasons, which are noticeably distinct from one another. Winter, spring, summer, and fall all feature different weather. Whatever the elements are in your setting, the weather can be used to your story's advantage. You will need to know the particulars about the environment you're creating, and the details you choose to include will enhance the authenticity of your story.

It wouldn't be unusual to see me writing in the rain, under an awning on Chinatown's main drag. This is what I'd see.

The rain starts to pound down and it affects everyone on the street. There is a fresh sense of urgency as Chinese people walk faster; deliverymen have to hustle, even as truck and car traffic slows down. A few people don't mind getting wet and they proceed at their own pace. The sidewalk merchants roll out their carts of umbrellas for sale.

I've seen this stretch of street before, seen how it looks different under two feet of snow in January, with the locals going about their business around the piles of dirty slush and ice. But in July, when the heat ripples up from the black tar street, the locals move much slower from the oppressive temperatures and humidity. The same street is alive with celebration during the Chinese New Year. The colors of luck and good cheer—reds and golds—everywhere. Fireworks. Lion dancers and floats with beauty queens and marching bands. It's so crowded, you can't even walk down the street.

These observations give me a creative choice about how to use this setting. Plot-wise, does something dramatically different happen because it's subzero freezing cold, instead of heat-wave 105-degree hot? How does the change affect your character(s), who live in this environment?

In a key shootout scene from *Year of the Dog*, this is precisely what happens; the weather conditions have set off a chain reaction of violent and fatal events.

In *Red Jade*, the weather figures in everything, but for more on that you'd have to read the book.

EXERCISE

Select an exterior location that figures prominently in your story and observe that setting during various times: morning, noon, rush hour, evening, and so on. How differently do people act during those times? How could what's happening during those different times affect what your characters will do in a scene?

What does the location look like in winter? How does it feel in the summer, or in the fall? What happens there during a thunderstorm? What seasonal/traditional events (a street fair, a parade) regularly occur there? The answers to these questions will give you added creative flexibility to enhance your story components.

Always take notes, mental or otherwise.

Again, observe, but also engage all of your senses.

What colors do you see? (Bright and cheery, or muted?) Is it an emotional setting (like a funeral procession)?

What sounds do you hear? (Traffic noise, different languages, street music?)

What do you smell? (Savory aromas of food, the scent of flowers, the stench of garbage?) One reviewer of *Chinatown Beat* wrote, "You can almost smell the tofu cooking."

What does the air feel like? (Hot or cold, sticky, humid, wet?)

Are there any food items in the location that will allow you a taste of the setting? (A fruit market, a bakery, a sidewalk food vendor?)

These exercises will help you get an organic feel for your chosen environment, a visceral understanding of how that setting can be made to work for you and your story. Try to apply your imagination against the vivid background of the setting, which, it's often noted, can be a character as well.

PETER JAMES

The Importance of Research

PETER JAMES is the author of the internationally bestselling Detective Superintendent Roy Grace series, published in thirty-four languages with world sales of more than six million copies, and a further fifteen thrillers, which have also been highly successful. Three of his books have been filmed and his current series is in development for television. His novel *Dead Like You* was published by Minotaur in November 2010, and his latest, *Dead Man's Grip*, was published by Minotaur in November 2011.

For me, research is as important an element in writing my novels as character and plot. I view each of these elements as an inseparable trinity. Each of my Roy Grace novels has its genesis in a true story or in research facts—as indeed do all of my previous novels. My first Roy Grace novel, *Dead Simple*, came out of my fascination as a child with Poe and the terrifying notion of premature burial—and the research I did into whether such a thing as unintentional premature burial can happen today.

As a crime novelist, I am intrigued by seemingly normal people who do terrible things. Many of our worst monsters don't walk around with the words "Rapist" or "Serial Killer" tattooed on their foreheads; they wear suits and spectacles. They are often successful professionals or businessmen, most of them with adoring wives and children, and they are viewed by friends and neighbors as pillars of their community.

Dr. Harold Shipman, sentenced to fifteen life sentences in 2000, killed more than 250 people. Yet all of his patients and his wife revered this quiet family doctor, and one Greater Manchester detective described him as "the dullest killer I have ever met." Dennis Nilsen, convicted in 1983 for the murder and cannibalism of fifteen boys and men and known as "The Kindly Killer," had been a police officer and then a civil servant. Ted Bundy, a handsome university graduate and former law student who had worked for the Republican Party, was executed in 1989 for raping and murdering an estimated thirty-five young women. In 2005, Wichita's Dennis Rader, self-styled "BTK"—Bind, Torture, Kill—was convicted on ten counts of murder. A local government compliance officer, married, with two teenage daughters who worshipped him, he was a pleasant-looking man of fifty and, as a scout leader and a church warden, a much-respected man in his community.

I'm curious about what makes these people do the things they do. From the perspective of writing an intriguing novel, their intelligence, cunning, and ability to remain calm and methodical make them all the harder for the police to detect and catch.

Three years ago I attended a police forensics lecture on the latest advances in DNA and learned of a case, that of the Rotherham Shoe Rapist, which was to become the inspiration for my sixth Roy Grace novel, *Dead Like You*.

Between 1983 and 1986, a number of women, ranging from eighteen to fifty-three years old, walking home at night from clubs or pubs in Rotherham and Barnsley in South Yorkshire, were dragged off the streets and brutally raped by a man with a stocking over his head. He would truss them up and take their shoes as trophies, occasionally items of jewelry as well.

In 1986 he stopped, suddenly, and the police trail went cold. Detectives on the case believed that the attacker must have been a known sex offender who had either died or been jailed for other offenses, or as sometimes happens with serial offenders, who was simply having an extended cooling-off period. But in fact, James Lloyd, a divorcé with one child, stopped for a much less obvious reason: he had remarried, and was soon to father two more children.

Police files on rape and murder are never closed. By the early 1990s, DNA typing was being used on cold cases such as this one, but no matches to the "Shoe Man" were found. Then, in the early 2000s, there was a major breakthrough in forensic DNA analysis: familial DNA typing came into existence. Now a partial—or familial—match could be obtained from a relative of the perpetrator. U.S. law enforcement came up with the slogan "If you have a brother doing time, don't commit a crime!"

South Yorkshire Police reopened the case and had their first piece of good fortune. A DNA sample from a woman, who had been arrested earlier on a drunk-driving charge, produced a familial match with the rapist. When the police went round to her home to ask if she had a brother, she replied that she did, but he was a respectable businessman, the manager of a large printing works, who had never been in trouble, so it could not possibly be him. However, when she phoned to tell her brother of the police's interest, his immediate reaction was to phone his father and tell him to look after his family; he then attempted, unsuccessfully, to hang himself in his garage. His life was saved by his son, who cut him down.

Searching Lloyd's office, the police lifted a concealed trapdoor and found a cache of 126 stiletto-heeled shoes, individually wrapped in cellophane; numerous stockings and tights; and some of his victims' jewelry.

Lloyd, an attractive man of forty-nine and a Freemason, lived with his family in a $575,000 four-bedroom detached house in Thurnscoe, near Rotherham in South Yorkshire. The Senior Investigating Officer, Detective Inspector Angie Wright, said, "This man was to all intents and purposes a perfectly respectable businessman with a family, and a pillar of society." None of his family or anyone around James Lloyd suspected for one moment that he could be the notorious shoe rapist. His wife said, "He has always been a good husband, good father, and hardworking. I had never had any indication he had the capacity for anything like that."

The Lloyd story appealed to me for a number of reasons. I had wanted to write a crime story centered on rape for a long while. As with all my books, I desired to explore the subject from all perspectives: from the perpetrator, the victim, and the police—and this case, with the intriguing fetish of the shoes, ticked all the boxes. It also ticked another box—my central character, Detective Superintendent Roy Grace, is in charge of Sussex Criminal Investigative Unit cold cases as well as being a homicide detective busy investigating present-day crimes. I thought this story would give me a unique opportunity to show how attitudes had changed within the police toward rape and, in particular, victims of rape, in little over a decade.

Fifteen years ago, a victim would probably be questioned by a cynical male officer, who would as likely as not say: "You went out in that miniskirt? Well, you were asking for it, weren't you?" Today a victim would be interviewed by same-sex officers, in a dedicated, secure interview suite attached to a hospital, where she (or he) would be made to feel safe and would be cared for and treated sympathetically. Every police force in the United Kingdom now has such a suite.

A fact little realized by victims is that they themselves become "crime scenes"—it is on or in their bodies that much of the key forensic evidence lies, from semen or saliva to something as microscopic as a single skin cell or a clothing fiber. In the forensic examination of rape victims, Edmond Locard's pioneering principle "Every contact leaves a trace" applies more than for almost any other kind of crime.

Until recently, the impact of rape has been underrated by everyone except for the victims. Maggie Wright, who runs a charity rape crisis center in Winchester, told me, "For a person to be raped is like being in a bad car smash. One moment you are happily walking along, living your life, the next you are lying in the wreckage of it. You receive mental injuries that will never heal." Maggie went on to tell me of the distress suffered by many victims in the aftermath and how some will even maim themselves. "I've seen young women who have scrubbed their vaginas with wire wool and bleach to get rid of all traces of the perpetrator," she told me.

Although the rapes perpetrated by James Lloyd and those in my novel are "stranger rapes," this kind of rape is relatively rare. More than eighty percent of all rapes are inflicted by a person the victim knows—whether a relative or someone met in a bar or at a party or on a social networking site such as Facebook. But the damage can be bad or even worse when the victim is raped by someone the victim knows—many victims find themselves never able to trust any other human being again.

I was fortunate to receive a great deal of help during my research from DI Tracy Edwards and her colleagues at the Sussex Police Rape

Prevention Team. Her answer to one of my questions, "What does a rapist get out of it?" surprised me, because it is not the obvious one. "For many rapists it is power over their victim, rather than sexual gratification itself," said DI Edwards. "Some rapists find themselves unable to climax at all during the attack."

The explanation of what turns someone into a rapist is even wider-ranging. And there is no one simple explanation for a fetishist. According to psychiatrist and author Dr. Dennis Friedman: "It could be as simple as a young man whose mother is always leaving him to meet a lover, and the sound of her clicking heels fading terrifies him, because they are taking her to get love from someone else, and not from him. So he first associates the sound of heels with love, then the idea of shoes is connected to the sex act."

EXERCISE

A key result of good research is to be able to write in a rounded way that brings into play all the senses, rather than just, say, the visual one: "The dog bounded over"; "The woman bent down and patted it." This would include all five: sight, sound, touch, taste, and smell. "The happy-looking dog bounded over to her, smelling like a damp rug, panting like a steam engine. Its hair was wet and soft, and as the dog turned to lick her, she could almost taste the rancid flesh of the dead rabbit it had been chewing."

So my exercise is: Write the opening paragraph of a scary story, in which a woman is being followed along a street as she makes her way to her car. Bring in all five senses—sight, sound, touch, taste, and smell—into this paragraph. Include details from your research about the location; include as much information as you can to bring the woman alive. The more we know her, the more concern we will feel as we realize she's in danger.

CHRISTOPHER G. MOORE

The Cultural Setting and the Cultural Detective

CHRISTOPHER G. MOORE is a novelist who has lived in Thailand since 1988. His twenty-two novels appear in twelve languages. Published in 2011, *9 Gold Bullets* is the twelfth novel in the Vincent Calvino series, featuring a Jewish Italian-American private detective from New York City. A feature film based on the Calvino series is in development. Moore has also written seven stand-alone novels, the Land of Smiles trilogy, and is the author of three nonfiction books, including *The Cultural Detective* (2011).

I f you write a mystery set in a foreign land, the location becomes an important aspect of the story. Culture means the language, religion, customs, rituals, and history that everyone in that place largely accepts as the basis for their identity. So when an American detective appears in Bangkok, the story can't convincingly proceed as if it were set in Boston or Toronto.

When the detective walks along the streets of Bangkok, he notices "spirit houses" and the offerings left in front of them, motorcycle taxis, street vendors selling everything from food to pirated DVDs, and signs in the Thai language. These are the exterior, visual aspects of Thai culture. As soon as he talks with a Thai or enters a Thai office or house, then other aspects of culture appear.

Curiosity and close observation are essential for a writer of any kind. In the context of a foreign country, these skills or talents become vital if the narrative is going to succeed. Crime fiction relies upon a good grasp of the criminal justice system, conflicts that lay half submerged within the social and economic structure of a society, and understanding what drives some people to crime. Greed, ambition, opportunity, weakness, limited education, bad neighborhood, absent father or mother, abuse of one type or another are all possibilities.

You may think that people are people wherever you find them and you wouldn't be entirely wrong. We share more things than we'd like to believe. That said, the small differences from language, religion, culture, and history do matter in the ultimate identity of a person. People, in other words, are mostly generic. The task of a fiction writer is to bring a sense of credibility to the purpose of a character's life, his or her choices, and to represent the genuine obstacles a person in that culture would face.

Novels aren't sociology textbooks. They aren't history or language books, either. The goal of learning through observation, questioning, and research is to draw a character that is a product of such influences, without making the reader feel that they are reading long passages of background narrative. And the novelist, by creating characters that are authentic in the context of the culture in which they live and work, allows the reader a way to enter and experience that "foreign" world. Once inside that world, the reader also has the pleasure of reflecting on his or her own native culture and how he or she would have done things differently.

The cultural conflict between people can be drama or comedy. I have a good Thai friend who spent time in America as a high school student. He's very bright, and he speaks fluent English. I will call my friend Khun Daeng (*daeng* means "red"), though it isn't his real name. Two friends came to Thailand to visit him and his family. His mother invited the two Americans to her house for tea. She also speaks fluent English and has a noble-like personality. When they came to the door, both Americans, who must have done research about Thai customs, started to remove their shoes. This indeed is an old, widely practiced custom in Thailand. Everyone removes their shoes before entering a private household. As the Americans stooped down to remove their shoes, Khun Daeng's mother insisted that they shouldn't bother. Both looked up at her and said it was no problem to take off their shoes. But the mother again persisted and both Americans rose to their feet, shoes on, and walked into the house where they enjoyed a wonderful tea.

Later that evening Khun Daeng received a phone call from his mother and she was upset with him and his friends. Why was his mother upset? Because his friends were so rude to enter her house with their shoes on. Didn't they know anything about Thai culture? She was shocked that they would traipse through her house with shoes that may have stepped into the most vile of roadside excretions and drag those germs and bacteria into her life. "But Mother, I stood next to them, and you told them that they didn't need to remove their shoes. You told them not once but twice."

She was steadfast in her response. "They simply should never wear shoes into a Thai house."

Here is the classic cultural gaffe that makes for a story. The mother was being polite; Thais value politeness and hospitality above all else, and they wish to make a good impression on their guests. But the guests are supposed to understand that when a Thai hostess insists that they can keep on their shoes, she doesn't really expect them to follow her command. She expects them to ignore her and take off their shoes. Her offer of politeness isn't to be taken at face value. But how were the two American visitors to know? This isn't something that is spelled out in the Thai guidebooks.

Here is the main point of the story. A novelist should be able to bring into the story incidents that reveal cultural aspects of character that a reader would never find in a guidebook. The guidebook, like the Discovery Channel program on a Thai village, isn't going to give much more than a superficial picture of cultural life. If you want a reading audience to trust you enough to follow you into a foreign land, then you must take them into the heart of the matter, peel back the mystery, and reveal the way local people process their reality and make that part of the story.

In other words, you become a cultural detective. Rather than tracking down a missing person, your job as a writer is to track down the forces in a society that shape the psychology, beliefs, and underpin the actions of people who are shaped by it. A good cultural detective looks for clues in the behavior of others, in their relationships, and how they go about their daily lives from morning breakfast, to the office, to a restaurant or bar, to the nightlife. All the while, when you become that cultural detective, you are constantly weighing the evidence, evaluating it, and reexamining your deductions before moving on. Your readers are following your mental calculations as you take them through this process.

The challenge is to do this with a minimal amount of explanatory details, foreign words, or local slang phrases—because to overdo the foreign parts will likely cause confusion if not indifference. That's why the best writing absorbs the details into the story and character so that they appear naturally as the narrative moves forward. The reader doesn't expect you to make them an expert. They are reading a story. They come to the party for different reasons than people who read a guidebook, a memoir, a biography, a cultural history, or a language guide.

The next time you decide to set a book in Hong Kong, Saigon, Bangkok, or Tokyo, remember that there are many people who know these places very well. And not just the guidebook information on where is the best hotel to stay in or the best restaurant for sea bass. People who understand the culture, language, and history of these places are like musicians who immediately hear the missed note, the one-beat-too-long delay, and before you know it, they turn off the music and they close the book. Being a good cultural detective will go a long way to avoid disappointing your reader. And if you have friends from the place where you have set your story, they can also be good sounding boards as to whether you should take off or keep on your shoes.

EXERCISE

You want to write a scene set at a funeral that takes place in Bangkok, Thailand. The deceased is a long-time expatriate and he has left behind a Thai wife and two children. The funeral service includes Thais and foreigners who will come to the temple each evening at seven-thirty p.m. for a three-day period.

Keep a notebook record of what activity goes on inside the Buddhist temple. What is the role of the monks? Where does the food come from for the visitors? How do the foreigners and Thais relate to each other? Do they sit together, talk together; are they friendly to each other? What is the role of the widow and the children and how is that revealing of character, culture, and place? Find out what occurs on the morning of the cremation—who attends this service, who officiates, what does the coffin look like, and what is the ceremony? Detail the full sequence of events.

Assume that the central character of the story is the deceased's brother from New York. He hasn't ever been to Thailand before. He was estranged from his brother for all of these years. When he appears at the temple for the first day of the services, what will his impressions be? Will he understand the nature of the service? And importantly, what will he come to understand about his brother's life through his widow, children, and friends?

How will the brother's grief and loss be expressed in this setting?

ROBERT S. LEVINSON

The Truth Is in the Fiction

ROBERT S. LEVINSON is the bestselling author of nine novels, including
A Rhumba in Waltz Time, *The Traitor in Us All*, *In the Key of Death*, *Where
the Lies Begin*, and *Ask a Dead Man*. *The Elvis and Marilyn Affair* was a
Hollywood Press Club Best Novel winner. A regular contributor to *Alfred
Hitchcock* and *Ellery Queen* mystery magazines, his short story "The
Quick Brown Fox" won the Derringer Award. His fiction has appeared in
Year's Best anthologies six consecutive years and his nonfiction in *Rolling
Stone* magazine, *Los Angeles* magazine, *Westways*, the Writers Guild of
America's *Written By*, and *Autograph*.

The *National Enquirer* came calling when my first novel, *The Elvis
and Marilyn Affair*, was published a decade or so ago, wondering
how much truth there was to the romance that drove the mystery. Had, in fact, the two icons wrapped themselves in each other,
the reporter wondered, and, if so, how specifically did I know so?

She had done her homework and was aware of an extensive background in the worlds of movies and music that often allowed me to
rub shoulders with the high and the mighty of show business.

She knew I had hung a bit with Presley and some of his people,
although never often or close enough to be considered a member of
his inner circle, and I had dealt with people who'd been on a tighter-
than-tight, first-name basis with Monroe.

"Whaddaya say, Bob?" she said, pressing me for some answers
that would give her a strong hook and greater space for the feature
story she'd be cranking out. What could I reveal that might influence
her readers to race to their nearest bookstore and purchase a copy of
The Elvis and Marilyn Affair?

I built in some dead air, as if struggling with myself over how to respond, before I said, "The truth is in the fiction."

Her face screwed into a puzzle while she tried to figure out what she'd heard.

"So you're telling me they did have a hot and heavy romance that began when they were both filming on the Fox lot back in the fifties, correct?"

"My book is telling you that—the story, not me," I said.

"But isn't the first rule of fiction to write what you know?"

"It's been said."

"I'll take that as confirmation."

"About my writing, sure, but that's all."

"So, then—you're telling me Elvis and Marilyn didn't play patty-cake between the sheets?"

"You've read the book—you tell me."

She stopped me from saying more with an outstretched palm and pulled a copy from her stuffed tote bag. The book's spine was broken, pages littered with those little yellow pasty things. She picked one at random, opened to the section it marked, and read aloud from an underlined passage: "I wouldn't call it a real romance, and maybe affair would be too strong. A fling. It lasted a couple of months and then it was history. She came after him like a hurricane in a hurry. I don't have to explain what kind of an impression it made on a youngster like El, although he already could have his pick of the girls, to have this ripe sex goddess ready to park her body beneath his."

She elevated a perfectly shaped eyebrow.

I said, "That's not me speaking. That's one of the characters in the book."

"You write what you know, and the truth is in the fiction," she said, driving my words back at me with the speed and precision of a Wimbledon champion.

"I also write about people murdering people. I don't know any murderers, and I've never murdered anyone myself."

"You were involved at one time with Dr. Samuel Sheppard, who was convicted of murdering his wife."

"Sam's conviction was eventually overturned," I said. "He was tried a second time and acquitted . . . Besides, he's not in the book."

"In spirit, maybe? In your knowledge; writing what you know? Present under another name? You did blend real people by their real names with fictional characters who could easily be real people in disguise . . . What do you say to that, Bob?"

The best I could do was repeat myself: "The truth is in the fiction."

We went around like that for another half-hour or so, and she left no closer to learning from me if an Elvis and Marilyn love affair was any more than the figment of an author's overripe imagination, but—

She was back at me a year later, when *The James Dean Affair*, the second novel in my series featuring newspaper columnist Neil Gulliver and actress Stevie Marriner, "The Sex Queen of the Soaps," was published—

On the phone this time, challenging the root of the story, that Dean might be the link connecting the curious, often mysterious and questionable deaths of people who had been tight with the actor before he died in the fiery highway crash of his Porsche Spyder, "The Little Bastard," among them actor Nick Adams, supposedly a suicide; actor Sal Mineo, killed during what police logged as a random street robbery; and actress Natalie Wood, who drowned in a freak accident off Catalina Island.

"Your book is the only one I've found that ties the deaths together, to Jimmy Dean, and challenges how they happened and why. Is that the truth in your fiction or simply more fiction in your truth?"

"I wrote what I know," I said. "I know they all died."

"You were associated at one time with the Actors Studio, knew and dealt with many of Dean's fellow members who were his friends, as well as Lee Strasberg himself. Were they the source behind what you eventually wrote? Stories you picked up or overheard?"

"Then wouldn't it be nonfiction?"

"You tell me."

I didn't, and we sparred like that until she hung up, satisfied she had again reached a dead end in driving after some confirmation, any confirmation, from me that would make for a headline story.

A year later—

My third "Affair" novel, *The John Lennon Affair*, had Neil, Stevie, and other fictional characters engaged with dozens of legitimate music industry luminaries, as well as Mark David Chapman, the whacky misfit who murdered Lennon.

As in the first two books, I had blended who I knew with what I knew. Some of them played larger roles than others, who wandered in and out of the story in cameos or crowd scenes, adding verisimilitude to set pieces based on fact or wholly invented, explaining in an author's note a bit more than I'd ever let on to the *Enquirer*:

Readers may think they found truths encapsulated in the fiction, shards of reality that screamed out roman à clef *at them, but it isn't so, of course.*

Maybe recollections worth borrowing and building upon, a little bit here, a little bit there, a collage of events and people from the past— including my time running a news bureau in a desert town next to an Indian reservation, near a gambling casino—pasted into the marvelous world of invention and imagination.

Coincidence, that's all, if that.

Actually, as I've been confessing here, more than coincidence.

I'd been pairing reality to make-believe and make-believe to reality, investing my fiction with real names and authentic events, set down by someone who had lived the experience and didn't depend on research that too often saddled others with anecdotes originally created to burnish a celebrity's ego; hide, ignore, disguise, or shed a favorable light on some embarrassing truth; a lie by any name.

I gave readers examples of my process in an author's note for the fourth book in the series, *The Andy Warhol Affair* (originally published as *Hot Paint*):

The Warhol encounter built around rock idol Richie Savage that climaxes with Neil Gulliver leading Andy onto the stage at Madison Square Garden to observe Richie's SRO concert from behind the amps happened a lot like it's presented, except the rock idol was Shaun Cassidy and the author substitutes Neil Gulliver for himself.

For the longest time I went around thinking to myself I had invented something fresh and new, what I came to call "autobiographical fiction." Not so. Damn it. Turns out that was me and my ego applying self-serving fiction to the truth, but—

I was in great company that dated back at least to the 1800s, when authors such as Charles Dickens, Louisa May Alcott, and even Tolstoy wrote novels that mirrored their lives, changing names and locations and re-creating events for more dramatic punch. They and dozens more who followed to some degree likened their protagonists to themselves.

Their plotlines injected events pulled from their lives without exact truths, the events adjusted for artistic or thematic purposes. Autobiographical fiction was a proven, standard, and well-worn concept long before I came along.

Beyond that, there was a category christened "historical fiction" by the ubiquitous "they," where E. L. Doctorow and other authors paired real people with characters brought to life through the writers' wondrous imaginations.

In *Ragtime*, Doctorow borrowed the lives of Henry Ford, Harry Houdini, Emma Goldman, Booker T. Washington, Stanford White, and the beauteous Evelyn Nesbit. In *Billy Bathgate*, he had crusading New York Attorney General Thomas E. Dewey pitted against gangsters Dutch Schultz and Charles "Lucky" Luciano.

Unlike Doctorow and the other authors noted, I've incorporated a history I've lived and people I knew in leading roles more often than people I only knew about. That may be the one fresh element I brought to the genre in my four Affair books and the five mysteries/thrillers published since. I don't know if there's a name for what I've done. I don't know that it needs a name. What's in a name, anyway?

EXERCISE

Take a memorable experience from your life and apply it to a fictional protagonist, who doesn't necessarily resemble you otherwise. Introduce a secondary character by real name and description who, in fact, figured in that experience. Add other invented characters or composites of persons drawn from life to compose a scene that mixes truth with fiction and can leave readers questioning where one ends and the other begins.

AVOIDING BOOBY TRAPS

Story Development

REECE HIRSCH

The Most Common Mistakes in Plotting a Thriller
(from Someone Who Has Made Them All)

REECE HIRSCH's debut legal thriller, *The Insider*, was published by Berkley Books in May 2010 and was a finalist for the International Thriller Writers Award for Best First Novel. He is a partner in the San Francisco office of Morgan, Lewis & Bockius, specializing in privacy, security, and health care law.

When you start to write your novel, you may, with the hubris of the beginner, imagine that you are going to create something that the world has never seen before, a sui generis masterwork that changes the way mysteries and thrillers are read and written forevermore. And then you learn that there are rules.

Well, maybe rules is a bit strong; expectations may be more accurate. While writing and revising my first book, *The Insider*, I gradually learned that I had transgressed a few of those rules through feedback from beta readers and the agents who were consistently rejecting me. It was only after I learned to color within the lines that I landed an agent and a publisher.

A thriller is like a rock-and-roll song. Immediacy is one of the most highly valued virtues of both forms and, while the basic elements are well established, there is nearly infinite room for variation and expression within that framework. You can take a few basic chord progressions and a time limit of three minutes or so and get everything from "I Wanna Be Sedated" to "Strawberry Fields Forever." But if you stray too far from the rules, like, say, the Beatles' "Revolution 9," then it may be interesting, but it ceases to be something that will ever get played on the radio.

Here are six common mistakes in plotting a thriller, most of which I learned the hard way.

1. *Starting with a whimper.* In order to grab the attention of an agent and later an editor, your book needs to start quickly. Very quickly, with a bang. The first chapter will usually determine whether an agent reads further into your manuscript. If your book doesn't have a killer opening, it may not matter how good the ending is. And, of course, it's always nice to kill someone off early on.

2. *The passive protagonist.* A protagonist is most interesting when he or she is attempting to solve the conflict of the story through action, and least interesting when bobbing like a cork in the sea of events. Literary fiction is filled with characters that are paralyzed by indecision and ennui—thrillers, not so much.

3. *The unlikable protagonist.* If a reader is going to follow a character through the length of a novel, it helps if they like that character. As an author, you can help that bonding process along by actively thinking about ways that you can show the reader (preferably early on in the story) why they should care about your protagonist the way you do. Show your character doing something noble, brave, funny, or maybe just vulnerable. Sure, it's manipulative, but writing thrillers (and most fiction) is inherently manipulative.

4. *Writing only what you know (or only what you don't know).* Thrillers are somewhat hyperbolic by nature, relying upon velocity and pumped-up action. If you can ground your story in a milieu or a character that you know inside and out, then that aura of verisimilitude may rub off on other aspects of your story that are more invented.

For example, my protagonist is a corporate attorney in a big San Francisco law firm, a world I know very well. However, if I had stuck to the reality of that world, my thriller would have been about as thrilling as a Due Diligence summary. But hopefully, my portrayal of law firm life was credible enough that I earned a little suspension of disbelief from the reader when I ventured into the world of the Russian mob, which, I'm happy to say, I do not know so well.

5. *Front-loading the backstory.* When you introduce your protagonist in the first chapter, there is a tendency to want to tell the reader all of the many things you know about the character. Resist that impulse.

Nothing brings a first chapter to a screeching halt (see rule 1) faster than an extended character history. This information is more effectively shown than told and, if it must be told, it should be doled out gradually and not dumped on the reader all at once.

6. *Writing plot points, not scenes.* Thrillers tend to be plot-driven. Things happen, violently and often. Some thrillers can become overly mechanical if the author focuses primarily on moving the story from Point A to Point B to Point C and stops paying attention to the little details of setting and character that give a story life.

Although maintaining a brisk pace is paramount, it's just as important to make sure that Points A, B, and C are all entertaining places for the reader to be. When working out the plot of your book, it's helpful to think in terms of scenes. Make sure that every chapter stands on its own merits as much as possible as a freestanding scene. If you've created a scene that is interesting in terms of setting and character interaction and development *and* you advance the plot, then it's highly likely that the reader will keep turning the pages, which, after all, is what thrillers are all about.

EXERCISE

Outline the first five chapters of your book. These are the chapters that will have to do most of the selling for you when you're submitting your manuscript to agents and publishers. Ask yourself the following questions after you've completed the outline.

1. Will your first chapter grab your readers by the lapels and command their attention? And I know this sounds a little formulaic, but I have to ask, is there a dead body in the first chapter?

2. Is your protagonist acting or being acted upon?

3. By the end of the first five chapters, do we like the protagonist?

4. Have you convinced readers that they've entered an interesting world that you know and understand?

5. How much backstory have you conveyed about your protagonist? Hopefully, enough for readers to understand what's happening, but not so much that they feel they know everything there is to know about the character.

6. Does each of the first chapters stand on its own as a scene, with distinctive settings and character interactions?

SEAN DOOLITTLE

Road Trip

SEAN DOOLITTLE is the author of crime and suspense novels. *Dirt* was named one of the 100 Best Books of 2001 by Amazon.com; *Burn* won *ForeWord* magazine's Mystery Gold Medal; and *The Cleanup* received the Barry Award, an Anthony Award nomination, *CrimeSpree* magazine's Readers' Choice Award, a Spinetingler Award, and a Nebraska Book Award. His most recent book, *Safer*, received glowing reviews in *The New York Times*, *The Washington Post*, and *People* magazine. Doolittle's books have been licensed for translation into several languages.

Book critics sometimes make a distinction between plot-driven stories and character-driven stories. As readers, we basically understand what these terms are supposed to mean (plot = action, character = emotion). As writers of mysteries and thrillers, we understand the crucial importance of compelling plots.

But even in a good, twisty, hard-charging mystery or thriller, the best plots—the best stories—don't unfold at the expense of character. They grow from the characters. And if you are truly engaged with the story you're telling, the reverse can be true as well.

The playwright John Guare (*Six Degrees of Separation*) said, "I loved Feydeau's one rule of playwriting: Character A: My life is perfect as long as I don't see Character B. Knock Knock. Enter Character B."

I love the way this rule distills the plot and character relationship. If Character B never comes knocking, we have no plot. But why does the arrival of Character B put a kink in the life of Character A? Who are these people?

If you're writing a family drama, maybe Character B shows up with some emotional luggage in tow. If you're writing a mystery, maybe Character B walks in with a gun. If you're writing a thriller, maybe Character B walks in with a machine gun.

But any story line is strongest when the character threads and the plot threads are organically entwined. Try this exercise to flex some of the muscles that will help you achieve that union.

EXERCISE

PART ONE

Three characters are traveling somewhere in a car together:

MANDY (THE DRIVER): Mandy has a Ph.D. in art history but works in a corporate human resources department. She has tattoos but hides them under her clothes. She was married once but is single now. She has no children, though she believes she would like to be a mother one day.

RENÉE (PASSENGER SEAT): Renée is a waitress. She has tattoos and doesn't hide them. She thinks sometimes about going back to school but suspects in her heart that it's not going to happen. She recently quit smoking.

JUSTIN (HAS THE BACKSEAT ALL TO HIMSELF): He's younger than Mandy and Renée but not by much. He graduated high school but dropped out of college. He inherited a large sum of money when his parents were killed in a car accident, but so far he hasn't spent a dime of it.

Your task is to take this cast and no more than an hour of your life to develop a rough plot for a mystery or thriller story. Questions to get you started:

1. Where are they going?

2. How did these three characters wind up in this car together?

3. What do the characters want/expect out of this trip? Does what one character wants conflict with what the other character(s) want?

4. Do any of the characters know anything about the trip (or about each other) that the other characters don't know?

5. What are the obstacles between these three characters and their destination?

6. Are they going to get where they are going on time? Or at all?

These questions are only meant to get you thinking and plotting. It's not strictly mandatory to ask or answer all or any of them (though you'll no doubt answer some of them automatically). Just remember: If this car gets from Point A to Point B without incident, we have no plot.

As for what kind of plot you should create, keep the rules loose, but try always to answer the questions in ways that deepen your mystery (consider questions 1 through 3) or ramp up your thrills (consider question 5).

Tip 1: When considering question 5, think of obstacles both outside the car (flat tire, moose in the road, bad weather, military air strikes) and inside the car (see question 3).

Tip 2: If you get stuck, return to question 5.

PART TWO

In completing Part One, you've grown a plot out of characters. Now, take the plot you cultivated and return to the car. Change where everybody in the car is sitting. Most important: Put a different character in the driver's seat.

Without changing your plot—and without significantly altering the broad descriptions of our cast members supplied in Part One—take no more than another hour and see if you can make Mandy, Renée, and Justin fit into their new spots in ways that make sense.

Tip 3: To accomplish this, you'll probably need to know more about these characters than you know right now.

When you're finished, take a look at what you've done. Are the two versions of this story you've brainstormed plot-driven or character-driven? With luck, this will be a harder question to answer than any of the questions you've answered so far. . . .

WILL LAVENDER

The Hook: Killer Beginnings in Mystery Fiction

WILL LAVENDER is the *New York Times*–bestselling author of *Obedience*. His second novel, *Dominance*, was published by Simon & Schuster in July, 2011. He holds an MFA in creative writing from Bard College. He lives in Louisville, Kentucky, with his wife and children.

A lfred Hitchcock, that master of suspense, refused to film a true mystery, because there was so much emphasis on the end. As writers we can understand Hitchcock's objection: The endings of mystery novels are, by their nature, so essential that they can threaten other plot elements. How many of us have come to find that our writing has suffered in the middle of a book simply because the pressure of coming up with that final twist looms ahead like a dark cloud?

I was once asked to submit two pages of my first manuscript to an agent. Two! I immediately thought, *What can this person possibly learn by reading just two pages?* The reality is that this mind-set is how book buying is these days. How many pages is that person who picks up the book in a bookstore, reads the flap, then skims the first chapter of the book actually reading? One or two, at most. Our job as writers is to get that person from the shelf to the cash register. In the age of bookstore café browsing and e-book sample chapters, in the era of tough economic decisions, those first two pages have become crucial.

When I teach at workshops, I lecture on the necessity of the hook: a beginning that grabs readers and relentlessly pulls them into the rabbit hole of the story. After my lecture, my audience will look at me and usually ask two simple questions. The first is: "What's wrong with the beginning my working manuscript already has?"

To fix a problem, one has to first acknowledge that a problem exists. In my time reading student manuscripts and writing my own fiction, I have come to believe that there are three main problems with most beginnings in mystery manuscripts:

1. Nothing happens; or 2. Not enough happens; or 3. It happens in the wrong order.

If we assume that the beginning of a story, any story, is to provide the reader with information and dramatic conflict, these three points are key. Addressing the issue of action, as simple as it sounds, will almost invariably make the novel's hook sharper. Novels are often marred by the writer's belief that "things get going in the middle" or that their book "isn't an action novel, it's a mystery novel."

These are fallacies; all books need happenings, whether they are external or are in the characters' minds, to move the book forward in its first pages. Plodding, uneventful openings will almost always have me jumping to the next book in my queue.

The second question I am asked when it comes to beginnings is: "How?" How do you craft a beginning where interesting things happen in just the right order? What are the cardinal traits of good beginnings? How do you get your dream agent to bite and take a chance on your manuscript, and ultimately how do you change that book browser into a book buyer?

This, like all other pieces of writing advice, is multifaceted. There is not simply one trick to writing a better beginning, there are many. The writer's voice must be strong, the sense of pacing must be established, the main character or an important corollary character must be colorfully and acutely revealed—all of this in just a few hundred words. No one said writing fiction was easy.

There is, however, one easy trick to writing a better beginning: *Do not think of the crime; think about what the crime has done.* Mystery novels are essentially about crimes and criminals, and the weakness of many manuscripts is that they deal only with the crime and not with its fallout. Who has this crime affected? How have people's lives been changed? What has happened to people, physically and emotionally, because of this horrible deed?

Here's an example. In the great Thomas Harris's *Silence of the Lambs*, for my money the best genre novel written in the last half of the twentieth century, Harris uses two clever tricks to hook his reader. First, he provides a pleasing amount of action. This action is not explicit to the crime; that is, the main crime spree and the suspect himself are not revealed for another fifty pages or so. The action Harris gives his main character involves a task, and this task has to do only with the performance of a psychological evaluation. In just three pages, we get all this: the task, Clarice agreeing to said task, and her emotional qualms about undertaking it. Just like that: action without velocity. No explosions, no knifings, no blood, no body. Just the puzzle pieces scattered on the floor, and in Harris's hands that's enough.

But another interesting thing happens in these first few pages. Once we get inside the prison we learn, again implicitly, of the nature of Hannibal's crimes. We get who he is by the crimes he committed: what kind of person he is, who he ruined, what he's capable of. Harris is a brilliant writer, and he pulls all this off seamlessly by telling, inferring, implicitly hinting at these crimes. He shows nothing—not yet. He's too talented.

Too often writers want to jump into the procedural, into the whodunit itself. They want to show the body, introduce the cops who are to solve the crime, and get the plot moving toward the solution. I think a mystery novel's opening can be much more subtle, and can in fact be more about what has happened off-page than what happens on.

Below is an exercise that will help you to craft a stronger, sharper hook.

EXERCISE

Write the beginning of a story, novella, or novel about a policewoman interrogating a suspected arsonist. This beginning should be two pages long, but here's the twist: You cannot include anything from the interrogation room itself; this beginning must revolve completely around either what happens before the interrogation begins or what happens after.

Here is an opportunity to think about a story's hook in the framework not of movement and Hollywood-style velocity, but in the emotional complexity of the task at hand. Think about your all-important opening and how you will get the reader invested enough to ride along with you for what happens after these two pages.

And then, once you've written the story, think about how much happened in the tale. Is there enough action to satisfy that browser at the bookstore? Is that action in the right order? How, without the use of flashback (which I almost always warn writers to resist) and without any overt plot, do you include enough substance to hook that picky reader?

Best of luck and happy writing.

SOPHIE HANNAH

First Lines

SOPHIE HANNAH is the internationally bestselling author of the psychological thrillers *Little Face, The Truth-Teller's Lie, The Wrong Mother,* and *The Cradle in the Grave*. Those are the U.S. titles, anyway. Confusingly, some of her books have different titles in the United Kingdom, but they have the same first lines. Sophie is also a bestselling, award-winning poet. She lives in Cambridge, England.

It must have happened to me fifty times: People recommend that I read a novel, and then, when I ask for more detail about the book they're trying to press on me, they say, "Oh, it's incredibly gripping—once you get past page 157."

"Aha," I say, eyes narrow with suspicion. "Just so as I know— what's it like before you get to page 157? Gripping-ish? Mildly engaging? Or are we talking . . . bearable?'

"Oh, gosh, not even approaching bearable!" they say with glee. "The first 156 pages are turgid and tedious, and nearly made me want to slit my wrists—but I persevered and it was so worth it. From page 157 to the end, it's a masterpiece."

Er . . . no, it's not. If only the second half of a novel is brilliant, it's not a half-brilliant novel—it's a bad one. As my favorite crime writer, Ruth Rendell, once said, a novelist's job is to grip the reader from line one, page one. Rendell is strict with herself, as every author should be—every single line of a book counts, she believes; every line should make it more impossible for the reader even to contemplate putting down the book. Read any first line of a Rendell novel (or of any of the books she has written under the pseudonym Barbara Vine) and you will feel an almost physical pull as the first line reels you in.

Her novel *A Judgement in Stone,* for example, begins: "Eunice

Parchman killed the Coverdale family because she could not read or write." It's an incredibly risky opening line for a crime novel, because it appears to tell the reader all the things one waits in suspense to find out at the end of a book: who killed whom and why. However, in spite of this, the line works brilliantly, because it simultaneously tells you everything and nothing. You realize that knowing who did what and why is only the starting point—you need more detail; you crave the story summarized by those facts, in nonsummary form. If anything, Rendell increases the suspense by superficially telling the reader "everything" right at the start. *Hang on a minute,* the reader thinks, in a mild panic. *Slow down—tell me properly.* The authorial voice, by delivering the bare facts of the case in such a quick, perfunctory way, makes the reader feel almost as if she is being fobbed off, which increases the determination to find out the fullest version of the story.

Let me now make a controversial statement: It's more important that a novel—a thriller especially—should have a great beginning than a great ending. Now let me quickly qualify that before anyone gets cross: Obviously, in an ideal world, the whole of the novel one is reading or writing should be great, and that is what we should all aim for.

But this is not an ideal world, and so I stand by my statement: In a nightmarish impossible-choice situation, I would always choose a brilliant beginning over a brilliant ending.

One of my favorite mystery authors, who shall remain nameless, writes a series of novels which all have endings that make me sigh with disappointment. And yet, when her new novel is published each year, I rush out and buy it eagerly. Why? Because I love her beginnings more than practically anyone else's—her middles are pretty damn good, too—and for ninety-nine percent of the time I spend reading one of her books, I'm thoroughly enjoying myself. Yes, I'd prefer it if the endings were good, too, but you can't have everything. And if her endings were stunning and her beginnings mediocre, I would never get past page 10.

My own approach to writing the beginnings of my psychological suspense novels—and it starts when I'm thinking about the first line— is to be as neurotic as possible. I remember Ruth Rendell's wise words, and I think to myself, *Okay—there are millions and zillions of novels out*

there. Probably most of them are better than yours. Anyone who picks up one
of your books is going to suspect as much straightaway, and be looking for
proof that he or she is right and an excuse to toss your novel aside and read
one by a better writer. How are you going to stop that? What words can you
put into your book right at the very beginning that will act like superglue, or
crack cocaine, and make it impossible for anyone to stop reading?

A first line should be where a reader's addiction to a novel begins.
The second and third lines should then be equally addictive. Just as
we want every part of our roof to be leak-proof, we must make sure
every part of our manuscript is give-up-proof. The first line of your
novel should be a bold display of the best you can do, promising more
and better to come. It should say, "Look at me! If I'm this good now,
at first glance, how much better might I get if you spend more time
with me?"

To refer again to the opening of Ruth Rendell's *A Judgement in
Stone*, another great thing about it is that it's effectively boasting to the
reader, "If I can afford to give you up front all the stuff that other writers have to save until later, how many more goodies must I have up
my sleeve for later in the novel?"

Once you're sure you're feeling neurotic enough, the next step is
to add a dash of pessimism to your neurosis. When crafting the perfect
first line to win over readers, do not imagine those readers to be warm-
hearted, open-minded types, willing to give a book a fighting chance.
Assume your readers will be surly and impatient, with incredibly low
boredom thresholds. Those are the people you have to please—which
means you have to try even harder and do more pleasing. Usually, a
writer's harshest critic is him- or herself, so monitor your own reactions to your work. If you found a book that had the first line you've
just written, would you carry on? Be aware if you're starting to bore
yourself, and, if you are, stop.

As well as gripping the reader, a first line should pose a question
and/or give a sense of the flavor of the novel. The first line of *A Judgement in Stone* does this brilliantly—I can't think of a more effective way
for Rendell to have signaled to her readers that they're reading a psychological crime novel. The elegant, poignant, sinister first line of
Daphne du Maurier's *Rebecca*—"Last night I dreamt I went to Mander-

ley again"—tells you so much about the book. It tells you that a particular house, Manderley, is central to the novel; that a key theme is the way the past haunts the present; that the tone and mood will be atmospheric and haunted, not wisecracking and frivolous.

Writers should always try to make their first lines work as hard as possible: yes, they must grip, but they must also inform, and withhold, and tease, and sound good rhythmically to the inner ear. A first line should scare its author by promising more than it can possibly deliver—and then it should deliver. A book's chances of securing a perfect ending for itself are massively enhanced if it has a perfect beginning.

EXERCISE

There are several stages to this exercise. You have to do them all. If you skip any, it won't work.

1. Write the blurb of the novel you would love to write, in an ideal world. A blurb, not a synopsis—in other words, you don't have to tie up ends or resolve anything. You can promise the earth, and end your blurb-promise with a dot-dot-dot, a "Wait and see what happens next." Ask questions you can't answer, make promises you fear you won't be able to keep. All you need is the beginning of the idea, not the whole idea.

    Your imagination is likely to be more ambitious if it isn't terrified of failing to live up to expectations before it starts. For the time being, forget about the danger of disappointing people—if necessary, you can always run away and hide from the hordes of angry readers. Use your blurb to create massive expectations—you'll find yourself living up to them, once you stop feeling scared, and you'll be glad you didn't play it safe.

2. Once you've written your blurb, imagine you've finished your book and it's a masterpiece. (Don't worry about the precise details of how this character's going to have her plotline resolved at the

end, or not being able to think of a brilliant twist.) Write two reviews of your own book—the one you haven't written yet—by
two made-up reviewers. Give them names if you want to. Both
reviews should be praising your novel to the skies—and can be as
general or specific as you want.

You might find one of your fantasy reviewers writing, "This
book's heart-stopping final scene haunted me for weeks." And
there you go: you have part of your recipe. You now know that,
whatever else your novel might end up having, it's got that wonderful final scene. Which wonderful scene, exactly? Well, that's up
to you—but it'll help you to know that it's there, waiting for you
to think of it.

3. Now for writing your first line. Don't sit down and try to write an
awe-inspiringly brilliant first line, even though that's what you're
hoping to end up with. If you do, you'll be staring at a blank screen
for months. Try, instead, to write an average-to-bad first line. Or,
if you feel like it, a really terrible one. What line, at the start of your
wonderful novel, would really wreck everything you're hoping to
achieve. Write it down, or type it up. Then ask yourself what's
wrong with it. Improve it. Keep improving it, which—at some
point—will mean changing it altogether.

4. One of two things should happen now. Either you'll keep improving and improving and end up with your brilliant first line, or (and
this is more likely) while you're busy trying to do this, a great first
line—crucially, one that you're not aware of having struggled
to come up with—will suddenly present itself. You'll be so sure
you love it and it's perfect that you won't care anymore what I'm
telling you to do. Your line will be so good that I can go to hell.
Congratulations—you've done it!

JUDITH VAN GIESON
Writing the First Chapter

JUDITH VAN GIESON is the author of eight mystery novels featuring Albuquerque lawyer/sleuth Neil Hamel and five mysteries with Claire Reynier, a librarian at the University of New Mexico and crime-solver. Judith's books have been regional and Independent Mystery Booksellers Association bestsellers.

Time is of the essence in a crime novel and a writer needs to establish the protagonist and any sidekicks right away. Villains can take a little longer. Setting is also of the essence and needs to be described in the first chapter. In a series, if presented well, setting can become almost another character in the books.

Readers need to know what will bring the protagonist into crime-solving. If criminal investigation is the sleuth's profession, then show him or her at work. If you're writing about an amateur sleuth, a profession may still be what leads that person into investigating a crime. Even mild-mannered fictional librarians come across crime in their work. If it's not the character's profession, then show the reader what does get the sleuth involved in solving a crime.

Often sleuths have sidekicks who work with them and help them. Sidekicks can provide a balance to the sleuth, and it's helpful to introduce them in the first chapter, too. When the sleuth is tense and serious, the sidekick can relieve the tension by cracking wise. Or vice versa. Demonstrating the interaction between the two is a good way to reveal character in the first chapter as well as to show character development later on.

Just as you'll want to give the reader good place description, it helps to describe your characters. It isn't absolutely essential since characters can reveal themselves through dialogue and action. But if you are going to describe them, do so early on. If you wait, readers will form their own impression. You don't want them thinking your sleuth has short dark hair only to find out later that it's long and blond.

It's also important to establish the tone of your mystery right away through the voice you use. A first-person narration can be quick and sharp. Often it sounds like the narrator is speaking to the reader and it helps to have the rhythms and vernacular of speech. The third-person-narrator and omniscient-narrator points of view can be more leisurely and reflective.

Dialogue is essential as a way to reveal information and character and to keep the story moving along. You'll want to include some in your first chapter.

The exercises that work the best for me are a matter of observation and experimentation.

EXERCISE

1. Take a good look at your setting. Even if it's a place you know well and/or have lived in for a long time, drive or walk around it making use of all your senses. How does it smell? What colors do you see? Ask yourself what will make this particular setting unique, interesting, unforgettable to the reader.

   Since a crime is going to take place here, you'll need to explore the bad side as well as the good. And while you're exploring, think about what your setting is going to mean to your sleuth.

2. If you listen carefully you will notice that speech is linked to setting. People in different places have their own lingo. Eavesdropping is not a bad habit for a writer.

   Spend some time in the food court of your local mall listening to the words and the rhythms people use in their speech. In many cities you will hear languages other than English being spoken separately or mixed in with English. Text what you've heard to your cell phone or take notes. If you're writing in the first person, it helps to read your work out loud, and it's good to do this with dialogue, too. Does it sound authentic? Does it have the rhythm of speech? Is this the way people in your chosen setting talk? Are you using the kind of slang they use?

3. If you don't already work in your sleuth's profession, spend some time around people who do. One way to do this is to join professional organizations or go to meetings those people attend and listen to how they talk. Are there any words, phrases, or attitudes that are unique to that profession? Any dynamic in the way they interact that you might be able to use in the relationships between your sleuth and a sidekick? Are the professionals wary of each other or at ease? Notice what kind of cars these people drive and how they dress. When I started writing about lawyers, I learned about them by temping for law firms, but not every writer will be willing to go that far.

4. If you're not sure what voice you want to use to tell your story, then experiment. Do you want to get into the minds of more than one character or is one enough? Try writing a couple of paragraphs and reading them out loud. Which is the best way to express the thoughts of your sleuth? For me, reading my work out loud is always a good exercise.

GAR ANTHONY HAYWOOD

You Can't Cheat an Honest Reader

GAR ANTHONY HAYWOOD is the Shamus- and Anthony-winning author of twelve crime novels and numerous short stories. He has written six mysteries featuring African-American private investigator Aaron Gunner; two starring Joe and Dottie Loudermilk, retiree crime-solvers and Airstream-owning parents to five grown "children from hell"; and four stand-alone thrillers. Gar has written for *The New York Times* and the *Los Angeles Times*, and for such television shows as *New York Undercover* and *The District*. His most recent novel is the thriller *Assume Nothing* (Severn House, 2011).

I hate cheaters. Not because they never prosper, as the old saying goes, because we all know some cheaters actually do quite nicely for themselves. No, I hate cheaters because they're lazy. They sidestep the rules the rest of us abide by as a shortcut to what they want; they lie to your face and expect you not to notice.

Cheaters who write mysteries may not be the worst offenders of the lot, but they're close, and discerning readers often treat them with the same level of disdain card sharks were shown at Old West poker tables. Because a mystery author who cheats breaks the unwritten contract between writer and reader that demands he always play fair, that he not stretch the boundaries of what is probable, let alone possible, simply to make Tab A fit into Slot B.

Keeping readers guessing what's real and what isn't is, of course, what a successful mystery novel does best, but this is true only if its author has given such things as logistics and credibility their proper due. The key to leaving a reader marveling at your skillful sleight of hand, rather than your inattention to detail or, worse, your bald-faced dishonesty, is anticipating every question your reader might have about your plot, and then making sure each of these questions has been answered in a straightforward and reasonable manner.

The alternative to doing such grunt work—and it is grunt work—is cheating, as in committing the following crimes against nature:

Contradiction. Establishing a fact or pattern of behavior at one point in your book, then doing a one-eighty on yourself just to satisfy a need of your plot. Example: Having a character referred to throughout your novel as "Johnny," only to have someone at some point call him "John," for no reason other than to make him look more innocent or guilty than he really is.

Neglecting to answer obvious questions. "What kind of obvious questions?" you ask. Here are just a few examples:

Why would she do that?

Where did that come from?

Shouldn't he have done A instead of B?

Part of your job as a mystery author is to outthink your reader, and that involves anticipating all the questions he or she could possibly come up with about the story you're trying to sell. Refusing to explain something that demands explanation is inexcusable. Here's a rule of thumb: The more improbable a scenario, the more obligated you are to offer your reader detailed reasons to believe it.

Defying logic. Pigs can't fly, dogs don't talk, and an assistant prosecuting attorney can't hot-wire a late-model car with a chopstick no matter *how* badly you need her to drive off in it. If you've created a problem for your protagonist that neither of you can solve in a believable fashion, scrap the problem and replace it with something more manageable. Don't just fake your way out of it and hope your reader won't notice, because he or she will. Trust me.

Dropping red herrings out of the sky. This is the act of making something or someone appear out of nowhere (and then disappear again) without adequate explanation. Like contradiction, this cheat is usually committed to force-fit a plot point or to misdirect the reader's attention. Example: In a suspect's dresser drawer, your protagonist finds a red rubber frog, the incredibly specific calling card of the serial killer he or she is after—but in the end, the suspect isn't the killer, and no explanation is ever given for the frog's presence in the suspect's home.

Overreliance on coincidence. Yes, it is a small world, and sometimes two people who've met at the post office only once will share the same birthday and first four digits of their Social Security number, but try to hinge the solution of your mystery on such a flimsy unlikelihood and no reader in their right mind will forgive you. A coincidence or two is okay as minor plot points, but if you can stay away from them altogether, do so.

Treating your reader like a character. Example: Harriet is a psychopath who has been pretending to walk with a limp all book long to throw off the reader and your protagonist. You write a scene in which she's alone in her kitchen, making dinner, and she's *still limping.* Why? For whose benefit? The reader's, of course. You've made Harriet aware of the reader's prying eyes in her kitchen, and hell if she's going to give herself away as long as your reader's around. New rule: Don't put anyone in a room alone if you don't want the reader to see how he or she is likely to behave there.

Resorting to hackneyed devices. A phone number scribbled inside a matchbook, a loaded gun that jams at a crucial moment, a killer who confesses all without sufficient reason—these are all cheap stunts that mediocre mystery authors have used since Holmes dropped his first "Elementary" on Watson, and they're as glaring an indicator now of amateurism as ever. Don't go there.

Giving up. You've written yourself into a corner you can't find your way out of, lost interest in your story, or run up against a deadline that can't be extended. For whatever reason, you're all done wrestling with this beast and you want it over with, so you just slap an ending on it and walk away, leaving your reader wanting for more. Think a reader won't recognize a rush job when he or she reads one? Think again. The best way to avoid writing a book that falls flat in the end is to treat each one like a bar fight: Never start what you aren't prepared to finish.

Cheating as outlined above is more glaring in a mystery than a crime novel because of the complexity of the former's structure and how focused readers are upon its every point of stress. But cheating in a crime novel is no less unforgivable. The suspense of unanswered questions is still the name of the game, whether "Who done it?" is among them or not, and if you don't answer these questions satisfactorily—that is, without thumbing your nose at reality—your failure is just as great. Perhaps even more so, considering the less restrictive space in which a crime novelist has to operate. With so few rules to worry about (no clues, suspects, or red herrings required), surely it isn't too much for your reader to expect a little honesty and fair play from you?

To repeat my original complaint, as surely one former teacher or another once told you, cheating is the sign of a lazy mind. Leaving a gaping plot hole open in error is one thing; deliberately plugging it with chewing gum is another. Get in the habit now of checking your work for cheap fixes and eliminate them, no matter how much work this involves. Pros do; amateurs don't. 'Nuff said.

EXERCISES

SITUATION 1

Though it won't be revealed until the end of your book, Doreen has murdered her husband's mistress, Sheila, and hidden the body in the trunk of her car. She's driving her husband, Joe, to the train station when a tire on her car goes flat and she has to pull over to the side of the road.

YOUR MISSION: Write a two-page scene using the third-person narrative during which Doreen talks Joe out of opening the trunk to fix the flat himself, while planting seeds of her guilt the reader can refer to later.

THE CHEAT TO AVOID: Having Doreen say or do something inconsistent with her culpability in Sheila's murder.

SITUATION 2

Homicide cop Lou Gray is searching the dark garage of a murder suspect when a gunman hiding in the shadows steps forward to shoot him dead. The last thing Gray sees before he dies is the highly distinctive necktie the killer is wearing—a tie he's seen his partner, Will Bennett, wear many times.

YOUR MISSION: Write three rational explanations for the killer wearing this tie if Gray's partner Bennett is NOT the gunman in the garage.

THE CHEAT TO AVOID: Overreliance on coincidence.

SITUATION 3

Your P.I. Angie Wentworth is examining the scene of a crime following a double homicide. The police have already gone over the place with a fine-tooth comb without finding any link to the murderer, but Angie discovers something they missed, something that points her to a specific location where the killer might be found.

YOUR MISSION: Come up with four things Angie might stumble upon that (a) the police may have logically overlooked; and (b) could indicate the killer's hiding place.

THE CHEAT TO AVOID: Resorting to overused and hackneyed devices.

SITUATION 4

Your first-person narrator, Harry Childs, suffers from occasional blackouts, and isn't at all sure he's not the serial killer of young women the police have been looking for.

YOUR MISSION: Think of at least five questions your reader would be likely to ask in order to buy into the scenario above.

THE CHEAT TO AVOID: Failing to anticipate and answer an obvious question.

MICHAEL SEARS

A Feeling for Location and Culture

MICHAEL SEARS is a professor of computer science at the University of the Witwatersrand in Johannesburg, South Africa, and is one half of the writing team Michael Stanley. The duo has written several mystery short stories and three novels set in southern Africa. Their latest novel is *Death of the Mantis* (HarperCollins, 2011).

E lsewhere in this book (and in others on writing), you will see the phrase "Show, don't tell." What this means is that one wants the environment, culture, sense of place, and so on to be revealed through the characters and the plot. The reader of fiction doesn't want a travelogue or a tour guide. It's the story (especially in a mystery) that holds the reader's interest, and it's the characters that make it come alive. So sense of place and culture is really the background to a picture that shows real people engaged in doing interesting things.

The protagonist in our novels is a large, overweight detective in the Criminal Investigation Department in Botswana. His nickname is Kubu, which means hippopotamus in Setswana—the language spoken by almost everyone in the country. Right away we have a small start to the sense of place. Kubu is easy to pronounce (koo-boo) and remember, and more evocative than Hippo would be.

Returning to the theme of telling versus showing, telling is usually a narrative giving the reader pieces of information or descriptions that the writer thinks are interesting in their own right, will build up background, or will help with plot. But characters can tell, too. Take a look at this:

On his way to the scene of the murder near Ganzi, Kubu stopped his vehicle under a tree in a dry riverbed. He had a long drink of water and ate a sandwich.

He turned to Sergeant Nledi. "Most rivers in Botswana are actually dry," he said. "But it's interesting how the trees still grow along the river verges because their roots go down to the water table—not that far below the surface—and they can get moisture there." He glanced up into the rolling dunes that headed out from the riverbed. "There's no moisture up there," he continued. "You'll find nothing but hardy succulents, hoarding the moisture from dew, growing in that loose sand."

Kubu was interested to see many animal tracks in the riverbed— even some from birds. One could follow those to where the animal had gone, *he thought. The sand is a sheet on which the past is written.*

One could probably get away with the first two sentences followed by the last three—assuming that following tracks in the sand is going to be important for the plot. As for the rest, it's a lecture on desert ecology. If readers were after that, they'd have taken a course.

The next piece is adapted from our first Detective Kubu novel, *A Carrion Death*. The environment is the same as the last piece. Bongani, an ecologist, and Andries, a game ranger, discover a body partially eaten by wild animals. Andries believes it's the result of a tourist getting lost in the desert; Bongani thinks otherwise.

Bongani looked at the area around the corpse. Acacia thorn trees, typical of Kalahari stream verges, scattered along the edges of the dry river. The riverbanks consisted of mud baked to hardness by the sun. From there scattered tufts of grass spread away from the bank, becoming less frequent as they battled the encroaching sand.

The two men stood under one of the trees, its canopy cutting off the heat, its roots sucking moisture from the subterranean water. The body sprawled on the edge of a mess of twigs, leaves, and branches, which had fallen to the ground over the years. Behind it lay the sand bed of the long-vanished river, patterned with tracks of animals, some old with the edges of the imprints crumbling, and some as recent as the hyena they'd disturbed.

Bongani focused further up and down the river. The wind, animals, and the hard stream verge could explain the lack of footprints, but a vehicle track would last for years in these conditions.

"Where's the vehicle?" he asked.

"He'll have got stuck in the dunes and tried to walk out," Andries replied.

Bongani turned to stare at Andries. "So let's see. Your tourist has enough knowledge of local geography to realize that following the watercourse will be the easy way back to camp. However, he doesn't realize how much dangerous game he may encounter in the river. And, by the way, he's working on his suntan at the same time because he sets off naked."

Andries looked down. "What makes you think he was naked?"

"Well, do you see any cloth scraps? The animals wouldn't eat them, certainly not with bone and bits of sinew still left. And what about shoes? Animals won't eat those either."

If this piece works, it's because we are interested in the interplay between the two men, and in what the environment surrounding the body is telling us about what happened. Inevitably we are led to it being murder, and Andries's theory is rejected. The issue of the tracks is of immediate importance to the story.

Culture is a harder issue than environment because readers make comparisons with what they know—their own culture and background—and inevitably make value judgments. If they have identified with the character, this may produce conflict rather than understanding.

For example, witchdoctors play a powerful role in southern African tribal culture, and this is reflected today in the urban environment as well. There is nothing surprising about a woman shopping for potions in a traditional medicine store in downtown Johannesburg while speaking on her cell phone, yet this strikes a Western reader as quite odd. When you analyze it, however, the woman has only the faintest idea how the cell phone technology works and similar understanding of how the magic of the potion works. If anything, she probably feels more comfortable with the traditional remedy. Again, the reader is likely to be more convinced by being shown this than by being told.

The term "witchdoctor" itself is contentious and is often used to cover a wide range of professionals from traditional healers to sorcerers who use human body parts for black magic. (Would you have chosen the word "professionals" to use in that sentence?)

Later in *A Carrion Death*, Bongani is hounded by a witchdoctor he knows only as the Old Man. His Western education and scientific training battle with his inherent beliefs shaped by his upbringing in a small rural village. Here is a selection from a scene:

> The Old Man closed the door and sat opposite Bongani. He nodded in terse greeting. Suddenly he took the lion-skin pouch in his right hand and, before Bongani could pull back, grasped his right hand. Bongani stared at the Old Man's hand. It felt like dry bone, warmed by the sun.
>
> Then the Old Man reached across with his left hand, took Bongani's left, their arms crossing over the desk. Bongani felt the hand suddenly cold as death. Colder. As though the witchdoctor had been carrying something frozen. The chill spread to Bongani. With a small cry he jerked both his hands free and jumped up.

Some Western readers have found the reactions of such an educated person to a witchdoctor hard to believe; yet these are everyday occurrences in southern Africa.

EXERCISE

Choose a country or an area other than where you live or grew up—preferably one which is not too similar to your own, but one in which you have spent some time, perhaps a few visits or perhaps you were there once for a reasonable length of time.

The body of a murder victim is discovered by a local, and the police arrive. Write a short piece describing the scene from the point of view of the person who discovers the body. Try to show some aspect or aspects of the country and its people in the ensuing events. You'll probably find there are some important pieces of information that you need and don't have. Research on the Internet to help fill those gaps.

ROBERT BROWNE

The Parts People Skip

ROBERT BROWNE has written several novels under his own and other names. His most recent work, *The Paradise Prophecy*, was published in July 2011 by Dutton.

One of our best American writers, Elmore Leonard, has famously said that when he's writing he tries to "leave out the parts that people skip."

But what exactly does he mean by this?

Readers start skimming when they lose interest. When they want you to get on with things. When they're not as engaged by the story as they should be.

Your job as a novelist is to make sure they're always engaged. You want them to pick up your book at ten p.m. and not be able to go to bed, because they just have to find out what happens.

So how do you do this?

First, you have to know what those skippable parts are. . . .

EXERCISE

We learn more by simply reading other authors' work than we do from a hundred of these exercises, but if you're reading with an eye toward learning, you have to do it with a critical mind.

This is difficult if you're reading an author you thoroughly enjoy. You often find yourself wrapped up in the warmth of a familiar embrace—the comfort of his or her prose—and forget that you're here to learn. So what I'd suggest is that you look for books by authors you've never read before and get to work.

When you start, read only for pleasure. Don't let your inner critic come out until you find your mind straying from the page. And when that happens, ask yourself, "Why?"

Why am I suddenly losing interest here?

There are a number of things to consider as you read; things that you should apply to your own work when you finally sit down to write.

Here they are in no particular order:

Is the prose style simple and economic and clear?

An author can certainly be clever and artistic, but should never sacrifice economy and clarity for the sake of art. Much of that art, in fact, is writing in a way that the sentences and paragraphs and pages flow from one to the next, giving the reader no choice but to hang on to every word. And clarity is always important. If a reader is confused about what is going on, he or she may well give up on you.

Is the story bogged down by too much description?

Descriptive passages can be quite beautiful, but an author's job is to weigh whether or not they're necessary. Are they slowing the story down?

Gregory MacDonald, the author of the Fletch books, once said that because we live in a post-television world, it is no longer necessary to describe everything. We all know what the Statue of Liberty looks like because we've seen it on TV. We've seen just about everything on TV, and probably even more on the Internet. So, an author should limit descriptions to only what's absolutely necessary to make the story work.

Let's face it. Saying something as simple as "The place was a dump. Several used syringes lay on the floor next to a ratty mattress with half its stuffing gone" is often more than enough to get the message across.

Is the author teasing his or her readers?

One of the biggest mistakes I see aspiring writers make is that they try to reveal too much about character motivation and story too soon. An author's job—as crass as it might sound—is to manipulate the reader. To keep the reader reading. Turning those pages.

Imagine meeting people for the first time, and they tell you everything there is to know about them. Where they were born, where they went to school, how many affairs they've had, how many brothers and sisters, their favorite color, their favorite food, and so forth. What makes people interesting to us is that all of these things are revealed over a long period of time. We get to know them gradually, rather than all at once. They are a mystery that must be unraveled.

The same holds true with storytelling. You manipulate your readers by constantly creating questions in their minds. Why is she doing that? Where is she going? What happened to her in the past that makes her afraid of confronting him?

If we know it all up front, we'll lose interest fast.

Do the characters have a series of goals?

Most stories will involve a central character who wants something. In a thriller, for instance, that may be something very big. The hero wants to stop the bad guy from, say, blowing up the federal building. But if that's all the story is about, then the reader is probably yawning already.

If you give the hero a series of goals—smaller points he or she must reach (both internally and externally) before finally reaching that ultimate goal, then your reader will never lose interest.

Does the author create compelling characters?

If we don't create characters who are interesting in themselves, who have internal struggles we can relate to, who have fears we understand, who have a goal that makes sense to us on a personal level, then it doesn't matter how cleverly we plot our novels.

The readers won't care.

There are many different ways to approach characterization, and no single way will work for every author, but the old axiom "Character is story" will always apply.

Hopefully, all of the above will help you understand what "leave out the parts that people skip" means, and when you sit down for a critical look at your own work, you'll find ways to make it more compelling.

The number-one rule of writing is this: Don't be boring.

HARLEY JANE KOZAK

The Telling Detail

HARLEY JANE KOZAK's debut novel, *Dating Dead Men*, won the Agatha, Anthony, and Macavity awards, and it was followed by *Dating Is Murder*, *Dead Ex*, and *A Date You Can't Refuse*. Her short prose has appeared in *Ms.*, *Soap Opera Digest*, *The Sun*, and *Santa Monica Review*, and in the anthologies *Mystery Muses*, *This Is Chick-Lit*, *A Hell of a Woman*, *Butcher Knives and Body Counts*, *Crimes by Moonlight*, and *The Rich and the Dead*, edited by Nelson DeMille.

Mysteries and thrillers are famous for their large casts of characters. Typically, you need a victim, a good guy, a bad guy, some allies for the good guy, friends for the bad guy, survivors for the victim, enemies of the good guy, maybe a romantic interest or two, a couple of cops, and a bunch of potential killers. Perhaps a pet. Unless your reader is accustomed to Dostoyevsky, that's a lot of people to keep straight.

Of course, other literary genres can be densely populated, too, but mysteries and thrillers call for a snappy pace that's rarely compatible with long character biographies and lengthy descriptions of, for example, shoes—stuff that might feel right at home in literary fiction or romance.

Enter the Telling Detail. This is a description of a character (or a place, state of mind, weather) that takes up relatively little space on the page, but is disproportionately delightful. Or creepy. Intriguing. Evocative.

I find the Telling Detail useful for dealing with two very different problems.

First, there's the TMI (too much information) syndrome. When you give a lot of page time to someone, or even just a name, you're telling your reader, "Listen up. This girl's important to my story."

But if that girl is there only to drive the cab that transports your Hero from Point A to Point B on page 22, you don't want the reader to expend any extra energy on her, subliminally waiting for—let's call her Ursula—to reappear in the story, Ursula with the mother who died of scurvy when Ursula was in kindergarten, leading to the years in foster care, community college, an abusive marriage, a move cross-country, and ultimately her own cab company.

Unless Ursula's going to die in chapter 5, or reappear to rescue your Hero in chapter 34, save that reader's emotional investment for your Hero, or your Hero's cat. Maybe all we need to know about this cab-driving girl is that she's wearing a Mets baseball cap, when the story is set in Salt Lake City.

On the opposite end of the spectrum, there's the "Steve who?" dilemma. Let's say Steve, whom you introduce early on, walks into the plot every hundred pages to do something important, then goes back to Brazil. If your reader says, "Steve? Who the hell is Steve?" at these key moments, it pulls her out of the story.

But it's mind-numbing to read identifying tags such as "Steve, Harriet's sister-in-law's brother" every time Steve puts in an appearance. Not all details are telling; some are dull. Learning someone's age, eye color, or height, in inches or centimeters, is not compelling, which is why we don't consider drivers' licenses literature.

Ditto stock descriptions and overworked adjectives. For instance, you can tell us that a woman is blond and beautiful, or you can tell us—if you're Raymond Chandler, writing *Farewell, My Lovely*—that she's "blonde. A blonde to make a bishop kick a hole in a stained glass window."

So perhaps Steve, Harriet's sister-in-law's brother, is middle-aged, plain to the point of invisibility except for one small detail: his nails. Steve has a French manicure.

Or let's take William. William has a lot of body hair, peeping out from beneath his shirt collar and all over his arms and the backs of his hands. Sarah is transfixed by his hair, stares at it while he snaps on latex gloves, is so distracted by it that she can hardly hear what he's saying about cervical cancer. With that much hair, she thinks, William should be an auto mechanic or a big game hunter, something other than a gynecologist. This gives us a mental bookmark, so that when we encounter gynecologist William later on, we stand a chance of remembering him, or at least remembering Sarah's feeling about him, without having to flip back through the pages to find him.

EXERCISE

Here's the exercise: Find some people. Real people are best (as opposed to TV people) standing in a line, riding the subway, waiting on you at Starbucks. Jot down as many Telling Details as you can, one per person.

Avoid these words: pretty, handsome, beautiful, ugly, cute, awesome, or anything you'd see in ad copy or a political campaign. Brevity is fine, but not critical. Sometimes the Telling Detail takes a single word and expands on it. "Underweight" becomes "She was thin. Not just 'I watch my carbs' slender, but 'I swallowed a tapeworm' skinny." "Elderly" becomes "She had grandmother hair, so fragile and fine and soft it might have been lint plucked from a clothes dryer and stuck atop her head."

The world abounds with singularity, often better than what our imagination can supply when we're sitting in front of our computer screens. The purpose of this exercise is to find fresh ways of describing human beings in an age of e-mail, tweets, and online profiles ("Likes family values & walks on the beach"). To paint a better picture. To surprise ourselves.

ANDY STRAKA

Sea of Troubles: The Art of Outlining

ANDY STRAKA has published five novels. He is the Shamus Award–winning and Anthony- and Agatha-nominated author of the Frank Pavlicek mystery series featuring a former NYPD detective turned Virginia private investigator and falconer. A licensed falconer and cofounder of the popular Crime Wave at the annual Virginia Festival of the Book, Straka is also the author of *Record of Wrongs*, which *Mystery Scene* magazine calls "a first-rate thriller." He lives with his family in Virginia.

That incredible idea for a crime novel has finally begun to take shape—at least in your head. What do you do now?

Call your mother? Talk to your writers' group? Rack your brain to come up with a great logline or blockbuster title? Jot down some poignant thoughts? How about just sit down and start writing the story?

Many would argue—especially when it comes to writing the mystery—that your first task is to build a detailed outline of your book, fleshing out each of your characters and meticulously planning every plot twist. After all, you can't build a house without a blueprint. A detailed outline allows you to anticipate any potential conflicts or difficulties, to think globally without being weighed down by the minutia of each scene, and to avoid wasting precious time on subplots that turn into dead ends. Indeed, a simple online search will uncover dozens of tools, from books to software programs, purporting to help you accomplish this apparently critical yet daunting task. It all sounds logical, doesn't it?

Not so fast.

There is a great deal to be said for the value of outlining. I outline some myself. But just as often I don't, and in my experience if you ask published crime novelists, many of them quite successful, whether they outline, you may be in for a surprise: their answers will be all over the board.

The late great Donald Westlake, for example, was once asked a question about outlining at a prestigious book conference affiliated with a major university. In the audience were scores of literary writers, each looking to glean precious bits of information to help them with their own fiction.

"I subscribe to a technique I like to call 'narrative push,'" Westlake deadpanned.

"Narrative push?" The questioner sat forward in her seat. "What's that?"

All around her other members of the audience—the serious writers at least—sat a little taller in their seats as well, papers at the ready, pens raised. They were hoping the questioner had uncovered Westlake's magic formula, the secret that allowed him to pen over a hundred novels and books of nonfiction, winning the Edgar Award three times, and earning the distinction as a Grand Master of the Mystery Writers of the America.

"It's quite simple, actually," Westlake explained. "I make everything up as I go along."

Whether Westlake's technique will work for you, the truth is we've all read books or seen movies where the action appears to clip along in picture-perfect cadence, the characters seem pulled straight out of central casting, and everything is supposed to blend together in some grand and glorious scheme guaranteed to leave us dazzled.

Except it doesn't. Not only does the story fail to dazzle, it falls flat. Overscripted and overwritten—we the audience sense that the life has been drained from the story. We feel duped. Living, breathing characters don't behave like that, actions and events don't pile up so neatly, and we've been cheated of the spontaneity that breeds sleight of hand and the element of surprise.

So, to outline or not to outline, that is the question. Whether (as Shakespeare more skillfully put it) "'tis nobler in the mind to suffer the slings and arrows of outrageous fortune, or to take arms against a sea of troubles."

The answer lies within you.

This is the real alchemy of creating a novel—each writer must take blank sheet in hand and through trial and error come up with the technique that works best for them. Some writers will use a series of note cards. Some will use a storyboard. Some will just dive right in and write until they can write no more. While others may sit in a dark room for hours imagining the tale and then craft a meticulously detailed outline before ever starting the story.

Still others, such as myself, may use a hybrid technique, writing a little, then outlining a little, mixing in organizational notes with the prose, using the story as driver but stepping back on occasion to outline a few chapters ahead.

Whatever method is used, the details you map out must serve to make the story stronger. A finely crafted mystery will build tension and suspense, layer upon layer, without the reader being aware. The best crime novels contain surprises, maybe a startling twist, and for good measure a red herring thrown in. They do not achieve this magic in any formulaic manner, but in a way that is true to the characters and setting. If a plot point is not organic to the story, it must be eliminated.

Many ask if I have an ending in mind as I write, and I always answer yes, but it is often a murky generality that is best characterized by E. L. Doctorow's oft-quoted trope about writing a novel: "It's like driving a car at night. You never see further than your headlights, but you can make the whole trip that way." In my novel *Cold Quarry*, for example, all I had starting out was the opening line: "The ski-masked man balanced the business end of the twelve-gauge Mossberg Persuader against my temple with a shaky hand." I had an idea that the man might be young and might be part of some extremist or paramilitary group, but nothing more. Even the details of the shotgun-toting character's life were unclear at the start—he was behind a mask, after all.

As the writer, you will need to know your own mind to discover what works best for you. In the beginning all you may have is a silhouette—a special character and an inciting incident, maybe a great surprise ending. To go from vague shape to rich Technicolor will not be an easy journey, but it will be worth the effort.

In the end you will find yourself the author of a crime novel that works.

EXERCISE

1. Pick a chapter or an entire section of a novel that has been giving you difficulties. Try making an outline using note cards to fill in the details of each scene. Also use the cards for character sketches.

2. Next, take the same chapter and try outlining the action using the old-fashioned format of headings that break down into greater and greater detail.

3. See if you can find an outlining or writing software program that you like. (Most of these have free trials.) Try outlining the same chapter using this program.

4. Still working with the same chapter, try writing deeper into the story—making it up as you go along—stopping to fill in details of an outline any time you feel stuck.

5. After you have finished the above, decide which one of these techniques works best for you, or make up your own hybrid technique.

6. Try out this technique on a favorite novel or bestseller. See how the outline you create from the bestseller's chapter differs from your own, and look for clues to help improve your own story's outline.

PLOT THICKENING

Compelling Story Structure

NANCY MEANS WRIGHT

Discover Plot and Character
Through the Journey Quest

NANCY MEANS WRIGHT has published sixteen books, including five mystery novels, most recently, *Midnight Fires: A Mystery with Mary Wollstonecraft* (2010) and its sequel, *The Nightmare* (2011). Her children's mysteries received both an Agatha Award and Agatha nomination for Best Children's/YA Novel. Short stories have appeared in *American Literary Review*, *Ellery Queen's Mystery Magazine*, Level Best Books anthologies, and elsewhere. Longtime teacher and a Bread Loaf Scholar for a first novel, Nancy lives in Middlebury, Vermont, with her spouse and two Maine coon cats.

I've been fascinated by mythology ever since I studied Greek and Roman myths in ninth grade and then read Homer's *Odyssey*. In college I rediscovered these myths in art and literature, and in the archetypal images of the psychiatrist Jung. Later I came across the philosopher Nietzsche, who claimed that in our sleep and dreams "we pass through the whole thought of earlier humanity." I was amazed to think that my fears, doubts, and desires had already been experienced by my forebears in their quest for fulfillment. To know that in my dreams I'd been dipping into some Great Unconscious!

But it wasn't until years later, when I completed my first mystery novel, that I fully understood this quest. I had gone through a traumatic divorce and left my Vermont family and friends to teach in a small liberal arts college in New York's mid-Hudson Valley. I felt like a pariah, dropped into a kind of limbo. I wanted to write—but I had to have a day job. The novel I'd started before the divorce sat in an unpacked box. I didn't know where I was going with it anyway—why continue? I could write only short poems that ended (as T. S. Eliot wrote) "not with a bang but a whimper."

Then, for my birthday, a friend gave me a copy of Joseph Campbell's *The Power of Myth*. I read, and reread, the chapter titled "The Hero's Adventure." In it, Campbell wrote: "Where we had thought to travel outward, we will come to the center of our own existence. And where we had thought to be alone, we will be with all the world."

Was it possible? I went on to study this journey quest, in which the reluctant hero or heroine finally accepts the call, despite the hardships involved, and sets out on a series of adventures beyond the safe, known world—often in search of something missing or lost. The journey is both physical and interior: a search for answers inside the self. As the seeker journeys into this mysterious "underworld," he or she meets with trials, tests, temptations to overcome and monsters to subdue. There are moments of doubt and despair. Yet with luck, the hero will encounter an altruistic person, male or female—perhaps a romantic counterpart—to help achieve the goal. (I did soon after, as it happened, but that's another story.)

The seeker ultimately prevails, and returns "home" with a renewed understanding of self, the world, and of his or her place within it. The hero has been thinking one way, and now must discover a new way "of being or becoming." Campbell cites the trials of seekers as diverse as Buddha, Odysseus, King Arthur, Jesus, Jonah and his whale, Martin Luther King, Jr., and protagonists in novels by Thomas Mann and James Joyce, even in *Star Wars*.

Intrigued, I thought: *Why not apply this archetypal journey quest to my abortive mystery?* Before my divorce, I'd read about a pair of farmer-brothers who distrusted banks; one night they were assaulted and left for dead. The police found the assailants after they'd thrown the stolen cash about in bars and diners—and the money reeked of barn. I felt I had to write a mystery—though, at that point, I'd published only mainstream fiction. I changed the brothers to a wife and husband and opened the novel with the break-in. I introduced a feisty dairy farmer neighbor, who, as amateur sleuth, determines to find the villains. Then came the divorce, and I abandoned the novel on page 26.

Now I couldn't wait to work on it again. This time my primary concern was not the story line, but my farmer Ruth. I would let the plot unfold through the passions, strengths, and flaws of her character. Though initially reluctant to take time from her never-ending barn work, Ruth is pulled into the story through anger at the husband who left her, the injustice of the attack on her neighbors, and concern for the loss of Vermont's farms. As time goes on, she is severely tested: her barn on fire, a family zealot who undermines her sleuthing, the bullying and disappearance of her young son, the mounting pressures to sell farmland to eager developers. A former love comes to her aid, and together they overcome the evils and return to "normalcy." But the trauma has altered their thinking: "Those are pearls that were their eyes," as Shakespeare wrote in *The Tempest*.

With the journey quest in my head, I didn't need to outline—I let the novel develop organically, like Ruth's farm, and named it *Mad Season*. St. Martin's Press published five Ruth Willmarth novels in all, ending the series with Ruth's cows quarantined for mad cow disease (not all adventures end happily). I continued my quests in two middle-grade mysteries. Now I have embarked on a series in the persona of fiery Mary Wollstonecraft, who in 1792 wrote the groundbreaking *A Vindication of the Rights of Woman*, for which many called her "a hyena in petticoats." Her life was a continual quest for women's rights, social justice, and recognition as a serious writer. Yet it was filled with adversity: the childbirth death of a beloved friend; abandonment during the French Revolution by a lover whose child she bore; two suicide attempts; and then death at age thirty-eight, just after she'd found fulfillment with writer William Godwin and given birth to the future Mary Shelley, who wrote *Frankenstein*.

Mary Wollstonecraft was possessed of such a brilliant, inquiring (yet conflicted) mind, so intolerant of injustice and sham, that I felt she would make an extraordinary sleuth. Combining true history with mystery, of course, has been a challenge—in a sense, two journey quests in one. But to date I've completed two books in the series, and, in the process, the writing has transformed my own thinking. As I hope it might alter yours.

EXERCISE

Create a mysterious journey quest of your own. Think of it as departure, initiation (misadventure), return, and transformation. As you go, consider the thoughts and questions below.

DEPARTURE: Where is "home" at the start of your novel? Describe it lovingly and keep it in mind throughout the novel. What is your protagonist's personal quest? To find a killer, or is it more than that? To recover a job, health, a former love, an estranged family member, faith, or self-confidence? Something, that is, to draw the seeker into the quest, so that the journey is physical and mental (spiritual). What does this person desire most of all? (Each scene should renew this question.) Will your novel open with these dramatic *quest*-ions to pull in the reader?

Perhaps, too, the object is tangible, one that might bring about more deaths (think of Arthur's holy grail). Let the seeker use an object, or prop in the search, a talisman of sorts, a good luck charm. And don't forget the secrets the sleuth holds and must unravel during the journey. Finally, how long should this opening be? If the book is to be some three hundred pages, the opening might be only ten or twenty pages at the most.

INITIATION: Now the tension starts to rise, along with the obstacles thrown in the seeker's path. What trials will the seeker encounter? What adversaries will the seeker encounter during the quest, and who are they? Perhaps the killer? Others with motives and secrets of their own? A pain-in-the-butt relative, boss, or colleague who torments the seeker and tries to sabotage the quest? Might the protagonist, too, become a suspect? Will someone try to maim or kill the seeker? Harm that person's loved ones? Will the seeker be plagued by self-doubts to the point of almost giving up?

This might be the time to introduce a helpmate, perhaps a romantic one who has been present all the time but whom the seeker has just come to appreciate. The helpmate can support the seeker through the black moments, and be sure to lace those moments with torments, pitfalls, plot twists. Give each scene a forward motion, a raison d'être, a hook ending. Some writers think of a novel as a series of acts (as I do, from my theater past). Let the seeker's "underworld" expand in each of three or four acts, come to climax each time, with a reversal, and then remission (rather than intermission); then climb again until the final dramatic climax, what I call "the obligatory theatrics."

RETURN AND TRANSFORMATION: Now the tunnel leads upward toward the light. Let the denouement scene, the unraveling of plot, be quick, no more than a dozen pages, with perhaps a final twist to delight and surprise the reader. The seeker must have a moment of enlightenment, an epiphany of sorts: *So that's how it happened! That's who it was! If only I could have seen....* The epiphany concerns not only the killer revealed, but a change in the sleuth's consciousness. In what way? Naïve at first, he or she has now seen the dark side of the world, and perhaps internally as well? Could the seeker, too, have killed (come close to killing)?

Finally, remember to show all this, with a minimum of telling. Above all, the seeker should come home a different person. Even home will not be the same. To quote Longfellow, "Things are not what they seem."

SIMON BRETT

Controlling the Flow of Information

SIMON BRETT is the author of over eighty books, many of them mysteries. He has written the Charles Paris, Mrs. Pargeter, Fethering, and Blotto and Twinks series. His stand-alone thriller *A Shock to the System* was adapted into a film starring Michael Caine.

A s a writer, you have one enormous advantage over your readers or audience. You know the whole story, and they don't.

Except in very rare circumstances, you don't start off knowing the whole story. You begin with an idea, which hopefully leads to other ideas, which in turn act as springboards for further ideas. Characters begin to develop, as do conflicts between those characters. Settings become more solid and pertinent in your mind. A plot emerges. Gradually your story takes shape.

There's no right or wrong way of building a story. Some writers don't start the actual writing until they have the whole scenario worked out in their minds. Others begin with a sentence that intrigues and see where it leads them. Some regard the first draft as the exciting part of the process—telling themselves the story—and resent any changes that have to be made afterward. Others find the first draft a terrible bore, creating a great block of material from which, rather like a sculptor with a mass of stone, they will carve out and perfect their work of art. For them the fun of writing lies in cutting away the dross, refining and reshaping.

But by whatever process a writer arrives at it, there comes a point when the whole story is known to them. And what they then have to decide is how much of that story they want their readers or audience to know at any given point in the narrative.

This is true in all writing, but particularly so in the two areas in which I specialize, crime fiction and comedy. The effect of both is weakened by giving out too little or too much information. For example, I remember my sister once saying to me, "I've just heard this very good joke about the Lunchpack of Notre Dame." I asked her to tell me more and she gave me the setup question: "What's put in a plastic box and swings from a bell-rope?" I said I didn't know and she told me the punch line: "The Lunchpack of Notre Dame!" She was disappointed at my lack of reaction to the joke, but then, she had given me rather too much information too soon.

And that's how storytelling works. The writer feeds out the narrative gradually, withholding clues and details until the optimum moment of revelation. A lot of a writer's planning will involve thoughts like: *If that's going to happen there, then it must have been set up earlier.*

For this reason, one of the most difficult parts of any book, play, or screenplay is the exposition. A lot of information has to be conveyed in as short a time as possible. In the visual media it's easier. How people look, the environment in which they live, their clothes, their possessions can all increase viewers' knowledge of their character. And all that information comes across the moment most characters walk onstage or appear on the screen.

In a book you don't have that shortcut. Everything needs to be described, but it's up to the writer to decide how much is necessary. And here the general rule is: Go for the minimum. If a character's height is going to be important to your story, tell your readers how tall he is. If it isn't, don't bother. Two-page descriptions of every new character in the manner of Charles Dickens are completely unnecessary. The same goes for where they went to school, what their parents did for a living, how many siblings they had, whether their childhood was happy, and an infinite number of other details. Let your readers do some work for themselves; let them create their own pictures in their minds. Supply only the kind of information that is going to be relevant in the story you're telling.

Some writers, I am aware, say they cannot begin a novel without knowing all the characters in detail, without having built up lengthy dossiers with all their personal data. In my view that's just another displacement activity—and no one is more skilled in displacement activity than writers. Anything that puts off that dreadful moment of actually having to *write* is fulsomely welcomed.

The importance of exposition generally means that the opening of any piece of writing is the bit that gets most rewritten. As new ideas emerge in the course of creating the story, new information has to be injected into the already set-up chapters or scenes. And it's a task with which most writers have difficulties. If you ever feel uncertain about your own skills as a writer of exposition, I recommend that you take down from your bookshelves the *Complete Works* of William Shake-speare and turn to *The Tempest*. In act 1, scene 2, of that classic play you will find one of the worst pieces of exposition you will ever encounter. The first 284 lines set up the backstory to the action in what is effectively a monologue by Prospero, with brief interjections from his daughter, Miranda, along the lines of "What happened next, Dad?" It is inept and tedious. So even the greats had their problems with exposition.

But there's no way around it. Your readers or audience have to be given that information somehow. And it is in that "how" that the writer's skills are really tested. Particularly in a crime novel, the plot is often dependent on a detail that the readers cannot claim they haven't been told of, but which is slipped into the narrative in a way that doesn't draw attention to it. Something apparently trivial can frequently turn out to be of pivotal importance.

The skill required to shuffle in this kind of information can be compared to that of the conjuror. As he uses his patter to distract the audience from what he's doing with his hands, so a crime novelist has to find his own means of distraction to disguise the importance of certain details. All you have to do is to obey the basic rules of storytelling. Make your scene so dramatic—or so funny, or so intriguing—that your readers have an emotional response to your writing and almost unconsciously assimilate the facts that you have so subtly shoehorned into the narrative.

Never forget that a book is an interactive medium. The relationship between writer and reader may develop and change, but it never disappears. And a skillful writer will be constantly aware of the effect that his or her words have on the reader at any given point in the action. That's what storytelling is about.

EXERCISE

A good way of honing your skills at controlling the flow of information is to write a page of dialogue that contains the fact you are trying to hide. Say, for instance, the fact is: "The pastor had once been a professional footballer." Think of the various ways in which, without actually stating it in so many words, you can get that information across. The aim of the exercise is to make the little scene of dialogue you write so compelling that your readers become more concerned about the drama of the situation than about listening for the facts it contains. And the only restriction placed on what you write is that you are not allowed to hide your important fact in a catalogue of many.

This exercise works even better with a group of writers. The tutor or moderator of the group writes different pieces of simple information on separate scraps of paper, and each participant then picks one slip out of a hat or bag. Each person writes a section of dialogue. When everyone has finished, the pieces of work are read out in turn, and the other participants have to try to guess what the hidden snippet of information is. The exercise combines the fun element of a party game with a useful lesson in writers' diversionary tactics.

JIM NAPIER

Putting Your Protagonist in Jeopardy

JIM NAPIER is a crime writer and reviewer of crime fiction and a former teacher of crime fiction and creative writing. His Deadly Diversions website features reviews, articles, and interviews with many of today's leading crime writers, as well as resources for readers and writers.

The phrase "It's a real page-turner" is one of the highest commendations a crime writer can receive, and is sweet music to the ears—often accompanied by that other delightful sound, the melodious jingling of cash registers!

Certainly it's important to have interesting characters immersed in a believable plot grounded in a colorful setting, but the heart of every page-turner is *suspense*, the fear that something terrible is about to happen, and likely on the very next page. In a way, reading a thriller is like driving by a highway accident: we don't want to look, something tells us not to, but we do anyway.

The difference is that you don't have to feel guilty after reading a thriller.

Creating fear in your readers that something terrible is about to happen to someone they care about means creating a character they can relate to in a positive way (which is not to say the protagonist has to be likable). Then you must exploit some vulnerability of the character, which could be physical or psychological, or simply a matter of circumstance—being in the wrong place at the wrong time.

Just think of Daphne du Maurier's timeless masterpiece *Rebecca*, and the tension between the young and naïve bride of wealthy widower Maxim de Winter and the menacing housekeeper and self-appointed keeper of the flame, Mrs. Danvers.

In its most effective form, suspense or fear is *cumulative*, playing off the readers' own phobias in ever-building increments, foreshadowing what is just around the corner.

Two examples. In the film SLEEPING WITH THE ENEMY, Laura (the character played by Julia Roberts) flees her abusive and obsessive-compulsive husband, Martin. Laura fakes her own death at sea and moves to a small town, establishing a new identity. She even tentatively begins to forge a new relationship. But her husband suspects his wife is not dead and sets out to find her. When she returns home one day she notices that the canned goods in the kitchen cupboards have been meticulously arranged, their labels uniformly facing the front. Alarmed, she hurries to the bathroom to see whether the towels she'd so casually thrown down that morning are still strewn about. They are all immaculately arranged on the towel bars. There is no room for doubt: Martin has tracked her down.

In similar fashion, consummate thriller writer Peter James sets up the central premise of his thriller *Dead Simple*: a young businessman, Michael (not the protagonist, but a great example nonetheless), is about to be married. Four of his closest friends throw him a stag party, but with a difference: he's a practical joker, and at one time or another they've each been his victim. Now it's payback time. After getting him pleasantly sloshed, his mates drive him to a secluded site in the countryside, where they place him in a coffin and bury him in a shallow grave, with a breathing tube running to the surface. Then they set off for a nearby pub to let him sweat for a few hours. But fate has a way of upsetting the best of plans; as they enter a nearby road the driver is distracted, and the van is hit head-on by a large truck; three of the pranksters are killed outright, and the fourth lies in a hospital in a coma, unable to tell anyone what they have done. Michael is utterly alone. While Michael awaits their return, confident they will not abandon him, fate deals him another surprise: the coffin—a cheap second they stole for the occasion—begins to leak groundwater. . . .

Each of these fine tales begins by establishing a sympathetic character, then sets up a threatening situation, and heightens the suspense in layers, drawing the reader into the victim's terror. In SLEEPING WITH THE ENEMY, Roberts's character is alone and vulnerable. By the time she realizes that her husband has tracked her down, it's night-time, and she must cope with a maniac who insists, "I can't live without you. And I won't let you live without me."

In Peter James's *Dead Simple*, Michael confronts a litany of many people's phobias: he's confined in a small space, it's dark, water is seeping in, he's alone and helpless, and no one knows where he is. In each case the writer explores the vulnerability of a sympathetic protagonist who is utterly isolated in a seemingly hopeless situation.

Effectively creating suspense, then, is more than a matter of creating one particular aspect of a scene. A person hearing an unfamiliar noise is not, in itself, going to send chills up the reader's spine. But establish a recent history of such events, make the person blind and alone, cut her off from the outside world (a psychopath has severed the phone lines), and *then* make the floorboards just outside her door squeak, and you're well on your way to holding your readers firmly in your grasp. (For a classic, gripping example of this, see the superb Audrey Hepburn film WAIT UNTIL DARK.)

EXERCISE

1. Everyone has phobias. Imagine your absolutely worst fear, and build a scene around it. Is it fear of fire? Water? Heights? Snakes? Imagine yourself in that situation, and then ask yourself what would make it *worse*.

   Suppose, for instance, you were lost in the woods, night was approaching, it was getting dangerously cold, and no one knew where you were. Now crank it up a notch: you are responsible for another person with you—a small, terrified child. Make a list of the sounds and sights and smells unique to that situation and combine them in a paragraph or two, adding them one by one to build the suspense. Don't forget to include your protagonist's reactions to each of these elements. Does she tighten her grip on the child so much that it hurts? Does she break out in a cold sweat, or try to put on a brave face and reassure the child? Does the child see through her act?

2. Imagine a setting that is familiar and pleasant—for example, a drive in the country on a clear, sunny day. Now introduce, one by one, unexpected events. A large black pickup truck appears in the mirror. The windows are tinted, and your protagonist can't see the driver. It gets closer, until the only thing visible in the protagonist's rearview mirror is the grille of the pickup. No one else is on the road. The truck behind him is relentless, pressing him on, nudging his rear bumper. Your protagonist tries to slow down, but the truck is more powerful. He picks up the cell phone on the seat beside him, only to discover that he's in a dead zone. Then, as he rounds a corner, his worst nightmare comes true: a road crew is working just ahead of him, and the way is completely blocked by a large, unyielding earthmoving machine. . . .

My final words of advice: Writing is (or should be) a vocation, not a job—have fun! Remember, if you're not happy with what you created, you can always hit the delete key. That's one huge advantage writers enjoy over sculptors!

HENRY PEREZ

Conflict! Conflict! Everywhere!

HENRY PEREZ is the author of the critically acclaimed thrillers *Killing Red* and *Mourn the Living*, a number-one Amazon Kindle bestseller. His latest book is *Raise the Dead*. He has worked as a newspaper reporter for more than a decade and as a television and video producer before that. Born in Cuba, he immigrated to the United States at a young age, and lives in the Chicago area with his family.

When in doubt, have a man come through a door with a gun in his hand.

—RAYMOND CHANDLER

You've written thirty to forty thousand words, and so far your manuscript is filled with complications and possibilities, but now you've hit a wall, and the narrative is beginning to slow, or possibly even stop. This can happen to new and veteran writers alike, often somewhere in the second act.

When it does occur, the cause is almost always the same—conflict—or rather the lack of it. This is a common problem for new writers who've spent a great deal of time polishing their core story, only to realize that no matter how strong it may be, there's just not enough there to sustain an entire novel. This can also signify that the story, and quite possibly its characters, are not layered and developed enough to engage a reader for four to six hundred pages. You need to add conflict.

There are two basic ways to remedy this. The first is to place new obstacles in the path of the protagonist. Doing so can give your story a spark, but if it's done too often or in a heavy-handed way, it can feel contrived and antagonize your readers. The other is to add a subplot or two to complicate your protagonist's life, and hamper their efforts.

The best option is a combination of the two, in which the subplot generates those complications that become obstacles for the protagonist. In this way, the problems that arise will seem more organic.

In my first thriller, *Killing Red*, newspaper reporter Alex Chapa must track down a woman who has been marked for death before her would-be killer finds her. That is the core plot that drives the story and sends Chapa off on his primary mission. But there are also two significant subplots. The first concerns Chapa's struggle to stay connected to his young daughter, from whom his ex-wife is keeping him. The second involves his ongoing issues at work, in an industry that is dying a painful death.

There are several points in each of my books where the main character's everyday life issues get in the way of his achieving the primary goal. These complications, and how my protagonist responds to them, help to build a more layered character, one who is not solely defined by the task at hand, while also helping to keep the story moving.

Secondary problems and the conflict they create can also be useful in revealing the character's backstory in a way that avoids clunky exposition or page-long info dumps—those annoying, seemingly endless paragraphs that bring the story to a screeching stop while the author tells the reader everything they need to know about a character.

EXERCISE

On more than one occasion, I've heard struggling writers say that they don't know how to add conflict to a plot that, in their minds, is already fully formed. They have created a terrific setup, know what their resolution will be, but have suddenly run out of dots to connect between one and the other. This exercise is designed to spark your imagination while using real-world situations and problems to add conflict to your story.

STEP 1
Keep a journal of your daily activities, focusing specifically on the conflicts you experience every day. I don't mean just disagreements with your significant other or arguments with a neighbor (though

those would be included), but all kinds of conflict, big or small. Anything that gets in the way of what you want or need to do.

Did you have to rush to work because you overslept this morning? That's conflict. Did you have to stop and think about whether to use a credit or debit card to pay for gas, because one is maxed out and there's not much cash left on the other? That's conflict. Write it down. Did you hear an office rumor that several jobs, perhaps even yours, may be lost to budget cuts? Write that down, too.

Just about all of us experience various forms of conflict every day. And while it may, hopefully, not be as large-scale or as life-threatening as the situations that fuel crime novels, these everyday complications can form the root of those larger problems.

Keep the journal for at least a week or two, perhaps as long as a month. Do not hesitate to write something down because you believe it may be too trivial. There's no reason to edit yourself in this process.

STEP 2

Now go back through your journal entries, pick out at least a half-dozen, and embellish them. Let your imagination go wild as you create mini-scenarios to explain the possible reasons behind each bit of conflict.

Maybe you overslept that morning last week because the strange noises coming from your next-door neighbor's house kept you awake all night. And now you realize that though you've seen the wife rushing to and from her car since then, you haven't seen the husband.

Perhaps the reason you have limited funds left in your account is that you loaned a few hundred dollars to your deadbeat cousin. That was two months ago, and you haven't heard from him since. And why does it seem there's more money gone from your account than the amount you lent him?

Could be you know the reason for those budget cuts everyone's worried about might have something to do with that young woman you saw getting into your boss's car a few weeks ago. And you recall the look of desperation on the boss's face when you walked into his office last week and caught him in the middle of a hushed telephone conversation.

Everyday issues have now been transformed into a neighbor who might have a murderous streak, a shady cousin who may be stealing from you, and a philandering boss who could be the victim of a blackmail scheme.

Do this with as many of your journal entries as you wish. And have fun with it.

STEP 3

Now let's apply this same approach to your protagonist. For the moment, don't concern yourself with what you already have on the page, in an outline, or in your head. Instead, let's go back to a month before your story begins.

What was a typical day like for your protagonist? What conflicts did they have to deal with? Which ones were resolved, and which lingered? Here's the key question: Which conflicts can you develop into subplots that can then be weaved into your narrative?

Creating a backstory for everyday events is also a useful approach to develop complications for, and give greater depth to, antagonists and to secondary characters as well.

You may be wondering whether you can skip the personal journal portion and go straight into your character's background. Of course you can. But using your own life experience as a template will often yield more useful and more inventive results.

JANE K. CLELAND

Avoiding Saggy Middles

JANE K. CLELAND is the author of the IMBA-bestselling and Agatha- and Anthony-nominated Josie Prescott Antiques Mystery series. The books are often reviewed as an *Antiques Roadshow* for mystery fans. *Consigned to Death* was named by *Library Journal* as one of only twenty-two core titles recommended for librarians seeking to build a "cozy" mystery collection, alongside novels by Agatha Christie and Dorothy L. Sayers.

Saggy middles are the bane of most mystery writers' existence. You've started with a bang (or a poisoning or a clunk on the head); you've introduced your characters and laid the groundwork so that key suspects with credible motives are on your readers' radar; and your detective has begun his or her investigation. You're somewhere about a quarter of the way through, and the pace has slowed to a crawl: the action has become predictable, and you can't think of how to pep it up.

The answer is to ratchet up the tension three separate times in the middle two quarters of the book. Kill someone, introduce suspense, or add a plot twist. This is easier said than done, of course, because nothing you do can be contrived or coincidental. All incidents must develop organically based on the characters; likewise, all character development must evolve naturally as a result of the incidents.

The best tension-inducing incidents involve ordinary events. While you're putting away groceries, for instance, you notice that a knife is missing from your knife block. The doorbell rings in the middle of the night, but when you peek out the peephole, no one's there. You're alone in an elevator with the doors closing, when suddenly an arm pushes in.

If you structure your novel in quarters, planning how to increase tension in the middle half is easier. In the first quarter, introduce the characters, set the scene, and kill someone. In the last quarter, weave all the plot threads into one cohesive whole, solve the crime, and resolve any outstanding issues. In the middle two quarters, increase tension by adding danger—three times.

For instance, let's say your book is 300 pages long. Between pages 75 (one quarter in) and 225 (three quarters in), add three incidents designed to pep up the 150 pages in between. For example, in the center chunk of my sixth Josie Prescott Antiques Mystery novel, *Deadly Threads*, I do the following:

1. Terrify Josie by having her hear weird noises while walking alone in a shadowy, cold warehouse;

2. Shoot Gretchen, Josie's employee, as Josie stands next to her—leaving the reader wondering if the bullet was intended for Josie; and

3. Burn Gretchen's home down while Josie, thinking Gretchen's inside, tries to rescue her.

Consider the first incident. Long before the middle of the book, you meet a gung-ho intern named Ava. She loves learning the antiques appraisal business, and is especially enamored of the vintage clothing collection Josie's just been hired to appraise. I've also planted (i.e., mentioned earlier) that Ava, like most of her college-age contemporaries, listens to music on her iPod every minute she can.

In the excerpt that follows, Josie is walking alone through her cavernous, dimly lit warehouse when she hears something odd, soft rustlings followed by tinny scratching sounds.

"Hello!" I called. "Is anyone here?"

Silence, then a scrape, followed by soft sounds, footsteps maybe, then another rustle and another scrape.

Why wasn't whoever was inside responding? I wondered. Maybe

a small animal had snuck in, a squirrel, perhaps. I wasn't scared ex-
actly, but it was eerie, standing there alone in a quasi-dark place,
hearing odd, unfamiliar noises. I told myself not to be silly, that I was
in my own building during working hours, that nothing could pos-
sibly be amiss. Still, as I started down the central aisle, I shivered as
if a cold breeze had blown through the warehouse.

The tension builds as Josie tiptoes past shadows that resemble people, her heart pounds and her pulse spikes because she knows that a killer is on the loose. The situation is relatable—we can imagine how we'd feel in those circumstances. When she discovers Ava going through the racks of plastic-enclosed garments while listening to her iPod, we all breathe a sigh of relief. Mission accomplished—I've added tension in the middle section of the book.

To help you think of spine-tingling, tension-inducing incidents that will resonate with your readers, consider the effect of the unexpected on the ordinary—and describe it sensually. In *Deadly Threads*, the first twist involves Josie seeing unexpected and mysterious shapes in a dim, gloomy environment (i.e., seeing); the second involves hearing pops, shots, but not knowing where they were coming from (i.e., hearing); and the third involves seeing smoke gush from an apartment while breathing in acrid fumes (i.e., smelling).

Thinking of how events will feel to your characters will help you select incidents that are realistic, significant, and meaningful, and that create deliciously dangerous tension.

EXERCISE

The first decisions you need to make in writing your mystery or thriller involve the setting, timing, crime, protagonist, suspects, villain, and clues you'll plant along the way, as well as any subplots you plan on integrating. Delineated chronologically, this is your plot. Once that's done, to avoid a saggy middle, add in three plot twists, surprising or suspenseful incidents, or elements of danger, as described above.

What can your protagonist see that would startle or frighten her?

What can your protagonist hear that would startle or frighten her?

What can your protagonist taste that would startle or frighten her?

What can your protagonist smell that would startle or frighten her?

What can your protagonist touch that would startle or frighten her?

GRAHAM BROWN

Humanizing the Character Arc

GRAHAM BROWN has been a pilot, an attorney, and a ditch digger (it's a long story). An avid reader, he decided to write a novel, thinking, *How hard can this be?* Ten years later, Random House bought the rights to his first book, *Black Rain*. The sequel, *Black Sun*, offers a unique twist on the concept of a 2012 apocalypse. Currently, Graham is at work on his third novel and a pair of screenplays.

There are many important facets to a successful novel, and by successful I mean interesting, memorable, enjoyable, not necessarily bestselling.

In general we have to focus on a broad swath of the entire project, even as we fine-tune the details of the writing. And while we all know that concept is "king," plot twists need to "astound," and pacing must be "breathless," we often get so busy focusing on these things that many writers seem to forget about character.

Sometimes it's intentional. I have spoken with authors who insist the story is "what happens" and not how the people feel about what happens, or how it affects them.

Other times it's unintentional. We know our characters so well that we end up not articulating their human nature. They become devices, just there to propel the plot along, to discover the clue at the right moment, and so on. . . .

Perhaps some minor characters can fit that description, but your major characters should never be that way, not if you want them to resonate with people. Not if you want them—and your book—to be remembered.

If readers connect with your main characters, identify and mentally put themselves into the place of those characters—in other words, feel their pain—then, when your heroes overcome whatever deadly and impressive obstacles you've put in their path, your readers will feel the great endorphin boost that goes along with succeeding, as if they'd done it themselves. And that's what makes them remember your book, because the triumph of your novel is the reader's victory as well as the character's.

Just think of sports fans talking about the year "They won it all"—even though they did not play a down or throw the ball. Writing is the same.

"Okay," you say. "That's great advice, now how exactly do I do that?"

Lesson One: Take the characters you already have and break them. You have to make them less than perfect. You have to give them flaws, errors, and regrets. You have to give them a past with a few marks in the loss column. In essence, you have to make them human.

I'll use some movies to illustrate, only because with 150 movies out per year, versus 60,000 books or more, movies are more universal. And, because an average script is basically 110 pages of mostly dialogue, the hits and misses can be more easily spotted.

A perfect example is one of my all-time favorites, James Bond. I love the movies: a lot of great stunts and action scenes; some fantastic one-liners; extremely attractive women; and a fast, relentless pace. It's a formula that has been good for nearly five decades and a couple of billion dollars. It also influences a lot of novels, including mine. But for the most part, many of the recent Bond movies are just kind of a hazy blur to me. They were fun while I was watching, but I can't say they really stuck with me long after the credits rolled.

Enter new writers and Daniel Craig as the new James Bond. Suddenly we have a Bond who isn't perfect anymore. He's more of an outcast, not exactly at the top of his profession and even considered a thug by M, who feels she made a mistake promoting him to 00 status.

So Daniel Craig's Bond starts out with a chip on his shoulder and something to prove. Things go downhill from there, until this Bond, unlike any of the others, falls desperately in love with the female lead: Vesper Lynd. He almost dies for her, only to find out that she's betrayed both him and country. The bitterness he feels literally seeps from the screen (in a book, of course, it should literally seep from the page), and this Bond, with his flaws and weaknesses and failures, strikes a chord in us. We remember him. We remember perceiving him as if he were a gun ready to go off, not because we were told this but because we can feel what he feels.

Lesson Two: Make those flaws matter to the plot. A perfect example of this comes from one of the best thrillers of all time: *The Bourne Identity*. Everyone has seen the Matt Damon movie, and it's fantastic. No less fantastic is the original novel by Robert Ludlum.

The threat in this story is not all that unique: a master terrorist is going to kill a bunch of people in New York. What is unique is the character of Jason Bourne. Not only is he flawed. He is ALL flaws.

His main flaw, of course, is that he has amnesia. That becomes hyperrelevant because people are trying to kill him and he doesn't know who they are, or why they're trying to kill him. This makes him vulnerable, another flaw. He is also on the tragic side because if he doesn't remember who he is, something terrible will happen (the terrorist shootings), but if he does, the truth may drive away the only light in his life, the woman who has befriended him.

There is little success in Jason Bourne's life, but because he is essentially good and trying to do the right thing, whatever he once was, we identify with him. Who isn't trying to make up for a few past wrongs? So the readers pull for him and feel his success with him and they don't forget it.

That's what you want character to do for you.

EXERCISE

1. Take your main character. Come up with three ways to make him or her flawed, tragic, vulnerable, and more likely to fail.

2. Make these flaws integral to the plot, in that your character must at least partially overcome them to succeed in overcoming the antagonist.

CATHY PICKENS

Character Motivations

CATHY PICKENS's first mystery, *Southern Fried*, won the St. Martin's Press Malice Domestic Award for Best New Traditional Mystery. She teaches law in the McColl School of Business at Queens University of Charlotte, is president of the Mecklenburg Forensic Medicine Program, and currently serves on the Mystery Writers of America board and as president of Sisters in Crime, two national mystery writers' organizations.

In a cemetery one day, I watched a tall, gray-haired man unfold himself from a lumbering Buick, open the trunk, pull out a broom and clippers, and solemnly set to clearing around a bronze memorial plaque on one of the graves. He clipped and swept and studied his handiwork.

Caring for the memory of a much-loved wife, I surmised.

But the writer in me asked what other reasons, besides romantic devotion, might have brought him to the graveyard. An insurmountable grief? An obsessive-compulsive disorder that, in life, drove his wife to distraction? Guilt because he had killed her? Or caused her to kill herself? What if it's not his wife but a longtime lover with whom he tormented his wife?

Different motives drive the story in very different directions.

Motivation is the reason why a character does something. Motivation—and how another's actions affect it—is what drives stories. To create compelling characters, a writer must understand what motivates every character on every page.

In deciding what drives characters, "Why?" is the most important question a writer can ask. The more times you ask your characters "Why?" the deeper into their motivation you can delve. Don't take the first easy answer. We each have multiple reasons for our actions; the most interesting are often deeply buried, hidden even from ourselves.

In addition, a writer should consider the reader's motivation. What brings a reader to this book? Characters with strong, compelling reasons for what they do attract readers. Crime fiction readers like to solve puzzles. They want to wrestle with good *and* evil. Most of all, they like heroes (even dark ones), and they want to understand *why*. We seldom get satisfactory answers about why in real life, so we look to fiction to help us understand why people do what they do.

To answer why, I like to build on this structure: My character wants X because of Y, but can't get it because of Z. Y is the motivation, Z is the conflict. Every character, every scene, every story arc needs to have this structure.

Most critical in a crime novel, the detective or puzzle-solver must have a reason to be involved in the case. A plausible motive can be more difficult for the amateur sleuth than for those who have professional reasons to be involved in criminal cases (attorneys, police officers, P.I.s, reporters, and others). Moving forward in a series (which crime fiction readers love), what motivates the detective to get involved may change, especially if the detective isn't in the business of solving crimes.

Rather than just strolling through the story, characters need to be driven by something strong and at every stage. For a detective, the goal is to solve the crime. But why? Wouldn't it be easier to go get a doughnut and hope things work out? Real detectives get paid to solve crimes, but is that what really interests readers? Or what really motivates a good hero—in fiction or in real life? "I do it because it's my job" sounds better coming from a guy or gal who risks it all, puts it all on the line, who is motivated not by a paycheck but by pride or fear or vigilantism or the desire to protect the innocent (a particular innocent person is more compelling than an amorphous or unidentified lump of innocent people).

Why does your detective want to be involved? Because someone asked for his help? Not very compelling, but it's a start. Better than a detective aimlessly wandering into dangerous situations. Maybe he wants to be involved because someone asked him . . . and because he wants to redeem himself from a past failure. Or he wants to help because someone he loves is accused. Or . . .

The more specific, the more personal; the more individual, the more tied to that detective and those characters, the stronger the motivation.

Strong motives should also face strong opposition. If your character wants something important but it's easy to get, that's not much of a story. Every character must have something he wants *and* some reason he can't get it. Conflict is linked to motivation. That's where the bad guy or the antagonist comes in.

Motivating the detective or hero is critical, but what drives the villain or lesser antagonists is also important. While a writer may easily identify with a hero, identifying with the villain may not come as naturally. Some antagonists are truly villainous. Some are accidentally so, but all need believable motivation that equally matches the hero's. Anything less leaves the story more flat and less developed than it could be.

Spending time in the antagonist's head (and this may be someone who isn't a villain but merely an obstacle in a scene), deciding what she wants and why, will yield a richer story for your readers. Remember, too, that the villain or antagonist also faces obstacles; for the villain, it is the detective, or victim, or others who stand in her way.

Why does the murderer choose to commit the crime? Any criminal prosecutor will tell you that motive isn't required to prove guilt; however, that same prosecutor will try his darnedest to weave for the jury a story that explains why, because juries want to understand what could have motivated someone to commit a crime. Readers want to know, too.

Spend time asking "Why?" of your villains and victims as well as your detective. Don't create cardboard cutouts you can easily pick up and move from one place to another. You want flesh-and-blood characters readers can understand, even if they don't like them very much. Ask "Why?". . . and keep asking until they tell you the truth.

EXERCISE

1. Choose a favorite book, movie, or television show and map out the characters' motivations: this character wants X because of Y, but Z gets in the way.

   The characters should have motives that carry the story arc but also motives within each scene. In Anthony Powell's *A Dance to the Music of Time*, Nick wants his uncle Giles to leave because he's an embarrassment *and* will get Nick in trouble for smoking in his dorm room; Uncle Giles wants Nick's help getting money. Both characters have motivations that make an otherwise simple scene—an uncle visiting his nephew at school—worth reading.

   In your sample, why is your favorite detective involved? It should be more than idle curiosity. Why did Perry Mason take on daunting cases? Clearly, it wasn't because it was just a job. Sometimes he didn't even get paid. So why did he accept difficult cases? Because the girl was attractive and helpless. Because he wanted to be a hero. Because he wanted to rescue the underdog. Because he wanted to torment Hamilton Burger. Because he wanted to test himself. Detectives need to have compelling, believable—even heroic—reasons for being involved.

   Why is the villain willing to kill someone, to violate one of the most basic contracts with other humans? Pride is described as the ultimate sin, the sin that got the shining angel Lucifer cast from heaven. Ask a villain "Why?" often enough and you will uncover pathological pride in its many forms: fear or loathing or greed or . . .

2. Now look at your own characters. How often have you asked them "Why?" Have they told you the truth about what they want and why? Keep asking, dig deep, find what drives them. Their inner drive is what delivers great fiction.

JAMES SCOTT BELL

Maintaining Suspense

JAMES SCOTT BELL is the bestselling author of *Deceived, Try Dying, Try Darkness, Try Fear,* and several other thrillers. He served as the fiction columnist for *Writer's Digest* and has written three bestselling craft books: *Plot & Structure, Revision & Self-Editing,* and *The Art of War for Writers.* He lives and writes in Los Angeles.

W *hat happens next?*
    That's the question you want in your readers' minds. That's what keeps them flipping pages long into the night. That's suspense.

And every novel needs it.

Suspense in fiction is a feeling of pleasurable uncertainty. That feeling must, of course, permeate a thriller or mystery, but it is just as essential for a character-driven or literary novel. Unless readers feel pleasurable uncertainty the story drags. Books get put aside that way.

Here are two ways to keep that from happening.

Death Overhanging. Physical death, of course, is the norm for most suspense fiction. The serial killer on the loose, the villain with a strong motive to kill the protagonist, the malevolent conspiracy out to silence those who know too much—variations on these themes abound.

In *The Protector* by David Morrell, the threat of death is established from the start. Cavanaugh, the protagonist, is a professional protector who saves a man named Prescott from a hit squad over the course of a fifty-page chase scene. If they're caught, they're dead, so we keep reading to see if they make it. Those stakes remain throughout the book.

But there are other kinds of death. One of these is professional death. If the hero does not perform his duties, he's through in his livelihood. He simply must succeed.

Consider the down-and-out lawyer who gets one last case, a final chance at redeeming his professional life, as in Barry Reed's *The Verdict*. The same conflict is present for the shamed cop, or the failed detective, or anyone else whose work is crucial to society.

Then there is psychological death. This sort of overhanging threat can turn literary fiction into a suspenseful read. Unless the character finds a reason to go on living, or solves a dark question from the past, or heals a wound from childhood, she will die inside. Life will become intolerable.

In Janet Fitch's *White Oleander*, young Astrid must escape the lethal influence of her strong-willed mother, Ingrid, as well as the emotional challenges in each of her foster homes. The threat of Astrid dying inside infuses every page.

The key to selling any of these forms of death is to create scenes early on that show what the central problem means to the protagonist. If such a scene is not in your book yet, put it there now. Get the readers to feel what's at stake.

A Sympathetic Protagonist. Death may be overhanging the story, but unless we care about the protagonist we won't really worry too much about it. For that we need sympathy for the lead character.

Beyond mere empathy—the ability to understand and relate— sympathy places us emotionally alongside the hero.

Sympathy begins, first, with a fully rounded character, one who has flaws as well as strengths. No one can sympathize with perfection.

Second, the character must, at some level, have guts. The number-one rule for lead characters is *no wimps*. A wimp is someone who sits around and takes it, who reacts more than acts. Get your characters moving against the forces arrayed against him.

In John Lutz's *The Night Caller*, ex-cop Ezekiel Cooper is a man who roams his neighborhood, "without employment, social life or purpose." He's fighting cancer and his only daughter has been murdered. After the funeral, he is alone in his apartment, with "his grief to keep him company . . . along with his self-pity."

But Lutz doesn't let Cooper stay there. By the end of the chapter he's going to get an old friend to help him find out what the cops are doing. "Not tomorrow. Today. He couldn't rely on tomorrows."

The more emotional investment the reader has, the better the reading experience.

EXERCISE

1. What is the death overhanging your story? If it isn't physical death, it must be either professional or psychological. If the stakes aren't that high, find a way to ratchet them up. You can do this for any story. Then justify the high stakes with sufficient backstory.

2. Analyze your protagonist. Is she human and flawed, yet strong? Does she have someone to care for without whining about it? Is she action-oriented? Make those changes and the readers will truly care what happens next.

AILEEN G. BARON

Plausibility

A retired Near Eastern archaeologist, AILEEN G. BARON is the author of the Lily Sampson series, set in the Middle East during World War II and featuring archaeologist Lily Sampson. The series includes *A Fly Has a Hundred Eyes*, *The Torch of Tangier*, and *The Scorpion's Bite*. The first book in her contemporary series about the intrigue and deceit in the antiquities trade, *The Gold of Thrace*, features Tamar Saticoy, a professor of archaeology and an archaeological consultant for Interpol.

What bothers me the most in mysteries, what jars me beyond tolerance, is to find something implausible, improbable, and unreasonably unlikely sticking out of the page and shrieking at me.

It's only fiction, you say. Sometimes, bestselling writers get away with destroying any hope of verisimilitude. Maybe they can, but you and I can't.

You have to know what you're doing. Early in the nineteenth century, two of the most famous American authors were Washington Irving and James Fenimore Cooper. Washington Irving used implausibility as a weapon, to create sharp humor and satire. Cooper, on the other hand, wrote adventure stories.

In his day, Cooper's Leatherstocking Tales were bestsellers; his characters were larger than life. As in many of today's thrillers, plot and characterization were based on the improbable. No one could have Natty Bumppo's extraordinarily sharp marksmanship and eyesight; no one could have Chingachgook's ability to track footprints underwater in a streambed.

In his delightful essay "Fenimore Cooper's Literary Offenses," Mark Twain lists eighteen out of a possible nineteen literary offenses that Cooper committed in the space of two-thirds of a page in *The Deerslayer*. Among them was a requirement that "the personages of a tale shall confine themselves to possibilities and let miracles alone; or if they venture a miracle, the author must so plausibly set it forth as to make it look possible and reasonable."

Research and accurate observation are essential for plausibility. According to Twain, Cooper "saw nearly all things through a glass eye, darkly."

Like the Leatherstocking Tales, certain types of thrillers depend on the implausible, in which if such-and-such happens, the world as we know it will end. Sometimes the assumptions are so preposterous that you want to strangle the author. That may be all right for these books, just a form of romantic escapism.

But in a well-crafted mystery, all must be plausible, or alarms go off in the reader's mind. Especially in a key scene, the protagonist can't suddenly come up with unexpected expertise at the last minute.

I ran into this in my book *The Gold of Thrace*. In the climactic scene, Tamar disarms her adversary by throwing a pot of paint at his hand. In order to make this believable and show that she could hurl an object that forcefully and accurately, I had to go back and create an earlier scene in which she saves a colleague from an attack of a venomous snake by throwing a rock at it. And to show how she developed that skill, I had to include a small flashback early in the book, showing her learning to pitch a baseball hard and fast, to compete with her brothers.

Try this technique in your own story.

EXERCISE

1. For your story, write a climactic scene in which the protagonist demonstrates a unique ability or skill to overcome an adversary.

2. Now ratchet up the suspense. Have the protagonist fail at other attempts to defeat the adversary. Make the adversary more formidable. Careful. Don't overdo this and make him or her a cartoon

character. Bring in the particular skill of the protagonist at the last minute, just as disaster seems imminent.

3. Write an earlier scene, in which this same ability is used to a lesser extent to rescue an ally. Feather it into your story.

4. Write a short, one-paragraph flashback showing how and why the protagonist developed and honed this ability. How would you place this in the story? How would you go into and out of the flashback? What inspires the memory? An object? A scent? A chance remark?

SLEUTHS

Know Your Detective

DOC MACOMBER

Finding the Key Strengths and Weaknesses
of Your Detective Character

DOC MACOMBER's writing career spans over two decades and includes several one-act plays, screenplays, short stories, young adult fiction, and adult mysteries. Doc serves with an Air Force Special Tactics unit and lives aboard a yacht on the Columbia River. He has contributed articles to the *Blood-Letter* and the *Mystery Readers Journal*, discussing the development of his Vietnamese investigator, Jack Vu, and the history of the ethnic detective. His Jack Vu series includes *The Killer Coin*, *Wolf's Remedy*, and *Snip*.

Years ago, as a fledgling writer, when I decided to create a fictional detective, I made a common novice mistake. My P.I. was a tough loner, disenfranchised from society, always in and out of relationships, barely scraping by, and, of course, he drank too much.

At the time I was reading Robert B. Parker, John D. MacDonald, and the hard-boiled detective series featuring Mike Hammer. These detectives were Robert Mitchum–strong, shining their hardened knuckles on bad guys' jaws, the romantic dream of every woman, each a real man's man. I patterned my detective after them. My early attempts didn't go anywhere with publishers. They'd seen this guy before. And, others were doing a much better job. I soon realized that I needed to create my own unique character, a step some writers took straight out of the gate.

In creating his protagonist, Jack Reacher, Lee Child stated, "I looked at what everyone else was doing—especially Michael Connelly because I'd read him and knew at once he'd be a huge success. Why compete with success? So I did everything that the others weren't. I created a character that wasn't a drunk or a cop. He wasn't damaged by women, work, or booze. He was just a man who one day walked away from it all and wandered the landscape with no particular need to help his fellow man. But Reacher will never back down from a fight."*

Since I was serving in an Air Force Special Ops unit, I decided to place my detective in a world I understood. I created a military investigator, based on an individual with whom I served. He was not your typical American soldier. He was a short Asian who had been in war as a child. His early life had been fraught with turmoil, suffering, and amazing struggles to survive. Yet you saw none of this on his serene face. As our friendship grew and he shared more of his life, I was captivated. I wanted to know more about him and slowly came to the realization that others would, too.

I created my fictive detective with distinctive Vietnamese traits, a diverse ethnic background, and made him an investigator in the Air Force Office of Special Investigations (OSI). Casting him as an ethnic fish out of water created conflict, which allowed me to show particular personality elements not familiar to American readers. And the series caught on.

I started by examining the key strengths and weaknesses I wanted this detective to possess. Using several of the basic core values of the armed forces—integrity, service before self, and excellence, I also gave him some unique elements. Being Buddhist, he believes in reincarnation and a karmic path. This allows him to have a new slant on crime scenes and murder. He has weaknesses that grew from his past as well, such as a strong need for isolation, hardheadedness, and a sensitive gut. For characters to be effective they should embody traits we admire, but they also need feet of clay—weaknesses that humanize them and with which we can identify.

Your detective may have a military background or be a cop or a P.I. He could be a college graduate or a high school dropout. She may be an amateur sleuth in her seventies living in a retirement home, a kick-ass female bounty hunter or a tough black dyke.

However you write your detective, in order to forge the key ele-

---

*Bouchercon Conference, San Francisco, October 16, 2010.

ments of their character, you need to discover what experiences shaped them, so they emerge from the page fully formed. What happened in their childhood? Who raised them? Parents, grandparents, or foster care? Who did they admire? Who hurt them and how did they cope? What series of events lead them to become detectives?

To create a fresh literary face, you need to decide the good and bad aspects that make up your sleuth. Strengths might include a sense of morality, courage, intelligence, wit, confidence, solid core beliefs, tenacity, toughness. Weaknesses that humanize your character could include selfishness, cowardice, laziness, alcoholism, clumsiness, short-sightedness with poor impulse control, indifference, alienation.

Notice some traits that could fall under either category? Some may think of hard-drinking as character strength. Likewise, being a loner, a long tradition found in the detective genre, could be either a strength or a weakness. For example, your solitary detective could be in a committed relationship, which creates conflicts between the need to be alone and the desire to share one's innermost thoughts with someone else. Humans are emotionally complex creatures, so feel free to mix it up.

EXERCISE

1. Visit an outdoor plaza or a Starbucks. Observe and make notes of the people. Do any of the people look strong or weak just from what they're wearing? From their expressions? Their voices? Their actions? Write down what triggers your impressions.

2. List ten strengths and ten weaknesses. Then narrow the list down to your top five. Now see if you can reveal these through the actions of your protagonist.

3. The next time you're reading your favorite detective novel or watching TV, note how other writers reveal strengths and weaknesses of their detective characters. Does the writer use a backstory to reveal their actions, motives, or behavior? Or does the viewer get this information from somewhere else?

4. Think about the people you've admired or looked up to. What do you recall about them that revealed their strength of character?

5. Try mixing genders. Think about your male lead or female lead and imagine changing their sex. Does this change what you know about them? Is this new character different than what you imagined?

6. Contrive three different ways your main character could react to the antagonist. Did you discover a new strength or weakness that you didn't know before about your protagonist?

7. What characteristic do you most dislike in others? Create a character that embodies this. Give them purpose. Perhaps use this trait in your antagonist, but also investigate how your hero might possess an unlikable trait in a way that your readers would sympathize.

8. Your character may be asked to do something that goes against his or her belief system. For instance, if your hero's job requires doing something that crosses the line and violates a sense of honor, how does the protagonist deal with it?

9. How are ethnic characters different from the all-American type of hero or antihero? Do they reveal their strengths and weaknesses differently?

By asking these questions you may get a better handle on the key elements of your detective character. What you don't want is a cardboard cutout. A detective that embodies both the best and worst traits is a riveting one.

DEBORAH COONTS

The Offbeat Protagonist

DEBORAH COONTS has been a storyteller from an early age—something that used to get her in trouble. After a stint as a humor columnist for a national magazine, she authored *Wanna Get Lucky?* a *New York Times* Notable Book for 2010. The sequel, *Lucky Stiff*, came out in 2011, with the third in the series, *So Damn Lucky*, to follow.

Las Vegas is about as idiosyncratic as cities come—perfect fodder for a novelist. I've lived here ten years and have come to understand that those of us who find our place in Sin City are square pegs. There isn't a normal person in the bunch. Of course, while this presents all kinds of wonderful storytelling opportunities for my mystery series, it also presents its challenges. One of the most critical, I found, was my choice of protagonist.

Now, protagonists are interesting creatures. Not only are they the door through which your readers enter and become invested in your world, they are also a function of the tenor and tone of your tale. Ideally, protagonists are recognizable to your readers—people they can relate to or feel empathy for. Their conflicts should strike a common chord so the reader starts to root for these characters, to care what happens to them.

For storytelling purposes, the protagonist also reflects or embodies the world the writer creates. Since I write stories about Las Vegas, there was no way my protagonist could be normal, a run-of-the-mill straight arrow. However, she needed to be normal enough so she wouldn't be off-putting or hard to relate to. It's a fine line: quirky yet normal. How's that for an oxymoron? But if you think about it, most of the people we remember are unique, yet normal enough.

As writers, how do we walk this line? What makes a protagonist memorable yet still accessible to your readers? The characters remember most are usually a bit eccentric, quite often with a finely honed wit that made me laugh, whether they intended that result or not. Often they are a bit unexpected. To me, this makes them more interesting and engaging, which is especially important in a protagonist.

It seems there are two different ways to make characters stand out: give them distinctive mannerisms or give them an odd but relatable conflict.

So, in building a backstory for my protagonist, I thought through all of the weird and wonderful things about Vegas. I thought about how someone would be shaped by growing up here. And Lucky was born: a woman in her early thirties who is extraordinarily good at her job as Head of Customer Relations at a Strip mega-resort, but who is completely inept in handling her personal life. She spent her formative years being raised in a whorehouse by her mother, a former hooker and current owner of the establishment. Lucky doesn't know who her father is. Through all of the bumps and bruises inflicted by this kind of upbringing, Lucky developed a keen appreciation for human frailties. She is tall, six feet, and large enough that she shops in the section where the transvestites shop—not a comfortable existence in the land of the beautiful people. Her best friend is a straight female impersonator, Juilliard-trained with a Harvard MBA, who wants to be more than friends. Lucky isn't too sure about dating a guy who looks better in her clothes than she does.

One of the difficult parts about creating a unique protagonist is you need to populate the story around them. In my Las Vegas stories, I had to resist the temptation to make them all totally over-the-top. If I did that, then my offbeat protagonist would blend in with the crowd—not a good thing. I had to choose carefully which particular traits or curiosities exposed by Vegas I wanted each character to represent.

Generally, what I like to do with supporting characters is to take the expected and turn it at least ninety degrees. Lucky's mother the madam? She's svelte, decked-out in designer duds, and a lobbyist for her industry. Lucky's boyfriend wears a dress for a living and her assistant is a fiftyish frump dating a thirty-five-year-old Aussie hunk.

She represents some of the dreams people come to Vegas to find, or the fantasies they play around in while here.

EXERCISE

So, how do you create memorable, quirky characters all your own?

Since the well of personal experience is what we draw from, think about the people in your life whom you remember. What traits or characteristics did they have that separated them from everyone else?

Did they have a particular physical trait that made them stand out? A cat's eye? Were they tall? Short? Fat? Thin? One leg longer than the other? Purple hair?

Did they have a particular skill that was unusual? Perhaps they played the piccolo? Or they drove a backhoe for a living? Or they rode circus horses when they were young or followed the Grateful Dead one summer? Perhaps they drive an unusual car or fly airplanes. Or they fold origami when they're nervous.

Maybe their job is unique: a sous-chef or a veterinary assistant. The shy desk clerk at the strip club . . . or the chicken girl at the Tropicana (don't ask).

Or perhaps their goals seem inconsistent with their lifestyle? A fifty-year-old frumpy secretary who dates a thirty-five-year-old Australian hunk. A woman who has serious trust issues yet longs for a mate. A straight guy who channels Cher for a living.

Let your imagination run wild, then tone things down, and mold them to your story. For me, a good laugh is golden, so I like to have some fun.

Caution: Don't go overboard. Give your characters one or two eccentricities. And pick and choose which characters will get them. Too many weird traits and too many offbeat characters and they all start blending together. This is the opposite of your goal: to make them memorable.

ROBERTA ISLEIB

Characters from the Inside Out

Clinical psychologist **ROBERTA ISLEIB** is the author of eight mysteries, including *Six Strokes Under* and *Deadly Advice*. Her books and stories have been nominated for Agatha, Anthony, and Macavity awards. Her first book in the Key West Food Critic mystery series (written under the name Lucy Burdette) will be published by NAL in January 2012.

B efore I began writing, I worked as a clinical psychologist in private practice. Beginning a course of psychotherapy with a new patient was always an interesting challenge. I often started a session with these questions: How can I help? What brings you in today?

A patient's answers would tell me a great deal about how they saw themselves in that moment. Had they suffered a crisis for which they needed urgent help, such as a sick child or a spouse asking for divorce? Had they been depressed for years but suddenly couldn't bear the weight of their sad feelings? Had someone close to them insisted they go for help?

Later on in that first hour, after I'd gotten a sense of the immediate circumstances leading to the appointment, I'd ask about family history. I'd explain that each person's understanding of relationships is shaped by what they experienced growing up. And I'd tell each patient that we tend to carry these old mental transcripts forward with us and apply them to new relationships where they don't necessarily fit.

Over time, of course, patients and I would learn together that the picture they had of themselves in the world wasn't completely accurate. Maybe the wonderful mother the patient remembered subtly preferred an older sibling. Or maybe hidden alcoholism in a family member skewed everyone's behavior. And we'd figure out how these layers of history had driven the patients' life choices, and then how their needs might change once they had been able to cut loose the old baggage.

My experience as a psychologist has turned out to be absolutely transferable to mystery writing. First of all, why is this character interested in solving a mystery? This question is easier to answer with a professional sleuth (it's their job!), but the most effective cop and P.I. characters are also driven by a complex history. Michael Connelly's Harry Bosch, whose prostitute mother was murdered when he was a boy, is a wonderful example—he's always looking out for the underdog.

With amateur sleuths, developing the character's reasonable and believable stake in solving the mystery is crucial. The writer must build an urgency to solve the crime into the character's history and psychology. Something that the character dearly wants—and maybe this isn't conscious—is blocked by the presenting problem.

For example, at the beginning of *Deadly Advice*, recently divorced psychologist Rebecca Butterman craves a normal, happy life. She wants to move forward, not look back at her failed marriage. After her next-door neighbor commits suicide, the neighbor's mother begs her to look into the death, which she believes was foul play.

Rebecca agrees. She feels guilty about not getting to know the neighbor, and because of something more subtle—this death taps into her feeling of being alone in the world. And feeling alone triggers a very old abandonment issue from childhood.

Yes, Rebecca Butterman wants to find out what happened to her neighbor, but she also wants to understand why she feels so lonely. And so she digs into a murder case further than any ordinary person might. See how it works?

In my forthcoming Key West Food Critic mystery, *A Taste for Murder*, the protagonist Hayley Snow is younger than Dr. Butterman, with a less dramatic family history. She moves to Key West to be with a new boyfriend who immediately dumps her for another woman, which leaves her feeling unmoored. So now she's searching for a way to find the self-esteem that she hoped would come with the new relationship. Then the other woman turns up murdered. Naturally Hayley is a suspect—and the upheaval in her interior life makes her particularly vulnerable to overinvolving herself in the mystery.

Over the course of your story, as with therapy, your character should learn new things about herself, and she should change because of what she learns. She may begin to understand that the things she thought she wanted are not what she really needs to feel fulfilled or loveable, or less lonely. So she can relinquish the old goals and set her sights on something more real.

EXERCISE

Answering these questions should help you develop a more rounded character.

- What brings this character into the story? (How can I help you today? Why now?)

- How would the character describe her goal at the beginning of the book? (The "How can I help?" question becomes "What does this character say she wants?")

- How will the character change as a result of what she faces, and learns about herself?

- What makes your character different from other people (inside and out)?

- What is this character's stake for getting involved in the solution of the mystery, both on the surface and inside?

- What about the character's family history shapes her stake in your story?

MARCIA TALLEY

Detectives Have Weaknesses, Too

MARCIA TALLEY is the Agatha- and Anthony-winning author of ten mystery novels featuring survivor and sleuth, Hannah Ives. Her short stories appear in more than a dozen collections. Like her sleuth, Marcia lives in Annapolis, Maryland, with a husband who loves to sail and a cat who doesn't.

It's a gift . . . and a curse.

—ADRIAN MONK

I've read a lot of novels in my time, published and unpublished, and there's one thing I'm sure of: Perfect characters are perfectly boring. To be interesting, your detective must have strengths, but flaws and vulnerabilities, too. Even Superman can be brought to his knees by kryptonite.

I'm not talking about the gun-toting, hard-drinking, chain-smoking detective who operates on the fringes of the law. Nor the badly behaved heroine in thigh-high boots who drinks, swears, and kicks plenty of ass. To stand out in a field of stereotypes, your characters need to be human, and human beings have faults.

Consider morose, brooding, introspective detectives like Sherlock Holmes, Adam Dalgliesh, Kurt Wallander, and Morse. Holmes is arrogant, self-absorbed, devoted to the science of deduction. So is Morse. "I don't think, Lewis, I deduce. I only ever deduce," Morse says in *The Wolvercote Tongue*. Yet Morse seems more real to me than Holmes. Perhaps it's because Morse is afraid of heights, cringes at the sight of blood, and, like his author, Colin Dexter, battles diabetes. Kurt Wallander, the modern melancholy Dane created by Henning Mankell, is dealing with high blood sugar, too. He's also separated from his wife, has an overbearing daughter, and a father suffering from Alzheimer's. P. D. James's detective, Commander Adam Dalgliesh, is a published poet haunted by the death of his wife and infant daughter. In facing life's challenges, Wallander, Morse, and Dalgliesh are more sympathetic than most to other people's pain and we, in turn, care more about them.

The challenges facing your detective can be physical. Wheelchair-bound by an assassin's bullet, San Francisco detective Robert T. Ironside continues to wage war against crime from his specially equipped van. Michael Longstreet, a New Orleans insurance investigator, is blind. In T. C. Boyle's fast-paced thriller *Talk Talk*, the main character, Dana Halter, is profoundly deaf.

The physical challenges facing our detectives can be temporary. In Hitchcock's thriller REAR WINDOW, Jeff Jeffries, a professional photographer, is confined to a wheelchair with a broken leg. Jeffries passes the time by watching his neighbors. When a neighbor's wife vanishes, Jeffries's quest to prove that her disappearance is the result of foul play puts his own life in danger.

In Josephine Tey's classic *The Daughter of Time*, Scotland Yard Inspector Alan Grant is in the hospital, also laid up with a broken leg. Bored senseless, he becomes intrigued by a portrait of the much-maligned Richard III and proceeds to exonerate him of the murders of his nephews, the princes in the Tower. A similar plot device was used by Colin Dexter in the 1989 Gold Dagger winner, *The Wench is Dead*. Inspector Morse is recovering from a bleeding ulcer in an Oxford hospital when he reads an account of an 1859 canal boat murder. Morse is convinced that the two men hanged for the crime were innocent and sets out to prove it from the confines of his bed.

Jeffries, Grant, and Morse are immobile, so they depend on acquaintances and friends to assist in their investigations. But nobody needs legs more than the quirky sleuth in Donna Andrews's series, Turing Hopper, an Artificial Intelligence personality trapped in a corporate computer. Turing has no body! When Turing's programmer mysteriously disappears in *You've Got Murder*, Turing suspects foul play and explores every avenue available to her microchips and processors to find him—surveillance cameras, credit card records, data files—as well as her human colleagues Tim and Maude.

Other detectives face mental and psychological challenges. Bo Bradley, who first appeared in Abigail Padgett's 1996 novel *Child of Silence*, is a San Diego Juvenile Court child abuse investigator. She's also a closet manic-depressive. Over the course of four novels, Bo's illness gives her psychological insight and deep empathy with her young clients. Readers empathize with Bo, too, as she struggles to work and live with manic depression.

There is no psychologically challenged character more popular in recent years than Adrian Monk, the obsessive-compulsive detective who suffers from—as he reveals somewhere in season six—312 phobias, requiring him to depend on personal assistants to shop, drive him to crime scenes, and keep a supply of wipes handy. According to his creator, Andy Breckman, Monk's attention to minute detail cripples him socially and sometimes hampers an investigation—Monk has to resist the urge to straighten overturned furniture at a crime scene— but it makes Monk a gifted detective and profiler. He has a photographic memory and can reconstruct entire crimes based on scraps of detail that seem unimportant to his colleagues.

Steve Hamilton's Edgar-nominated *The Lock Artist* is told in the first person by the engaging eighteen-year-old orphan Mike Smith, who is mute. Mike's a "boxman" who can open any safe, padlock, or locked door. No surprise that every criminal in the world wants to own him. Readers feel Mike's frustration—"You stupid fucking mutant freak. Say *something*"—as he struggles to escape a life of crime and unlock his silent world by revisiting the nightmares of his past.

"I am a mathematician with some behavioral difficulties," states Christopher Boone, the autistic fifteen-year-old narrator of Mark Haddon's mesmerizing *The Curious Incident of the Dog in the Night-Time*. Nearly overwhelmed by the vast amount of information and stimuli bombarding him, he nevertheless manages to solve the mystery of a murdered dog, travel to London to find his missing mother, and excel in his A-level math exam.

And continuing a trend for ever younger protagonists, eleven-year-old Flavia de Luce blithely ignores her dysfunctional family; mounts her trusty bicycle, Gladys, and solves the murder of a red-headed stranger in Alan Bradley's enchanting *The Sweetness at the Bottom of the Pie.*

The challenges that face some detectives border on the bizarre. The antihero of R. Scott Bakker's offbeat *Disciple of the Dog*, Disciple "Diss" Manning, has hyperthymestic syndrome—total recall: "The one thing you need to remember about me is that I don't forget. Anything. Ever." Diss can "freeze-frame and fast-forward, pause and replay things. . . . It's a kind of TiVo, only without the monthly fees." Diss replays investigations over and over, looking for nuances of meaning as he searches for a young woman amid the followers of an apocalyptic cult.

What if a detective had the opposite problem? In Christopher Nolan's brilliant MEMENTO, Leonard Shelby is so traumatized by a blow to the head after his wife's rape and murder that he's suffering from anterograde amnesia, which renders his brain unable to store new memories. In his search for his wife's killer, Leonard uses a system of notes and annotated Polaroid photos to keep track of everyone he meets, and he tattoos facts he wants to remember—like license plate numbers—all over his body.

Quirky, idiosyncratic, unpredictable, eccentric detective characters like these leap outside the box to break new ground in mystery fiction. Your detective can, too. I'm not suggesting that you make him a quadriplegic like Jeffery Deaver's Lincoln Rhyme, but whatever his strengths and weaknesses, he (or she) must be able to capture a reader's attention and hold it for three or four hundred pages. To do this, you—the author—must know your detective inside and out. Try testing your character: he locates a kidnapped child living happily within a loving family, while her real mother is a drug-addicted loser. What would he do? You need to know.

"When I got cancer, I decided I wasn't going to put up with crap from anybody anymore," my protagonist Hannah Ives says at the beginning of *Sing It to Her Bones.* Ten cases later, she's beaten cancer, but still isn't taking any crap.

Flaws and imperfections. They give your detective a place to go;

they are challenges to overcome, moving the story forward. If skillfully handled by both you and your detective, your detective's weakness can turn out to be his (or her) greatest strength.

EXERCISE

1. Ask yourself: What is the worst thing that can happen to my detective? Then ask: How can it get even worse? Write at least two pages explaining how your character solves this dilemma. For example: A woman struggling to support herself as a private investigator is engaged in a nasty custody battle with her ex. She's already late to pick up her children from day care when a client calls in distress. "Come now! I need you."

2. Up the stakes. A kidnapped fiancé, a missing child, a terrorist plot. Your detective is on the case, and time is running out. Now handicap him—a broken arm, a ruptured appendix, a summons to jury duty, an invitation to dinner at the White House. Writing in the voice of your detective character, take several pages to tell us how the character meets the challenge.

KAREN HARPER

Amateur Sleuths for Professional Authors

KAREN HARPER, published since 1982, is the *New York Times*–bestselling author of fifty novels, including contemporary suspense and a historical mystery series. *Dark Harvest*, with its Amish amateur sleuth heroine, won the Mary Higgins Clark Award. Harper's novels have been translated into many languages, most recently Russian and Turkish.

Despite the popularity of police, detectives, and forensic specialists as central characters in books and other mass media, amateur sleuths are always popular with readers and, therefore, publishers. As a veteran author of many books featuring amateur sleuths, I'd like to discuss how to create and bring them to life to propel and sell your work.

Amateur sleuths have worked well for me for eighteen years. My heroines, who have solved serious crimes (and made me a bestselling author), had such careers as rose grower, Amish teacher, scuba diver, farmer, camp counselor for at-risk girls, TV anchor, and a Ph.D. cancer researcher. And, oh yes, Queen of England in a nine-book mystery series featuring Bess Tudor, Queen Elizabeth I.

But first, what's the continued appeal of amateur sleuths? For one thing, many readers identify with them more easily than with a professional detective, and pulling the reader into your main character is job number one. The subconscious idea of *This could happen to me—this could be me!* is powerful.

This bond between the reader and the main character is also strengthened by the fact that, however much we love to see professional crime-solvers at their clever best, it is more compelling to watch an amateur sleuth solve a crime where something personal is at stake.

Amateur sleuths would not be investigating if something hadn't deeply affected them. Someone they know, possibly someone they love, has been abducted or murdered.

It makes for a good read to see a dedicated professional sleuth solve a crime, but it ups the ante if the sleuth has a huge stake in the investigation besides doing his job. Screenwriters of P.I. or police procedurals are aware of this ploy and sometimes go out of their way to work a detective's personal investment into a plot. How many times have you seen a police show on television where it happens that the investigator knows the victim or identifies with the victim for some reason? But when you write an amateur sleuth, you don't have to stretch for this, and the closer the crime victim is to the main character, the better.

Another allure of writing amateur sleuths is that many readers are overwhelmed with high-tech crime solving. They'd love it if the sleuth used good old deduction and brain power. Low-tech crime investigation is often more challenging and just plain fun for the reader and provides a break from his or her stress-filled, tech-loaded life.

Finally, amateur sleuths can provide a central character who has a fascinating hobby or career—hopefully one that provides the necessary investigative skills for the protagonist. In addition to the heroines mentioned above, I've used an Appalachian midwife, for example: she was skilled at observation and interviewing people, and nobody was going to steal her patients' babies. And amateur sleuths are easier to isolate for suspenseful scenes and often have to face the villain alone. (Which means it's good to avoid the common temptation to make the best friend or love interest of the sleuth a cop or detective.) Now, let's try to get some specific ideas together for creating your amateur sleuth.

EXERCISE

In either first person (amateur sleuth tells about herself) or in third person (you or an outside observer tells the story), write one to three paragraphs providing details about the crime:

- Who was harmed or killed?
- What is the sleuth's relationship to the victim?
- How did the sleuth find out about the crime?
- How did the sleuth react?
- Are the police involved?
- Why is the sleuth going to solve the crime herself?

Now, in first or third person, write at least one paragraph explaining what qualities make your hero or heroine a good amateur sleuth to solve this crime. A particular talent or career skill? A key clue? Inside information? Personal observation?

You now have the background to propel your plot and main character for your amateur sleuth novel.

DEBORAH TURRELL ATKINSON

Protagonist in Jeopardy

Inspired by Tony Hillerman's tales of the Navajo, DEBORAH TURRELL ATKINSON writes crime fiction novels that weave the legends and folklore of the Hawaiian Islands into suspenseful mysteries: a perspective of Hawaii the tour books never show. The series consists of four novels so far: *Primitive Secrets* (2002), *The Green Room* (2005), *Fire Prayer* (2007), and *Pleasing the Dead* (2009). At present, Atkinson is working on a new thriller series.

As writers, we have been told a thousand times that any tale worth reading deals with conflict. As readers, we know in our very bones when the conflict is good—we'd rather read that novel than sleep. When it's not working, we usually ditch the book. This exercise deals with certain kinds of peril and the effect this danger has on the protagonist—and the reader.

Real life demonstrates that people get into trouble, lots of it. Danger is all around us. How often do you read the paper (alleged truth) and marvel at the absurdity of a deadly situation? If an author wrote about some parents who claimed their son was in a helium-filled balloon for the sole purpose of appearing on reality TV, would readers buy the plot? There is a difference between truth and believability. As writers, we bear the burden of making both the danger and our protagonist's actions credible.

Traditional suspense novels have a protagonist who finds herself, in a spectrum that ranges from coercion to choice, committed to an action that places her in grave danger. The writer must lay careful groundwork and make choices. The main character, knowing danger exists, must have a reason to be drawn into it, and this reason must resonate

131

with emotion, desire, and urgency. The character also prepares for the peril.

In Michael Connelly's *The Poet*, Jack McEvoy, a Denver crime reporter, is assigned to write about the death of his twin brother, homicide detective Sean McEvoy, who apparently died of a self-inflicted gunshot wound. Smeared on the windshield of Sean's car, however, was a quote from Edgar Allan Poe. Jack cannot believe Sean committed suicide; he is convinced his brother was murdered. As a reporter, Jack has not just investigative resources, but contacts and informants as well, and he builds both his skills and his expertise in the course of his inquiry.

Connelly never allows the reader to doubt Jack's motives or abilities, even as he faces a diabolical, murderous villain. As Jack's peril increases, he may suffer moments of self-doubt, but the reader never doubts him. Except for his anxiety, the jeopardy Jack encounters is external, in the form of his brother's killer, and he faces his dangerous adversary with savvy and skill.

There are times when the protagonist's personality or mind-set endangers him more than outside forces. In Jack London's 1908 story "To Build a Fire," an unnamed newcomer to the Yukon sets out upon the long Yukon trail with a dog, a big native husky. When the man spits and ignores the fact that his spittle crackles before hitting the ground, readers know the man is going to make a choice that places him in jeopardy. His denial of the deep cold is dangerous. London's skillful writing makes watching the man's accumulating mistakes a painful experience. The combination of the external punishing conditions and the man's ignorant hubris is a recipe for doom.

Joseph Conrad gives us a sympathetic and tormented protagonist in *Lord Jim*. As a young seaman, Jim, along with his captain and the rest of the crew, abandoned ship and all the people aboard. Jim, however, is the only one who faces a judicial court of inquiry, where he is stripped of his certificate of command. It is at this point that the narrator, Marlow, meets Jim, takes sympathy, and helps Jim find work. Marlow identifies with Jim's desire to live a noble, adventurous life of good deeds, and he recognizes Jim's inability to forgive himself for his youthful mistake. Ultimately, it is Jim's failure to live up to his own idealism that leads him to sacrifice himself for what he sees as a noble cause.

By having his character's greatest peril come from within, Conrad is able to pose important questions about the meaning of honor and noble action. What are these man-made concepts? If a character's mind-set leads to self-sacrifice, does the action redeem him?

Putting your protagonist in jeopardy needs to accomplish more than keeping the pages turning. The most interesting conflicts usually combine internal and external threats and examine the reactions of humans under pressure. The protagonist learns skills and acquires wisdom throughout the story, so that she is prepared for the final confrontation. Sometimes the protagonist overcomes the obstacle, sometimes not, but he needs to grow and change. There is usually a dark moment of introspection, where the protagonist doubts her actions. As with London's unnamed traveler, the character sometimes realizes that he's ignored the signs he should have heeded. Oedipus ignored his oracles, and the tale ends as a tragedy, with both demise and wisdom.

The Greeks may have used deus ex machina, but it's a big no-no for today's writer. Help doesn't drop from the sky, the handsome beau doesn't bail her out, nor does the police car appear until the protagonist has solved the problem himself. You've taught your protagonist the lessons he needs, now turn him loose to use them.

Oh—remember to add the unexpected, too. Life does that.

EXERCISE

1. Working in a rough outline form, construct a situation whereby your protagonist is faced with a situation he or she cannot ignore. If you were working in the screenwriter's three-part structure, this would be the first part: establishing the problem. Your character has a dilemma.

2. Imagine an opponent worthy of your protagonist in every way, and think of three lessons your main character must learn in order to vanquish the opponent. These can be internal or external. These les-

sons shouldn't be easy; give your character some metaphorical—or literal—bruises. Draw on real life.

3. Think of three ways in which your character gains wisdom beyond the above lessons. Does she begin to listen to a character she once scoffed at?

4. Come up with three unexpected twists that no one could be prepared for. The cop goes into the meth dealer's den armed, but finds his partner has betrayed him and is collaborating. Turn the screws, and remember, these reasons should relate to the BIG issue.

5. Remember, your villain must be equal in smarts and strength to your protagonist. List three ways that this person or phenomenon will surprise your protagonist.

6. You're ready for your showdown and the conclusion. If you've done the steps above, your mind has already been working on this; you've imagined different scenes. Write two of them. You've got the bones of a novel!

JOHN WESTERMANN

Build the Cast for Your Police Procedural

JOHN WESTERMANN, a retired police officer from Long Island, is a novelist and nonfiction writer teaching at the Stony Brook–Southampton MFA program in Writing and Literature. His darkly comic second novel, *Exit Wounds*, was a major motion picture from Warner Brothers starring Steven Seagal in 2001. His nonfiction has been published in *Newsday*, *Writer's Digest*, and *The Long Island Pulse*. Two of his short stories have appeared in Otto Penzler anthologies.

There is something reassuring in a well-written police procedural. Evil is uncovered. Perpetrators are caught and punished. Curtains are lifted on crime and the flawed human beings who fight crime for pay. The reader gets deep inside the nightly news.

What I find comforting for the procedural writer is how seamless the plotting can be if the book is started well. Raise enough questions that must be answered and your characters are free to follow those threads to their logical solutions. No one has to grow up emotionally in a cop novel or change bad behaviors. They can, if the writer so desires, but making things right for somebody else excuses a lot of personal misbehavior. And, as Hayes Jacobs always said, good fiction is people misbehaving.

So get the cops in your story right. That's the first order of business. Since I was always more interested in precinct life than any individual crime or punishment, I set the bar low for the technical expertise of my heroes. But I wanted you to believe that they were real. They were precinct outcasts or dilettantes, stunned cogs in a larger machine that was beyond their control. As John Updike wrote accurately and ambiguously about policemen: "They were paid to care about you, but not that much." As a former cop, I had the advantage of a precinct roster to work from; I could mix and match the real and imagined. Most writers have to build this for themselves.

EXERCISE

Your exercise is to imagine any small mixed-gender group of adults you know well—the gang at the office, regulars at your coffee shop, or fellow parents at PTA meetings. Concentrate on their faults and weaknesses and exaggerate them. Do the same with their modest strengths. What divides them? Brings them joy or sorrow? Some will be brave, but some will have hands that shake and voices that break during confrontations.

Not everyone who has the cop job should have it. Maybe you know some folks like that. Maybe your boss is well-meaning but in over his head. Maybe he is not well-meaning. Now imagine your boss and all the other folks as uniformed cops, and hand them badges and guns and the power to cause great harm to themselves and others.

You have your believable police squad. Invent quickie biographies for them to lock them in your mind as characters and send them on a noble mission.

LIKELY SUSPECTS

Characters and Their Relationships

MATTHEW DICKS

Villains

MATTHEW DICKS is the author of the novels *Something Missing; Unexpectedly, Milo;* and *Memoirs of an Imaginary Friend.* When not writing, he spends his time teaching fifth grade in West Hartford, Connecticut; playing with his daughter, Clara; and wishing that his wife, Elysha, would dance more often. He is also a wedding DJ, an avid golfer, and basketball and poker player, and he is still looking for people willing to play tackle football with him.

The most compelling and most terrifying of all literary villains are those who appear the most human and the most appealing to the reader. They are the bad guys whom the reader might, on an especially dark day, find himself or herself secretly cheering for, despite the horror of doing so.

Annie Willkes from Stephen King's *Misery*

Hannibal Lecter from Thomas Harris's *Silence of the Lambs*

Bram Stoker's titular villain from *Dracula*

Iago from Shakespeare's *Othello*

These are villains whom the reader can't help liking at least a little. And the reason for this is simple: The writer did not abandon these villains to the darkness, but instead dared to step into the shadows in order to better understand the motivation of his characters.

As a writer, you must be willing to step into the darkness.

Three things that can help:

1. Understand that very few bad guys think of themselves as bad guys. In the book that I have just finished, *Memoirs of an Imaginary Friend*, one of my characters says, "Maybe we are all devils to someone else." I believe that this is true. Whether the villain is an ax murderer, a bank robber, or even the destroyer of kittens, he or she often has motives that seem fair and just in his or her own mind. And it is when those motives can be described honestly and fairly, absent of any preconceived prejudice, that your bad guy can come alive.

   Place yourself in the mind of the villain. Find sympathy for the villain's circumstances. Envision what the world must look like when one believes what your bad guy believes. Why is your ax murderer obliged to hack up old ladies? What are your bank robber's justifications for stealing from others? What does your kitten destroyer have against tiny felines that compels him to want them dead?

   The best of all bad guys have a reason for their villainy.

   The shark in Peter Benchley's *Jaws* eats human beings because this was what evolution has designed him to do. Dickens's Miss Havisham (*Great Expectations*) is swindled and left at the altar. Shakespeare's Edmund (*King Lear*) rises up against the injustices of illegitimacy and the tyranny of the first-born ("Now, gods, stand up for bastards!" he shouts). Stephen King's Annie Wilkes (*Misery*) hobbles writer Paul Sheldon in order to save her literary heroine, Misery Chastain. Even the Big Bad Wolf was simply trying to do what nature dictates all wolves to do: eat that which they can.

   They are all villains, but can we fault them for what they do?

2. This may seem rather obvious and simple, but try to remember that every character has a mother, and more often than not, a mother will love her child as villainous as he or she may be, and never give up hope that her child will eventually turn to the light.

   Assume the role of the mother. Be the mother of your bad guy. What might she say?

   Can't you see Captain Hook's mother attributing his villainy to the loss of his arm at the hands of Peter Pan (an often forgotten detail, the crocodile eats Hook's hand only after it had been chopped off)?

Or Moby-Dick's mother blaming her not-so-little whale's rampage on the incessant hunting by nineteenth-century whalers?

Or Big Brother's mom from Orwell's *1984* trying to explain to her country club socialites that her son's dictatorial inclinations were simply the result of his desire for order and civility.

Mothers have a nearly unfailing ability to see the righteousness in the most despicable of children. Do the same for your characters and you may find enough sympathy and compassion to humanize your villain.

3. Don't make life too easy for your bad guy. Flaws, foibles, and soft spots are often enough to make the worst bad guy seem slightly endearing or downright heroic to your readers.

    Robert Louis Stevenson's Long John Silver (*Treasure Island*) suffers the physical disability of a wooden leg and has a soft spot for Jim Hawkins that ultimately proves to be his undoing. Had he simply been able to cut young Jim's throat, he would have escaped with all of the treasure rather than three or four hundred guineas.

    Hannibal Lecter, one of the most frightening of villains in all of literature, is made almost heroic in light of his own tormentor, Dr Frederick Chilton (is there anything more villainous than an incompetent, jealous, ambitious psychologist) and his soft spot for Clarice Starling.

    Shakespeare's Lady Macbeth is tormented by guilt. Lewis Carroll's Queen of Hearts is constantly being subverted by the King of Hearts. Mr. Hyde must contend with the pestering reemergence of Dr. Jekyll.

A villain's life is never simple. And villains are not without villains. Remember this and your bad guys may not seem so bad after all.

EXERCISE

Choose a bad guy. One of your own making or one from literature. Imagine that the villain is standing trial for his or her crimes. Write two letters:

1. One from the perspective of the villain, asking the court for leniency, on the basis of the villain's more than reasonable motivations (which you will explain in full).

2. One from the perspective of the villain's mother, explaining the misunderstood nature of her child and asking the court for leniency toward the villain.

HALLIE EPHRON

Choosing Details to Reveal Character

HALLIE EPHRON writes suspense novels. Her latest is *Come and Find Me* from William Morrow. Her novel *Never Tell a Lie* was a finalist for the Mary Higgins Clark Award and was made into the movie AND BABY WILL FALL for Lifetime Movie Network. She is an award-winning crime fiction book reviewer for *The Boston Globe*. Her *Writing and Selling Your Mystery Novel: How to Knock 'Em Dead with Style* was nominated for an Edgar Award.

Think about a character in your book. Conjure in your mind what she looks like—her physical stature, her complexion, her hair, her eyes, her clothing, jewelry, posture, scars, and so on. Now, mentally set her in motion. How does she stand, sit, walk, or run? How does she show that she's anxious, upset, frustrated, elated, or surprised?

If you'd been taking notes, you could have generated a laundry list of details. Convey them all and you will overwhelm the reader. Instead, sift through the items on the list and pick the details that are the most potent at showing your character's personality and suggesting her backstory. Include some at the outset and layer in more as your story moves forward.

Showing with a few telling physical details. Your character's first appearance on the page is a critical moment that establishes that character in the reader's mind. Your challenge is to find the details that will create a compelling presence, rather than a checklist of physical details that constructs a lifeless, paint-by-numbers replica of the character you envision.

Take this example from *A Yellow Raft in Blue Water*. Author Michael

Dorris introduces the reader to Rayona's mother, an American Indian woman, as she plays solitaire on her hospital bed:

> *With the back moved all the way up and a pillow wedged under her knees, everything Mom wants is within her reach. Her round face is screwed into a mask of concentration, like a stumped contestant on Jeopardy! with time running out, and her eyes see nothing but the numbers on the cards. She wears her favorite rings, a narrow abalone, an inlaid turquoise-and-jet roadrunner, and a sandcast silver turtle. Dwarfed among them, the thin gold of her wedding band cuts into her third finger. She's on her throne, but her mind is with the game.*

Notice that Dorris has given us no vital statistics like height, weight, eye color, or hairstyle. We have no idea what Mom is wearing or whether her fingernails are polished. But still, with only her intense concentration on the game, her posture in the bed, and the rings that overwhelm her wedding band, she feels alive and intensely present to us.

In a second example from later in the same scene, Rayona's father appears in the doorway. Notice the details Dorris chooses to show the reader:

> *For a big man he's quiet, and I'm always surprised when he appears. He's tall and heavy, with skin a shade browner than mine. He has let his Afro grow out and there's rainwater caught in his hair. His mailman uniform is damp too, the gray wool pants baggy around the knees. At his wrist, the bracelet of three metals, copper, iron, and brass, has a dull shine. I've never seen him without it. He looks uncomfortable and edgy in the brightly lit room and wets his lips.*

Dorris uses quite a few physical details to establish the character's presence—his physical stature (*tall and heavy*), complexion (*browner than mine*), a long-ish Afro, and bracelet. The damp uniform shows him to be a mail carrier who's probably just come from work.

The contrast between Rayona's father and mother are striking. Where her mother feels relaxed and in her own world, the father seems ill at ease as he wets his lips, and the reader feels a dynamic, possibly a danger, beginning to build.

Fill the fictional world your character inhabits with props. Use them to suggest your character's backstory. Show, for example, that the sheets on just one side of her queen-size bed look as if they've been slept in, and you suggest a character who is recently separated from a lover. A funerary urn on the mantel suggests it's a separation due to death. The greeting on her answering machine is a man's voice— "Sorry we can't take your call"—suggesting that she hasn't begun to move on.

Which of these details would you show the reader first? If you carefully choreograph the details you choose to put on the page, you can reveal your character and her backstory in layers, deepening the reader's understanding as your story moves forward.

EXERCISE

1. Rule a page into two columns. In the left column, put the name of one of your main characters and list key elements of that character's personality and past. For example:

Jack Seever

   a. Impatient and ruthless businessman
   b. Trusts no one
   c. Is nearly broke and desperate to keep it a secret
   d. Still loves his high school sweetheart; they used to sing together in coffeehouses
   e. Gave up his dream of being a musician in order to fulfill his father's: making money

2. In the right column, make a list of every detail you know about that character—from physical attributes like eye color and height, to the settings that are his, like his office and home, to his personal possessions, like shoes and briefcase, home furnishings, and so on.

Don't self-censor. Try to get as many details down as you can so that this character, his possessions, and the settings that are uniquely his are etched in your mind.

3. Highlight in green any detail in the right column that reveals any of the key aspects of your character you listed on the left.

4. Highlight in red any detail in the right column that is nice for you, the writer, to know but not essential to convey to the reader.

5. As you write this character, use the green-highlighted details of person and place to reveal the character to the reader, building more details and depth of character as the novel progresses.

SOPHIE LITTLEFIELD

Creating Emotional Depth

SOPHIE LITTLEFIELD's first novel, *A Bad Day for Sorry*, won the Anthony Award and the Reviewers' Choice Award for Best First Mystery of 2009 by *RT Book Reviews* magazine, and it was nominated for the Edgar, Macavity, and Barry awards for Best First Novel. Sophie's first young adult novel, *Aftertime*, debuted in March 2011. Her award-winning short stories have appeared in a variety of publications. Sophie lives in Northern California with her family.

I'm always surprised when writers tell me they struggle with writing emotion. Humans are emotional creatures; most of us have experienced a full complement of emotions by the time we are adults, and gaps in our experience can be filled by observing others.

The difficulty does not appear to lie in understanding a character's emotions—writers tell me that they know their characters are feeling disappointment or joy or desire or grief or any of a hundred other emotions—but in putting them into words that will not get in the way of the story's momentum. There is a tendency to tell without showing: "Sharon was sad." Many writers know they need to improve in this area, but don't know where to start.

To write emotion effectively, a writer needs to first learn to pay attention to how emotions feel and look. Our bodies are reliable reflectors of emotion, and by noting and describing the sensations that result from feelings, you can teach yourself to write them believably. Just as important are external manifestations of emotion—changes in expression, skin tone, and voice; tics and gestures—and you can train yourself to observe these as well.

The quickest way to lose a reader is to present an unsympathetic hero. Typically, as we create characters, we rely on their actions to convey heroism or likability. But a character's appeal is just as dependent on his emotional motivations as on the particular choices he makes.

A detective who leaves his girlfriend because a difficult case demands all his time may come across as cold or selfish, alienating readers. But what happens if you explore the emotions behind his actions? Consider these two possibilities:

The detective is afraid that the killer is learning too much about him and may use that knowledge to hurt him through those he cares most about, including his girlfriend, so he pushes her away. His principal emotion is fear; he may also feel fury, protectiveness, and other emotions as the story progresses.

The detective's botched handling of the case leads to harsh judgment by a superior, which in turn dredges up feelings of unworthiness from the detective's past, stemming from a parent's neglect after the accidental death of a preferred sibling. The detective compensates by spending nearly all his time at work and by drinking and taking foolish risks. The principal emotion here is shame, followed by grief and anger.

In the first example, the detective is aware of his emotion and motivation; in the second, he is not. Both can be effective, but the second requires the author to communicate emotion to the reader indirectly.

Readers want to feel that they know and understand the characters in their favorite books. When judging whether an action is sufficiently motivated—whether a character would really do that—the reader is subconsciously measuring what she knows about a character against his actions and choices.

What she knows includes the character's backstory and relationships, but just as important are the reactions and feelings belonging to each character.

You must understand your characters' emotional palettes—what they feel most often; how they view emotions; what they allow themselves to experience and what feelings they block. Remember that repressing emotions is associated with physical sensations and external behaviors as well as expressing them.

Search your writing for emotion words ("Earl became enraged") and try substituting the experience of the emotion: "Earl's mouth tightened," "He gripped the wheel tightly," "His gut roiled," "He spoke with deadly precision." The result is often far more compelling prose.

The importance of emotion to genre fiction can't be overstated. It is key to building characters that readers care about; without vivid emotion there is no character arc. A character who merely goes through the motions—no matter how gripping the plot—cannot carry a story, while one whose emotions are well communicated can win readers' hearts.

EXERCISE

Becoming keenly aware of how emotions feel is the first step to writing them more effectively.

When you are feeling a strong emotion, take note of how it feels:

- In your head

- In your gut

- In your nerves

- How are you breathing?

- How fatigued or excitable are you?

- Are you sweating?

- Tearful?

- Are you blushing, ruddy, pale?

Keep a diary and jot down as much information as you can about how you experience emotion. Try to observe a full spectrum, from positive to negative, and to discern differences between related emotions. For instance, fear can be shaded by anxiety, trepidation, phobia, or other subtle differences.

After you have a good grasp of your own emotions, start observing others. Look for differences in how people express the same emotions. A timid person expressing anger is quite different from a bully.

Finally, using the list above, ask people to tell you how their emotions feel to them.

SHEILA CONNOLLY

To Whom Does Your Character Turn When She Needs Help, and What Do They Bring to the Equation?

After collecting too many degrees and exploring careers from art historian to investment banker to professional genealogist, SHEILA CONNOLLY began writing mysteries in 2001. Her Orchard Mystery series debuted in 2008 with *One Bad Apple*, followed by *Rotten to the Core*, *Red Delicious Death*, and *A Killer Crop*. Her Museum Mystery series opened with *Fundraising the Dead* in 2010, followed by *Let's Play Dead* (2011). She is a member of Sisters in Crime, Mystery Writers of America, and Romance Writers of America.

In a mystery, no one can do it alone. There's too much information that must be pried out of people and assembled to solve the crime, and that's where the other characters come in.

I write traditional mysteries, and in that genre the setting is usually a small town or community.

When I began writing the Orchard Mystery series, I was inspired by a real house, one built in the 1760s by one of my sixth great-grandfathers. It's located in a typical small New England town, one that is struggling to survive in the modern world with no industry and a declining population. It was a perfect setting, I thought, lots of history, and lots of conflict.

I took my protagonist, Meg Corey, stripped her of her Boston job and her boyfriend, and dumped her in this town, with no income, no friends, and no idea what she's going to do. Then she finds the ex's body in her septic tank. As the newcomer in town and the only one who knew the dead man, she's the obvious suspect for his murder.

But since this book started a series, poor Meg has to beat the rap.

Obviously she needs help, so I began populating her fictional town of Granford.

Next-door neighbor Seth Chapin came first. He's the go-to guy for any problem in town, personal or official (and he's also the plumber who installed that septic tank). Over the course of the series, he becomes increasingly important in Meg's life.

Then came the state police detective, who would like nothing better than to arrest Meg and close the case. He and Seth have an unhappy history that goes back to high school, so they're often at odds and that rubs off on Meg.

Meg needs an income, so she decides to try running the orchard that comes with the property, and she hires an orchard manager. Since Meg can't pay much, Brionna ends up living with Meg. She's not exactly a friend, but she does provide an alternative viewpoint.

Then I started to give Meg some much-needed friends: Seth's sister, the woman who runs the local historical society, a former colleague from Boston. With each successive book I've added more.

The process parallels the real-life experience of any newcomer. Meg meets people one at a time and gradually becomes part of the local community. But it's not random: each person you introduce has to have a reason to be there, even more than one reason. The person may appear to be a friend, but he or she may also be a murderer. A character can't take up space because you wanted to include your aunt Mabel or your best friend or a jerk of a former employer in a book, or because you had some sharp dialogue that didn't fit any of your other characters. And they can't just walk through, drop a clue, then vanish for the rest of the book.

EXERCISE

How do you build a town in your book? By creating characters, one at a time.

PROTAGONIST: What are his or her defining characteristics? Is this person gregarious or shy?

SIDEKICK: This person's personality should complement your protagonist's. Sidekicks serve important functions:

- a sounding board for your protagonist
- a second pair of eyes
- a connection to a broader pool of people who may know something relevant
- a backup when your protagonist inevitably gets into trouble

LAW ENFORCEMENT OFFICIALS: It's hard to solve a crime without them. Such characters can be antagonists, allies, love interests, friends, or all of the above.

SUSPECTS: Yes, more than one; readers like to be challenged to solve the crime, and that means you need multiple-choice suspects. How many is up to you, and remember, you have to create a three-dimensional personality for each of them.

Everyone who appears must serve the story in some way. They may:

- give insight into your protagonist's character
- offer clues
- divert attention from the real villain
- provide comic relief
- add local color

You can combine these roles, and the characters can evolve through the course of the book. Someone who appears as a buffoon in the beginning may turn out to be the love interest, or the killer. But whatever you do, make them believable, three-dimensional characters.

LYNNE HEITMAN

What Drives Your Character?

LYNNE HEITMAN worked for fourteen years in the airline industry, which makes everything else seem easy by comparison. She drew on that rich and colorful experience to create the Alex Shanahan thriller series, including *Hard Landing*, which takes place at Boston's Logan Airport, and *Tarmac*, named by *Publishers Weekly* as one of the year's best thrillers of 2002. Her current titles, *First Class Killing* and *The Pandora Key*, are available from Pocket Books. Her short story "Exit Interview" was recently published in the *Boston Noir* anthology, edited by Dennis Lehane.

I like characters. I like making characters. When I'm writing a book, I often have to declare a moratorium on new characters or else I never get to other necessary steps in the process . . . like plotting. Characters come easier to me than plot. Some writers see their books; I hear them. They get into my head and I hear their voices. It takes me longer to get to what they look like. Readers of my earliest drafts never had any idea what my characters looked like. I had to go back and try to create physical images that were as strong as the voices I was hearing.

I believe readers buy books for a lot of reasons. They might like the cover. They might have read a review or heard a recommendation from a friend. But they stay with the book because they connect with the characters. Voice is critical in developing a character, but what makes them relatable on the deepest level is not what they sound like or what they look like. It's their motivation. As human beings, we all want things, and we feel closest to the people and the characters who want things, too.

For a mystery writer, a character's motivation can seem deceptively easy. A homicide detective who gets handed a murder to solve doesn't ask what his motivation is. It's the same with private investigators. A client walks into the office, lays out a case, and pays money to have it solved. But to me, those are plot points, ways to set the story in motion. Just as your occupation doesn't say everything there is to know about you, simply being a cop doesn't make a character interesting. Sometimes you have to go back to why that character became a cop to find the good stuff. Cops and crooks often come from the same place—even the same DNA—and the motivation for each is not always that different.

Amateur sleuths can be trickier when it comes to motivation. What sane woman would walk into a dark basement knowing a murderer might be lurking there if she wasn't being paid to do it? Why not just call the police? Such is the mystery writer's challenge. In my first book, my sleuth was the manager of an airline operation at Logan Airport investigating the murder of her predecessor, someone she'd never met. Finding her motivation wasn't that hard at first. Curiosity in and of itself can be a powerful motivator. But if you want your character to have any brains at all, and I did, curiosity works only up to a point. Once the bullets started flying, I had to come up with a good reason for her not to do the sensible thing and bail. That's the thing about stories. The road has to rise. The stakes have to get higher and the character's motivation has to rise with it or else she seems at best like a moron and at worst, unrealistic.

There is often a point in your story where your hero will have the chance to bail out, will even want to give up because you've taken him to some dark places, places he doesn't want to go. Or maybe he's just worn out by the journey. You need to come up with a way to keep him in the game, because if he does the sensible thing, the obvious thing, and walks away, that's the end of your story. This is usually the point where the villain does something to make the fight personal. He kidnaps the wife or beats up the best friend or kills the dog. Whatever it is, it has to be strong enough to turn the hero around and propel him the rest of the way up a steep mountain where we know and he knows nothing good awaits him.

Some of the most powerful motivation comes from loss. Having something taken away can give rise to the strongest emotions. Grief.

Hate. Redemption. Self-loathing. A lust for revenge. Motivation can come from something basic, like wanting to live through the day, or it can derive from something more subtle and complex. Something internal. Sam Spade was supposedly on the trail of the Maltese Falcon, but his real motivation was to find who killed his partner. At the end of the story, he says, "When a man's partner is killed he's supposed to do something about it." It's a simple statement, but a powerful one. He didn't even much like his partner. He was having an affair with his wife. But the search reveals his true motivation—an unwavering commitment to his own personal code of ethics.

At several points during the development of your story, and particularly when you feel stuck, ask the question "What does she want?" Then ask, "What is she willing to do to get it?" If at any point in your story what she wants is not worth what she has to go through to get it, you have to fix something or your reader will stop believing. It's hard for a reader to relate to a character he doesn't believe. If he stops relating, he might stop caring and if he stops caring, he might put your book down and never pick it up again. Increase the value of what your hero wants or decrease the level of pain she has to go through to get it. I'm never in favor of decreasing the pain. Tests and obstacles on a rising scale of tension are what make your story go, so figure out how to make your character's motivation increase with each new test or obstacle. Here's one way to do it.

EXERCISE

STEP 1. CREATE YOUR CHARACTERS
Go to a place where you like to hang out. It could be the gym, Starbucks, or church. Observe the people around you. Find two people talking to each other, neither of whom you know. Observe them closely, but try not to get arrested. Look for details—how they sit or stand, the expressions on their faces, how they're dressed, and how they interact. If you're close enough, listen to their voices and how they talk. Jot down quick physical descriptions and give them names.

STEP 2. FIND THEIR MOTIVATION

Now assume one of them is planning to kill the other. Avoid making either one a vampire or a sociopath because the next part of the exercise is to find the motivation. Use any motive you want. Here's a list to get you going: jealousy, revenge, greed, lust for money or power. Once you've settled on one, write one or two pages of backstory to support it. Maybe one of your characters is having an affair with the other one's partner. Maybe it's a wealthy father telling his son he won't be included in the will. Find the circumstances that would provide one of your characters with enough motivation to kill the other.

STEP 3. LOOK DEEPER

Once you have the circumstances, go deeper into your character and find what is really broken inside. What happened to make him or her capable of taking a human life? When did it happen?

STEP 4. WRITE A SCENE

Once you have all that worked out, write a scene between your two characters. Figure out how to convey the most important elements of what you've figured out, without including backstory. Remember, no telling allowed. Show us.

JADEN TERRELL

Make 'Em Real: Reveal Your Characters Through Relationships

JADEN TERRELL is the author of *Racing the Devil* (2009) and *A Cup Full of Midnight* (2012), both featuring Nashville private detective Jared McKean. Terrell is the executive director of the Killer Nashville Thriller, Mystery, and Crime Literature Conference, and is a member of Mystery Writers of America, Private Eye Writers of America, International Thriller Writers, and the Tennessee Writers Alliance.

When I was in the third grade, I read a book called *The Silver Sword* by Ian Serraillier. I carried the book everywhere with me, reading and rereading it until it crumbled in my hand. I still remember tears streaming down my eight-year-old face as the Nazis invaded Poland and shattered the Balicki family.

Forty-plus years later, I'm still haunted by responsible Ruth, irrepressible Bronia, determined Edek, and orphaned Jan, who feared there would be no place for him once the family was reunited. The author didn't tell me Ruth was responsible; he showed me through her care for those she loved. He didn't tell me Edek was determined; he showed me a boy whose desire to find and protect his sisters was so strong that he escaped a Nazi prison camp by clinging to the underbelly of a train for hours. He didn't tell me about Jan's fears; he showed me through the boy's jealous behavior toward Edek and his possessiveness of the girls.

It was the characters who made this book remarkable—characters revealed through their relationships with others. When I became a writer, I knew I wanted to write about characters readers would remember and want to visit again and again. I began with my private detective hero, Jared McKean. I knew what he *looked* like—mid-thirties, buckskin-colored hair, Marlboro-man good looks. I knew he came from a law enforcement background and that he wore a leather bomber jacket that his father had worn in Vietnam, but these were surface characteristics. It wasn't until I began to explore his relationships with others that he really came to life.

As I asked myself questions about his relationships, a pattern emerged. Jared has a thirty-six-year-old quarter horse he's had since he was a boy. He has an elderly Akita. He's still in love with his ex-wife. His roommate is a gay man with AIDS, a man Jared has been friends with since kindergarten. Laying out these relationships showed me a key aspect of Jared's character: this is a man who doesn't let go of the things he loves. This characteristic is a driving force in the Jared McKean books, and I might not have discovered it if I hadn't taken the time to explore his relationships.

If I've done my job well, I won't need to tell my readers that Jared is a loyal man with a strong need to protect others. They'll see it when he defends his housemate against a bigot, when he cradles his son in his arms, when they learn that he once accepted disgrace and the loss of his job in order to protect a woman who betrayed him.

If you'd like to use relationships to add more depth and complexity to your characters, try using the following exercise. (Because my protagonist is male, I've used masculine pronouns. If your character is female, you should substitute feminine pronouns where applicable.)

EXERCISE

Answer the following questions. You can answer in your own voice or your character's, in as much detail or as little as seems appropriate. Don't be afraid to go deep. The more you learn about your character, the richer your story will be.

Is the character married? If yes, describe his relationship with his spouse or partner. If no, is he single (never married), divorced, or widowed? If divorced, what caused the dissolution of the marriage? What kind of relationship does he have with his ex-spouse? If widowed, under what circumstances? Where is he in the grieving process? Still holding on or ready to move forward? Is he a serial monogamist, a playboy, or celibate? If he's single, is he in a serious relationship, or is he looking for one, or does he play the field and like it that way?

Does he have a child or children? If yes, what sex(es)? How old? Describe the character's relationship with each child. What does being a parent mean to the character? If he has no children, why not? Does he want them? How does he feel about being (or not being) a parent?

Does he have siblings? How many? What sex(es)? How old? Describe the character's relationship with each sibling. If the character has no siblings, how has this affected his life?

Are his parents living? Describe his past and/or present relationship with each parent.

How was—and is—the character shaped by his family?

Does the character have a pet, perhaps more than one? How many? What kind? What are their names? How does he feel about them? How did he acquire each one? If he has no pets, why not?

Who are the character's friends and allies? Describe each major relationship in detail. Be sure to include any emotional conflicts and the implications of these relationships.

Does the character have any enemies or rivals? A nemesis? How did the animosity or rivalry begin? Describe what happened and how it affected the character.

Are there any relationships in which a friend, family member, or ally is also a rival? In these circumstances, how does the character balance love and tension, or love and betrayal?

If applicable, who are the character's employers, employees, or colleagues? Describe the character's relationship with each in as much detail as necessary.

Are you beginning to see any patterns? Do you feel like you're getting to know your character? Are you beginning to see his strengths? His flaws or weaknesses? How does the character interact with others?

Keep asking yourself questions until you understand your character. Each time you answer a question, you learn more about the character. You'll notice that each choice you make narrows the possibilities of future choices. Each new choice must be consistent with what has come before, or you will need to reconcile the apparent contradiction. For example, if your character is charming and charismatic with his colleagues, but cold and emotionally controlling with his spouse, you need to understand why and help your readers understand as well.

By eliminating choices or making (and explaining) unlikely ones, you begin to get a clearer picture of the character. By surrounding that character with people who bring out different facets of his personality, you end up with a main character of depth and complexity—one your readers will remember long after they've closed the cover of your book.

161

KATHLEEN GEORGE

Casting Your Characters

KATHLEEN GEORGE is the Edgar-nominated author of *The Odds*, the fourth in the Richard Christie novels set in Pittsburgh. Other titles in the series are *Taken*, *Fallen*, *Afterimage*, and *Hideout*. She is also the editor of the short fiction collection *Pittsburgh Noir*. George is a professor of theater and playwriting at the University of Pittsburgh, where she has directed many plays.

Human behavior is wonderfully complex and mysterious. Voices have distinctive prints. We know who is on the phone by the first half-word. And sometimes we recognize a person even from a distance by the way she walks. People have personal rhythms—of thought, of movement, of speech.

There are all kinds of ways of getting at character behaviors. Actors often use a chart that includes some fifty things to be determined. They must decide, among many other things, breathing patterns (shallow or deep, ragged or smooth), the state of digestion in the stomach and intestines, financial condition (how much money is in the character's pocket, how much in the bank, how much under the mattress), emotional tendencies (inhibitions and exhibitions), religious beliefs.

Writers, like actors, are trying to capture human behavior. And they need to know the same things. Writers of mysteries are especially dependent upon the ways characters move and speak—and pretend and conceal things that cannot be said—because those are the things mysteries are about.

"Do you see everything in your head?" I am often asked. "Do you see your characters and control their behaviors?"

I believe the ideal position of the writer is a changing one—both actor and director to what is on the page's stage. There are moments when I am my characters, feeling everything from the inside. And other moments when I step back and watch the characters—and help direct the performance. For this second step, I find it very helpful to cast characters, using professional actors from the stage or film or TV to find an image that works. I like to let the image of an existing actor begin to inform the way one of my characters speaks and moves. I love the point at which, with a strong image—a face, a movement, a pattern, a voice—I find the character capable of surprising me.

When I was a theater director and had to cast plays, I would notice that certain actors didn't make much sense in the secondary position. They had to be the doers, dominant. Other actors were especially right for whimsical humor and in some cases were not credible when the humor was harsh, satiric. There was constantly a need to get the dynamics right in a scene so that two dissimilar types got the action-engines going.

Aesthetic weights was a concept we talked about often. Some actors are naturally aesthetically heavy and others are light. A heavy actor (not in physical weight, but in aesthetic weight) moves less, and is more solid in opinions, while an actor of a lighter aesthetic weight is more changeable, flexible moment by moment.

When I first created my lead character, Richard Christie, I saw him as aesthetically medium to heavy. He looked a good bit like Liam Neeson. But he also had thought patterns that were calling up someone else. I found myself saying in several situations that to me he had a good deal of Gabriel Byrne in him, too. I couldn't explain easily what I meant, but the image and voice of Byrne kept coming to me, telling me something.

Christie, the character I wrote (and continue to write) is thoughtful, moody, smart, a bit self-effacing, egotistical, religious, guilty. I described him early on as the ultimate father figure. The other characters of each novel are drawn to him, even overly dependent on him; almost everyone falls in love with him. I had seen Gabriel Byrne only in MILLER'S CROSSING and THE USUAL SUSPECTS. What sense did my casting make?

The sense it made came a decade later when Byrne starred in *In Treatment* for HBO. His Dr. Paul Weston was in the mold of my Richard

Christie—paternalistic, moody, introspective, sympathetic, personally unsettled. He showed me the image I'd had all along. It was there, underneath.

My detective Colleen Greer has hair like Meg Ryan's and she looks a bit like her. She acts like a combination of Melissa George when she's impish, flirtatious, and Scarlett Johansson when she's tentative, thoughtful.

I encourage you to cast your characters and to do so from gut feeling. Images of people spark our imaginations, impel us to create. The following is an exercise in allowing known actors to inhabit your characters.

EXERCISE

Take something you have written and revise the scene with a specific set of actors in mind. Let's say you've written a confrontation scene that doesn't have all the layers and mixed moods you wish it had.

What happens if you imagine Josh Brolin confronting Larry David? You might discover humor you didn't know was there. Or you've got in mind a mother-daughter scene in which both characters are hiding something. How does this scene work if you cast Laura Linney and Ellen Page?

Allow yourself to add to the scene small details that come from the cast you've chosen. You can cast combinations of people. You can change your cast when something isn't quite working. To be clear— I'm not saying you should write that your character looks like or sounds like X. Just let them . . . be X.

DIANA ORGAIN

Putting Yourself in the Characters' Shoes

DIANA ORGAIN is the author of the Maternal Instincts Mystery series (*Bundle of Trouble, Motherhood Is Murder*, and *Formula for Murder*) published by Berkley. She holds a B.A. and an MFA in playwriting from San Francisco State University with a BA minor in acting. Diana has acted professionally in many theater roles and national commercials. She has written several plays that have been produced at San Francisco State University, GreenHouse Productions, and PlayGround in San Francisco. She currently lives in San Francisco with her husband and three children.

One of the most challenging parts about writing a great mystery is creating compelling characters. How does one create a believable killer when . . . er . . . hopefully . . . the author is not one! Fortunately, our imaginations can take us on exciting journeys, where one need not hurt anyone. One way to get into a character's head is to put yourself into their shoes by acting out the story.

When you put yourself in the body of a character, when you physically get up and play, things start to open up. For instance, if the character is powerful, where does their strength come from? The legs? The stomach? The chest? Are they reserved or shy? What part of themselves do they hold back? How the character carries their body, how they walk and move effects what they say. And that, of course, effects what you write.

Acting out the parts can also help you edit and move the story forward. You'll be able to understand not only what dialogue is necessary, but also what is motivating the character. Acting out different sections will help you with the conflict in the scene as each character should be moving toward their own objective while being blocked by another character or thing (obstacle).

And perhaps one of the most valuable aspects of running through this exercise is ensuring that each character is different and unique. That each character is serving your story. That each one is complex yet human and relatable.

Have fun with the following exercise. Let your imagination run wild and let go of your inhibitions as you step out from behind the page and onto the stage (even if it is only a stage in your own private living space).

EXERCISE

1. If you've written a scene with some dialogue in it, great: print it now. If not, move to step 2.

2. Get up on your feet! Select one of the characters to act out. If you are working with something you've written, read the lines and move as you say them. Find out how the character "feels" on his or her feet. (Yes, that's theater-speak.)

3. Try the following:

   a. *Walking in character:* Walk around as the character. What body part leads? Does the character walk on the balls of the feet or on the heels? Does changing that small detail change the feel of the character? Pick an emotion (e.g., anger, shame, fear, love, hope . . .) and walk around. How does that emotion feel in the body of the character? What emerges? Now pick a specific place to walk to or a reason for the walk. What happens in the body of the character?

   b. *Find a gesture:* Connect a gesture with each character you play. The gesture need not end up on the written page, but it can be helpful to trigger for you different elements of your character's personality. Does he or she fidget? Wring hands? Giggle? Repeatedly check the time? How does this gesture define this character and affect the other characters?

   c. *Slow it down:* Try to move through your scene, whether written or improvisational, in slow motion. Look for a connection between the words as you speak them and to the character you're working on. This will aid you with finding the character's motivation.

d. *Speed it up:* If you speed through the scene, you will discover if the character's motivation is sustained or if it alters. Hurrying through the scene can add urgency. Does that suit your character and his or her needs?

e. *Whisper or yell the scene:* Whispering or yelling will strengthen your character's need to communicate and will intensify the emotions. When you return to a regular voice is the need to communicate retained?

f. *Physical obstacle:* Pretend there is a physical obstacle in between the characters in the scene (a door, a chair, a lake, to name a few). This should again intensify emotion. How does this affect your character?

4. Now you're ready to rinse and repeat. You can use the various tactics above and others (feel free to create your own acting exercises) on various characters and scenes. Experiment to find out which tactic informs you most about each character, and understand that there may be different tactics for different characters, which hopefully will inform you even further about the character.

KENNETH WISHNIA

Getting Out of Your Comfort Zone:
Writing from Different Points of View

KENNETH WISHNIA's first novel, *23 Shades of Black*, was nominated for the Edgar and the Anthony awards. His other novels include *Soft Money*, a *Library Journal* Best Mystery of the Year, and *Red House*, a *Washington Post Book World* "Rave" Book of the Year. His short stories have appeared in *Ellery Queen's Mystery Magazine*, *Alfred Hitchcock's Mystery Magazine*, *Queens Noir*, and elsewhere. His latest novel is *The Fifth Servant*. He teaches writing, literature, and other deviant forms of thought at Suffolk Community College on Long Island.

Crime writers are often told to spend as much time on their bad guy as they do on their good guy, because you want the opponents to be more or less evenly matched, you want a villain who is compelling because he or she gives free rein to some of our own darkest desires and impulses (which are normally suppressed), and because, well, you want all your characters to be believable, not simply two-dimensional cardboard cutouts, don't you?

Another reason to write from more than one perspective is that it allows you to employ Alfred Hitchcock's formula for suspense: Tell the audience something the main character doesn't know. (Think of the scene in PSYCHO when Vera Miles tells John Gavin, "I can handle a sick old woman.")

My own series, featuring Ecuadorian-American detective Filomena Buscarsela, is written in the first-person present tense. One advantage of this style is that it lends tremendous immediacy to the narrative: Filomena is speaking directly to you, the reader, and she tells you everything that she is experiencing. What is lost, or at least weakened, is the ability to generate the classic Hitchcockian edge-of-the-seat, nail-biting suspense described above.

So I took a different approach in my latest novel, *The Fifth Servant*, a Jewish-themed historical thriller set in Prague in the late sixteenth century. The central character, an assistant *shammes* to the great Rabbi Loew (of the Golem legends), addresses the reader in the first person (past tense), but there are five other characters in the story whose points of view are presented in the third person (past tense). This approach helped me produce a narrative with a great deal of depth and complexity, as well as that crucial sense of ambiguity and ambivalence that makes for compelling drama.

In other words, if you take the time to show that an evil person is acting in a way that he or she somehow believes is completely justified; or, as opposed to most simplistic, big-budget action-adventure narratives, if there is no single, clear-cut choice that your protagonist must make, but a tangled web of conflicting, equally bad choices, then you will have created a much more meaningful and emotionally engaging drama.

Moreover, most beginning writers typically project some version of themselves onto the protagonist's persona, so it's always a good exercise to write from the perspective of someone else.

To that end, I employ the following exercise in my writing classes:

EXERCISE

Choose a newspaper or magazine article about a controversial topic and write a reaction to it in the voice of someone who is *not* you.

You can do this by opening the newspaper at random (or clicking on your preferred news source), but it's often best to choose political or celebrity scandals, since most people generally have strong opinions about such big media events.

The challenge is to create a monologue, with no descriptive passages or other external clues to the speaker's identity, which somehow gets across as much information as possible about the speaker's age, gender, social class, outlook on life, and so on.

The whole point is to get away from autobiographical self-projection. You have to create a person outside of yourself who reacts in a way that is appropriate for *that* person. You can't tell us right out who you are (e.g., "I'm a fifty-four-year-old bus driver . . ."). We have to be able to tell just from what you say and how you would say it if your character is old, young, rich, poor, or somewhere in between.

The results of this exercise are usually quite creative and fun. I've brought in articles about Hillary Clinton addressing the Democratic National Convention (which produced a monologue in the voice of a Latina janitor in the auditorium, watching from behind the scenes, who didn't know enough English to understand what Mrs. Clinton was saying, but who was still impressed with her obvious power, confidence, and authority); one about Miley Cyrus pole-dancing on TV (which produced a response in the voice of a five-year-old girl watching Miley on TV and who couldn't wait to imitate her idol's moves); and most recently, a story about a certain celebrity's latest release from rehab (which gave us a mom who couldn't believe that she had actually once thought the actress might serve as a role model for her own daughter; a disgruntled Vietnam veteran disgusted by the preferential treatment that spoiled celebrities get; and the voice of that celebrity's fictitious roommate in rehab, who resented all the attention her ex-roommate was getting).

It's not hard to take this further, into darker territory, and imagine the voice of a child who innocently tries to reenact a dangerous stunt seen on TV, or the parent who plots revenge on the offending celebrity for having been a bad influence on his or her child, or just where the jealousy expressed by that ex-roommate might lead. See what you can come up with.

FRANKIE Y. BAILEY

Creating Depth Through Character Relationships

FRANKIE Y. BAILEY is a faculty member in the School of Criminal Justice, University at Albany (SUNY). She is the author of *African American Mystery Writers: A Historical and Thematic Study* (2008) and *Wicked Albany: Lawlessness and Liquor in the Prohibition Era* (2009). The fifth book in her Lizzie Stuart mystery series is *Forty Acres and a Soggy Grave* (2011). Frankie is a former executive vice president of Mystery Writers of America and the 2011 vice president of Sisters in Crime.

Writing a mystery novel in which the protagonist is alone on a desert island, or a recluse living on a mountaintop, is possible. But if you do, there had better be a good story about how he got there and why he is staying and who may be showing up soon. In a mystery novel, character relationships are crucial to what happens—to the whodunit, whydunit, and, often, even the howdunit.

These relationships can and should be used to add depth to both the characters and the plot. In the course of interacting with other characters, the protagonist reveals who he is—his attitudes about life, what he believes, what he values. The protagonist reveals what he will fight for or die for.

Certain relationships are common to the genre. Some relationships are specific to subgenres. For example, what would a classic noir novel be without a tough guy and a femme fatale? In crime fiction, some characters support the protagonist (provide aid and comfort). Others are antagonists, who are out to destroy him, or who stand between her and the solution to the crime. In mysteries, as in other fiction, characters have families—or not. And the presence or absence of those family members is significant.

171

Sometimes other characters can serve as sounding boards that allow the protagonist to avoid Shakespearean soliloquies. The protagonist can complain to his secretary or his ex-cop drinking buddy about how there is no justice in the world. Instead of keeping her thoughts about what the villain deserves to herself, the protagonist can vent to her best friend or sidekick over pizza.

In a crime novel, conflict often leads to violence. But there is also verbal aggression, simmering or boiling over, cloaked in humor or downright ugly. Some verbal exchanges can be both more disturbing (for the characters) and more revealing (for the reader) than physical violence.

For example, in the fifth book in my series, my protagonist, Lizzie Stuart, is in a car with her fiancé, John Quinn. They are on their way to a reunion of Quinn's old West Point classmates on a farm on the Eastern Shore of Virginia. Lizzie has been trying to read a tourist guide to the area, but she realizes that before they arrive at their destination and she meets Quinn's friends for the first time, she needs to find out what has been bothering him. This chapter is titled "Talk to Me,"and in these few pages the two characters reveal themselves, as Lizzie probes and Quinn parries. The subtext to her questions about what he has on his mind is that she is concerned about the lack of emotional intimacy in their relationship. As the conversation goes on, Lizzie, the first-person narrator, shares with the reader her own sense of what the problem is between the two of them and why it makes her uneasy. And then something happens, and they are distracted from the conversation. But nothing has been resolved, and the tension between them—the things he hasn't told her and won't tell her, and her fears about this—play out as a subplot during the rest of the book.

I never feel that I understand what a book I am writing is about until I've gotten to know my characters. Before I dive into plotting, I like to spend some time thinking about their relationships. Those relationships will often take the plot in unexpected and rewarding directions.

In the exercise that follows, the object is to people your protagonist's world and then explore his or her interactions with the other characters.

EXERCISE

Who is in your character's world?

This will be determined in part by the subgenre of the novel you are writing, the setting, and the plot. Let's use a police procedural novel as an example. Let's assume you have a detective protagonist who carries the weight of your story. There are some basic questions you should ask and answer:

How does your detective interact with his coworkers? Is she laid-back, gruff, a wiseass? Why? Is this how she really feels or a cover for other emotions?

Is there someone she dislikes? Why does she dislike this person and how does she respond to him or her?

How does your detective respond to orders from her supervisor? Is she accommodating? Challenging? Disrespectful? Why?

How does your detective respond to victims? Is she empathetic and kind in dealing with some victims? Disdainful of others? Does she despise abusive men because her mother was abused? How does this play out when she has to question an alleged abuser or make an arrest?

What is your detective's home life like? What does your detective tell the people in her life about her work? What does she keep from them? How does that affect those relationships?

This kind of exercise works for any type of character. Think about who is in his life and why. Think about how the character responds to the different people in his life. Put him with those people and let them interact. Watch what happens. And ask yourself how this affects how the character responds to the crime or mystery that he has to solve, particularly his ability to rise to the challenge.

KELLI STANLEY

She Can Bring Home the Bacon

KELLI STANLEY is an award-winning author of crime fiction (novels and short stories). She makes her home in Dashiell Hammett's San Francisco, a city she loves to write about. She is the author of two crime fiction series, one set in 1940s San Francisco (featuring hard-boiled female P.I. Miranda Corbie), the other in first-century Roman Britain. Her novels include *City of Dragons*, *Nox Dormienda*, *The Curse-Maker*, and *City of Secrets*.

Women can run for president or hold up banks. They can fly space shuttles, invent new technologies, raise children, care for a household and family, run forgery scams, or mug little old ladies.

In other words, women are capable of the same acts—for good or bad, enforcing the law or breaking it—that men are.

So why do we need to think about women as detectives, as victims, or as killers? Because it has been only within the last half-century that women could even hope to hold some of the same careers as men. Legal battles, constant lobbying, and political and social pressure have opened new arenas for women, but the glass ceiling, according to the latest statistics, is still in place. Sisters in Crime, a nonprofit organization founded by Sara Paretsky in 1987, monitors gender inequalities within the crime-fiction publishing industry itself . . . and sadly, these are not going away.

Cultural traditions, lack of a voice in history text books, and the relative paucity of women in particular jobs or within certain professions throughout the twentieth century have led to gender stereotyping within our culture and entertainment media. Crime fiction writers need to be aware of these clichés in order to comment on them—or avoid them all together.

Woman as Killer. The murderess—a heartless killer devoid of the traditional virtues of mother-love who uses sex appeal to manipulate men—is a stock character in many hard-boiled and noir tales (think *Double Indemnity*), but really, her roots go back to Lady Macbeth and Medea. She is usually depicted as a sexualized being who uses sex but does not enjoy it. In other words, she is fully aware and in control of her allure but never allows herself to emotionally succumb to the man she hopes to manipulate. Her manifestly "unwomanly" nature is also sometimes conveyed through her disdain (and even murder of) children, as with Medea. She is often shown as strong and therefore identified as manlike. The relationship between Lady Macbeth and Macbeth is a perfect example of such traditional gender role-reversal.

Woman as Victim. You've all seen the movie. Young woman walks into basement (parking garage, abandoned house) alone, despite the fact that there's a killer roaming around and her friends have mysteriously disappeared. Maybe the oldest gender cliché on and in the books, the victim is usually young, and not as smart as the reader or audience who is watching her walk into a trap.

Women, of course, are disproportionately victimized by violent crime, particularly serial killer cases that usually make headlines . . . but it is too easy to fall into a trap of your own by constantly depicting them as the helpless, weak prey of predatory criminals.

Woman as Detective. The female detective is a relatively recent character in fiction—she certainly doesn't share the literary pedigree of murderess and victim. Though Nancy Drew and Agatha Christie's Jane Marple have popularized the female amateur sleuth for nearly a century, the female P.I. is of more recent vintage. Thanks to writers Marcia Muller, Sara Paretsky, and Sue Grafton, the hard-boiled woman detective has gained acceptance and respect.

However, just as in the other categories, stereotypes abound. Perky young women who date policemen, tough-as-nails female cops or private investigators, and elderly women who can dispense advice and catch criminals are all commonplace. So you must be deliberate about your character-building . . . tough doesn't always mean masculine.

Playing right tackle in football demands a certain kind of strength. Caring for an ill relative demands another. Women can be quite tough—anyone who's been through childbirth can testify to that. You don't need to resort to gender clichés to write a female detective.

So what do we do as writers? Not create any women victims, killers, or detectives? Not an option. Compelling fiction is published every year featuring every one of these categories. After all, women *are* victims of crime, as are men; women *are* murderers (the film MONSTER is an excellent portrayal of a female serial killer); women fight crime in the contemporary world as law enforcement officials and work as private detectives, and did so even in the past. The secret is to make your characters seem as real as possible—to make their motivations, actions, and behaviors believable and not gender stereotypes.

EXERCISE

Before deciding on the gender of your character, make out a list of characteristics you identify as feminine and masculine. Then make a list of a real person's traits—someone close to you, or even yourself, if you can be objective enough.

Most people consist of a mixture of characteristics we typically identify with one gender or another. Figure out what the narrative purpose of your character is, and what mixture of attributes you're looking for.

If you want to write about a female victim, killer, or detective, ask yourself whether or not you could switch genders without a problem. If you can, then either you need to develop a scenario in which the gender is intrinsic to the role as you envision it, or you could think about switching to a male point of view. And don't forget that sexuality itself can be stereotyped—try experimenting with a gay or bisexual POV for one of your characters. Expand and explore the vast diversity of the human condition!

If the female character is your protagonist, develop her as fully as you can. Write about her before you write with her—she should feel real to you, and her reactions should be based on what she would do. What are her favorite foods? What kinds of clothes does she wear? If she's a detective, women may notice details men typically don't, just because of familiarity—and vice versa. A male detective who has children may notice a clue in a child's broken toy before his childless female partner would. In other words, be aware of the stereotypes and clichés . . . and challenge them!

One of the most exhilarating aspects of writing crime fiction is living in your protagonist's shoes. Whether she wears stilettos, Nikes, or hiking boots, follow where she leads. She won't steer you wrong.

RACHEL BRADY

No Sloppy Seconds:
Write a Purposeful Supporting Cast

RACHEL BRADY lives in Houston, where she works as an engineer at NASA. Her interests include health and fitness, acoustic guitar, and books of all kinds. *Final Approach* and *Dead Lift* are the first two installments in her Emily Locke mystery series. *Dead Lift* was nominated for a Watson, an award presented for the best sidekick in a mystery.

Selecting the cast for your mystery or suspense novel is no trifling thing. Everybody agrees that it's important to have a well-formed, unique protagonist who is capable of carrying your story. And it's equally important to have well-formed, unique secondary characters. After all, these are the guys who will support your protagonist—or try to kill him. What good is the best hero in the world if there is nobody sinister or special enough to challenge his abilities?

I'm sure you can name someone important who helped you become the person you are today. If pressed, you might also be able to identify an individual who, in some way or another, tried to hold you back. There were certainly many people in between—folks who came in and out of your life without leaving a lasting impression one way or the other.

The pace required for mystery and suspense novels doesn't tolerate the inclusion of characters that fall into this last class. That leaves two main groups into which our supporting characters must fall. Secondary characters in your novel will either (1) help your protagonist or (2) hinder her. The ways in which this happens will not always be obvious to your readers, and that's okay. But you, the writer, must be clear about why each of your supporting characters gets the honor of being on your page.

Consider the people who bring out the best in you. Who makes you laugh? Calms or comforts you? Refocuses you? Choose one name. This is the person I'll call your Helper character.

Now think about folks who really push your buttons—the back-handed-compliment-giver, the overbearing know-it-all, or the consummately together soccer mom who unwittingly makes you feel inadequate when she simply enters a room. Got a name? That's your Inhibitor.

Imagine pulling into your driveway one evening, exhausted and stressed, muddy and wet, and for kicks, starving, too. A familiar car is waiting there.

How do you feel if the car belongs to your Helper? Contrast that with your reaction if the car belongs to your Inhibitor.

If we let them, the people we encounter every day can profoundly influence our outlook, mood, perspective, productivity, and ideas. It's exactly the same way for our protagonists. We can mess with them or throw them a lifeline simply by who we choose to put in the driveway.

Sometimes an antagonist will be disguised as a good guy, sometimes the reverse. A single character—take a love interest, for example—may serve both roles at various times, depending on what happens in the scene. The important thing to remember is that a good supporting cast member always does something to help or hinder your protagonist. Ambivalence is not allowed.

Fashion designers say, "Less is more." Similarly, a manuscript will be tighter if every supporting player serves to aid or divert your sleuth in some way, whether physically, intellectually, emotionally, or otherwise. Think about your cast in terms of less is more. If a character isn't moving the case forward or slowing it down, or boosting your protagonist or demoralizing him, consider deleting that role or combining it with another, more useful character. In this way, everyone on your pages will count.

Supporting characters don't always help or hinder on purpose. A sick child has no idea that his stomach flu is severely limiting his single dad's freedom to investigate a crime. Conversely, a random word of encouragement from an aunt or a sister could be the boost your amateur sleuth needs to shine up her magnifying glass and try again. These players may not be integral to your plot, but they should influence your protagonist in some fundamentally meaningful way, even if your main character doesn't recognize it. In every scene, ask yourself about the reason for the exchange or confrontation.

A main character should come away from every scene a little bit changed from the way she went into it. This could be a big external change, like interviewing someone and finding a clue or a small internal change, like feeling better or worse about her progress on a case. But if nothing has improved or grown worse for your protagonist, you probably don't need the scene, and you may not need the secondary character.

Like real people, secondary characters have their own agendas. Their motivations and goals drive their actions and their interactions with your main character. Ask yourself what each of your secondary characters wants in every scene. Your protagonist obviously has an agenda, too. When conflict arises, he'll have to be resourceful and creative to affect the outcome he wants.

EXERCISE

1. Identify your protagonist's main Helper and main Inhibitor. Go back to the driveway scenario you imagined earlier. Let your frazzled, depleted protagonist take your place. Write dialogue for each scenario, first for the case in which the Helper is waiting, then for the Inhibitor. Notice how your sleuth's mood and responses change depending on who steps out of the car.

    Secondary characters are helpful pacers. When you need to increase tension and raise the stakes, bring in the characters who present the biggest roadblocks. Make things miserable for your protagonist. When it's time for your sleuth to decompress and explore new clues, give him a Helper, a sounding board to offer fresh ideas and play devil's advocate in a nonthreatening way.

2. Few things confuse us more than unexpected behavior. Write a scene in which your character's main Helper inexplicably behaves in a way that slows your sleuth down. Write a page in which his Inhibitor strangely lends him a hand.

   Why did these secondary characters do those things?

Scenarios like these, in which things don't happen in an expected way, present all sorts of opportunities for you, the writer. Unexpected behavior leaves a story ripe for misdirection and misunderstanding, two critical ingredients in mystery and suspense.

VOICE
Tone, POV, and Dialogue

STEVE LISKOW

Voice and the Private Eye

STEVE LISKOW's *Who Wrote the Book of Death?* came out in 2010, and *Alfred Hitchcock's Mystery Magazine* published *The Stranglehold*, his 2009 Black Orchid Novella Award winner. He also writes short stories, and his current projects include mysteries about rock 'n' roll and roller derby. A member of Mystery Writers of America and Sisters in Crime, he lives in Connecticut with his wife, Barbara, and two rescued cats.

The problem," the agent told me, "is that publishers can count how many private eye stories they have. They can't do that with other books."

He's right.

An amateur sleuth can be a nurse, teacher, salesman, reporter, beautician, or dog trainer, and those different worlds offer variety for your stories. Private investigators, on the other hand —male or female— have a fairly constant pathology and get involved in certain situations over and over. That means certain plots appear over and over, too.

So how can you make your story stand out from all the others?

Style and voice.

Style refers to all the technical choices the writer makes to tell his story effectively. Those choices include setting, flashbacks, irony, dialogue, description, and everything else you studied in high school. Voice relies on three interrelated aspects of the story: character, point of view, and attitude, what English teachers usually call tone.

Your story and characters need an attitude, especially the point-of-view characters. If they have no attitude, there's no emotional stake, so your reader won't care enough to keep reading.

Many people claim that first-person POV is the most natural way to write. What they don't mention is how easy it is to do it badly. Repeating "I . . ." can bore your reader until she puts the book down. How do you fix that?

Years ago, George Garrett pointed out that the essential action of a first-person story is always the telling. Your character needs to tell his story. That means he has something at stake, and it creates an attitude that generates a distinctive voice. Think of Patrick Kenzie, who narrates Dennis Lehane's P.I. novels, Linda Barnes's Carlotta Carlyle, or Janet Evanovich's Stephanie Plum.

Omniscient POV allows the narrator to know everyone's thoughts and see all the story's events from the same distance. That's good if you have a complex story with several subplots, but it runs the risk of flattening the different characters' viewpoints into a homogenized sameness that muffles personality.

Multiple close third-person POV helps you pace scenes and create tension. It also helps create voice because the details and perceptions get filtered through different characters, who have distinct personalities and attitudes.

You convey your character's attitude—how he deals with the world around him—through imagery and rhythm. Imagery helps you capture the character's unique worldview and interests. A teacher, athlete, musician, or mechanic sees the world in terms of how he or she copes with it, and the imagery will show that. Children rely on senses other than vision more than most adults, and that can give them a distinctive voice, too. A small child may lack technical vocabulary, but he compares things with what he already knows: candy, animals, textures.

Rhythm is a product of vocabulary and punctuation. Short, choppy sentences (what my teacher used to call Hemingway style) with strong consonant sounds and sparse punctuation feel different from long lyrical sentences with commas, softer closing consonants, and parallel phrases and clauses. Modern open punctuation style favored by many publishers uses fewer commas between independent clauses, so sentences go more quickly, too.

Rita Mae Brown points out the differences between Latin-based vocabulary and Anglo-Saxon vocabulary. We think of the former as gentler and more cultured, maybe because the words often end in

STEVE LISKOW

vowels or softer consonants. It's a polite, erudite language. Anglo-Saxon, with its strong consonants, has most of the words we use to curse. It has more harsh monosyllables that interrupt the flow, too. These differences will help you imbue your character and writing with more attitude.

So will verb tenses. Present tense gives your prose more immediacy than past tense, and many contemporary editors discourage the use of past perfect, favoring the simple past because it creates less distance.

Subtext makes a difference, too. Don Winslow's present tense bristles with energy, and he uses urban settings and characters. As a result, his prose has a subtext that sounds like "Can you effing *believe* this crap?"

Janet Evanovich's Stephanie Plum is a big-haired Jersey Girl to the marrow, and her speech patterns betray her OMG vision of life so you can almost hear a question mark at the end of every sentence. Lisa Scottoline often tells her legal thrillers through Mary DiNunzio, a Nice Catholic Girl turned lawyer (speaking of paradox), and her take on the action adds more flavor than her mother's cooking.

Pat Conroy unspools sentences long enough to use for bungee jumping, full of exquisite description and parallel clauses. His majestic rhythms create a higher vision of the world, even if his characters have demons doing a kick line through their nightmares. Scottish author Kate Atkinson uses allusive puns and irony, referring to film, literature, and rock songs to give her characters a trenchant view of life, sort of *Macbeth* meets the Delta blues. Now look at Robert Crais, James Crumley, S. J. Rozan, or Laurence Block.

That's how you make your P.I. story stand out from the crowd.

Now let's practice.

EXERCISE

Write one page about a small incident that will have no lasting effect on anyone. No plane crashes, earthquakes, or tax audits, OK? No romantic breakups or lottery winnings. Make it as mundane as running out of milk for your breakfast cereal or leaving the dinner in the microwave too long and melting the plastic container.

Now rewrite that same event in at least six of the following styles. Keep the basic facts of the event consistent. Use vocabulary, sentence length, and punctuation to generate different rhythms and show attitude. Some styles will work better than others, and that's the point. You'll discover the voice for a scene, and maybe for your whole book.

1. Use no word of more than two syllables.

2. Use no sentence longer than ten words.

3. Make every sentence at least twenty-five words long.

4. Use present tense.

5. Use second person ("You open the door . . .").

6. Use allusions to the Bible, mythology, or Shakespeare.

7. Use tactile (touch) images or details.

8. Use references to any one of the following: baseball, music, chess, cooking, driving/cars, weather, or flowers.

9. Use only linking or passive verbs. (Every verb has a helping verb that is a form of "to be": *is . . . am . . . was . . . will be . . .* and so forth.)

10. Use no contractions (I'm, I'll, doesn't, don't, can't, he's, she's . . .).

TIM MALEENY

First Lines—An Exercise for Writers

TIM MALEENY is the award-winning author of numerous short stories and four bestselling novels, including *Stealing the Dragon*, which was recently optioned for film, and the comedic thriller *Jump*. He lives in New York with his family.

B*ang.*

How will your story begin? One of the most important decisions you'll make as a writer is how to grab your reader at the top of the page and never let go. As a novelist, I'm constantly rewriting, editing, and cutting and pasting until I have a draft that feels right, but first lines are an obsession. Some of my favorite opening lines appear in this article, words that have inspired me to rework that first sentence until it sings. Before any of my books go to press, I've probably rewritten the opening paragraph no less than forty times, agonizing over every word.

> *It's a lot of work being me.*
> —DON WINSLOW, *The Winter of Frankie Machine*

Is your first line a hook sharp enough to cut through the distractions, disinterest, and white noise buzzing around a potential reader's head? Before you answer, take a moment to consider the following sobering statistics. More than 270,000 books were published in the United States last year. Almost a thousand video game titles were released, along with a couple hundred major movies, not counting the DVD issues of the previous year's films. Enough newsweeklies, fashion magazines, and daily newspapers to create a tsunami of words that would take a lifetime to read. And that doesn't even begin to take into account the millions of websites and videos lurking on everyone's laptops, e-readers, and phones, each one a siren calling for our attention, promising entertainment and escape.

> *The cop climbed out of his car exactly four minutes before he got shot.*
> —LEE CHILD, *Persuader*

The question goes beyond storytelling, though as we'll see, the answer lies at the heart of that craft. One reason you want to open with a bang is that your words might be perused by someone standing at a random table in a chain store, your book sitting alongside a hundred other titles whose first chapters are about to be scanned. Or perhaps a curious online shopper selects "Look inside" for your book and jumps to the first page. They're hungry for a great read and want to taste the flavor of your writing. You get one shot, and if you miss, another book is just a click away.

> *It was the best of times, it was the worst of times.*
> —CHARLES DICKENS, *A Tale of Two Cities*

Now hold aside the grim reality of today's publishing world and relax for a moment, because the challenge is nothing new. Engaging your audience has always been at the heart of great storytelling.

Once upon a time—four simple words that instantly transport you to another world. A verbal cue to sit back, relax, and open your imagination. A phrase that has worked across centuries because it does the one thing any storyteller must do. Craft a great opening line to set things in motion.

> *In the bar, Karen drinking vodka-tonic, Ray on brandy to calm his nerves, she told him how people react to death and a stick-up in pretty much the same way: shock, disbelief, anger, acceptance.*
> —DECLAN BURKE, *The Big O*

Try thinking of your book as a film. Watch any of your favorite movies, especially stories of mystery or suspense, and study the opening scene. Nine times out of ten, the camera is already in motion when the first image appears on screen. Most important, something was happening *before* the story begins.

Call me Ishmael. —HERMAN MELVILLE, *Moby-Dick*

Great opening lines, like great stories, don't start at the beginning. They start in the middle and dare the reader to catch up.

As the writer, you are the eyes, ears, and nose of your readers. You hold the camera. They might find themselves gliding through the ocean, cutting through a crowd, panning across a landscape, zooming in on a couple sitting in a restaurant. The camera might stumble into a heated conversation or witness a murder, and suddenly they're right there, unable to look away. The train has left the station and they're on it, no turning back.

That's the kind of momentum you want to build with your opening lines.

The scream tore through the building like a pregnant nun on her way to confession. —TIM MALEENY, *Jump*

Writing is movement. Dialogue, description, even character development all stem from actions, motivations, choices, and conflicts. Tension that must be released. Words vibrating with potential energy. Think of your writing as a catalyst for something about to happen, a chemical reaction that generates heat between your characters and the person turning the pages.

Now sit down and write that first sentence. Make it a good one, and keep writing.

EXERCISE

1. Write an opening line or paragraph that transports the reader to a time and place:

Five hours' New York jet lag and Cayce Pollard wakes in Camden Town to
the dire and ever-circling wolves of disrupted circadian rhythm.
                                —WILLIAM GIBSON, *Pattern Recognition*

2. Introduce a character from another character's perspective, delivered with plenty of attitude:

If you didn't look at her face, she was less than thirty, quick-bodied and slim
as a girl.   —ROSS MACDONALD, *The Drowning Pool*

3. Open on something so abrupt and unexpected that it demands you keep reading to find out more:

Louie pulled off his bra and threw it down upon the casket.
                                —NICK TOSCHES, *In the Hand of Dante*

4. Write a complete opening paragraph that not only sets things in motion but also captures the flavor of your voice, so readers get sucked in, and know what to expect once they start turning the pages:

The last line of security was a big Basque built like a coke oven. He wore a
familiar face behind picador sideburns and a dozen-odd rivets in his eyebrows,
nose, and the deep dimple above his lip. In another Detroit, under a different
administration, he'd specialized in kneecapping Republicans. When the mar-
ket went soft in '94, he'd scored work in show business, playing a succession
of plumbers, janitors, and building superintendents in Spanish-language
soap operas. I couldn't approach him without glancing down at his chest for a
subtitle.   —LOREN ESTLEMAN, *Poison Blonde*

5. Write a first chapter, then edit it three different ways. Start with a description of the scene; then edit the chapter to open in the middle of an action sequence, or try beginning with a disconnected line of dialogue. Which version works best? Why?

REBECCA CANTRELL

Murder from the Point of View of the Murderer, Victim, and Detective

REBECCA CANTRELL writes the award-winning Hannah Vogel mystery series set in 1930s Berlin, including *A Trace of Smoke* and *A Night of Long Knives*. Her short stories are included in the *Missing* and *First Thrills* anthologies. Rebecca also writes the critically acclaimed YA iMonsters series, including *iDrakula*, as Bekka Black. Currently, she lives in Hawaii with her husband, her son, and too many geckoes to count.

I wanted the murder victim in *A Trace of Smoke* to have a voice in the book. I wanted us to know Ernst and love him on his own terms so we could understand what his sister, Hannah Vogel, lost when he died. The murderer took away his life, but I didn't want to let him take away Ernst's voice, too.

In my early drafts, Ernst talked from beyond the grave. Unfortunately, it was never quite right. My writing group struggled with it, and the first question my future agent asked was, "If I agree to represent you, would you be willing to consider removing the dead brother's voice from the manuscript?"

I was willing. I removed those sequences, but I knew that the facts and feelings from his passages needed to find their way into a novel written in the first person from Hannah's point of view. I discovered that my time on Ernst's murder, his life, and his experiences did give him a strong voice in the novel after all. I also made a surprise discovery: Writing the murder from the victim's point of view gave me a very clear picture of all the events surrounding it. It gave me the sights, sounds, and feelings for the very heart of the book.

The scene where Ernst was murdered revealed much about both

Ernst and the man who killed him. Plot threads spun there would weave through the rest of the book. You would think I would have learned my lesson. But I didn't. When I wrote my second book, *A Night of Long Knives*, I did not think to write the murder from the victim's point of view.

Only after I found myself repeatedly going back to the scene where Hannah discovers the body did I realize that I did not know enough about the crime that she works so hard to solve. So I sat down and wrote the murder from the victim's point of view. This time I knew that those words would not make it into the final book, but I also knew that the insights and clarity I gained by doing the work would.

EXERCISE

As a writing exercise, I suggest that you think carefully about the crime itself. I want you to focus on specific details and emotions. Try to be as present as you can in each scene.

1. Describe the murder from the murderer's point of view. Why is he or she killing the victim? Is the crime planned or unplanned? Does the killer leave any clues, either unintentionally or to deceive a future detective? What emotions does the killer experience? Exactly how is the crime committed? Step through every single action. Study every detail.

2. Write that exact same scene, but from the point of view of the murder victim. Does the victim know the killer? Is he surprised? Does the victim fight? Does the victim do something to leave a clue, either deliberately or accidentally? What does the victim feel both physically and emotionally?

    When, if ever, does the victim realize that he is going to die? If your murder victim does not realize that he is dying, as might be the case with poison, then write about the last things that the victim remembers.

3. Write the same scene from the detective's point of view. If the detective is at the crime scene, what does he see? What clues does he find? Have the detective imagine the murder, walking through the events physically or in his imagination. What things surprise him? How does the detective feel about the killer and the victim as he pictures the scene? How does it change him?

ELIZABETH ZELVIN

"Let Me Out!" Helping Characters Find Their Voice

ELIZABETH ZELVIN is a New York City psychotherapist. Her mystery series featuring recovering alcoholic Bruce Kohler includes *Death Will Get You Sober* and *Death Will Help You Leave Him*. Of her four short stories about the same character, two were nominated for the Agatha Award for Best Short Story. Liz's stories have appeared in *Ellery Queen's Mystery Magazine* and various anthologies and e-zines.

Voice is the most mysterious element of mystery fiction and one of the essentials for making a writer's work stand out from the pack. A memorable voice, whether it's a particular character's or the author's, draws the reader back. Because many mysteries are written in series, mystery authors need repeat business. Readers kept buying the late Robert B. Parker's work not because Spenser always blew away the bad guys, but for Parker's inimitable and immediately identifiable voice.

Whether painstakingly or intuitively, writers use a variety of techniques to distinguish between one voice and another. One of Parker's was never to use any attribution except "said." Another was the wisecracks for which both Spenser and his sidekick Hawk were famous.

Subtle differences in word choice and sentence construction distinguish Ruth Rendell's Inspector Wexford series from the novels of psychological suspense that she writes as Barbara Vine. One is a police procedural series with an ongoing likable protagonist and the other a succession of creepy stand-alones. But Rendell's brilliance shows in the utter dissimilarity of voice in the two bodies of work.

Distinctions of period and gender are among the easiest and, paradoxically, the hardest to make. If the voice isn't right, the character won't sound authentic.

One of my series protagonists is Bruce Kohler, a recovering alcoholic with a smart mouth and a good heart. The other is Diego, a young Marrano sailor on Columbus's first voyage. Suppose each of them is describing an incident in which someone is following him. Bruce might say, "I didn't want him to know where I was going." Diego would say, "I did not wish him to know where I went." Bruce's voice is colloquial, making use of present-day constructions. To create the historical voice, I avoid a contraction, choose a slightly more formal verb, and use simple past tense instead of the continuous past.

I established Bruce's voice as gritty and ironic in the first sentence of his first appearance, when he finds himself on skid row: "I woke up in detox with the taste of stale puke in my mouth." He looks at his surroundings and concludes, "I had an awful feeling it was Christmas Day." Diego talks very differently about the holidays: "It was the 25th day of Kislev in the year 5253 according to the Hebrew calendar, the second night of the Festival of Lights. It was also December 24th in what the others, including the Admiral, called the Year of Our Lord 1492: Christmas Eve."

A year later, in *Death Will Trim Your Tree*, Bruce is having a frustrating time with strings of Christmas lights. Bruce has a New York attitude, so I originally envisioned him using the F-word repeatedly. But the story was for a family-oriented anthology. Could I make Bruce's voice sound equally authentic without four-letter words? I wrote, "I sat on the floor . . . with a pile of blinking electrical spaghetti in my lap and ground my teeth. For this I'd stayed sober for 357 days and changed my whole life?"

Both of my series protagonists are male. Bruce's sidekick, Barbara, is a strong female character whose voice appears in dialogue. My authorial voice, too, must be different from Bruce's first-person voice when I write a scene in close third person from Barbara's point of view. Here's Barbara thinking about whether to keep an appointment with a plastic surgeon who's a murder suspect: "Barbara patted her nose. Why even pretend she wanted to trade it in? Most of the women her age . . . who had had nose jobs in their teens had ended up with identical, unmistakable little pinched-off snouts with too much nostril showing." Raymond Chandler wouldn't have written that passage.

Neither would Jane Austen. Not only the language but also the content and perspective contribute to the voice in which I write Barbara's point of view.

One of my female protagonists is Jenny, an eleven-year-old girl whose uncle is molesting her. In the story she appears in, I use both subject matter and vocabulary to establish her voice: "I've asked Mom over and over if I can have a lock on my door, but she says I'm not old enough." And later: "In the Middle Ages, my favorite period in history, the men wore armor and the women wore chastity belts. I bet they didn't even know how lucky they were." Jenny doesn't need teen slang or references to common adolescent issues for her voice to sound, to my ear, at least, neither adult nor male.

A fictional character's first-person voice does not have to be grammatical. The protagonist can say, "I locked both doors like I always did." But the third person narrator maintains credibility by saying, "He locked both doors as he always did." A character's vocabulary may be limited or specialized in a way that the author's need not. Voice is about breaking rules and taking risks in order to make the characters—and the writing—come alive.

EXERCISE

Below are lists of characters, settings, and situations. For each situation, put together the elements of two contrasting characters and settings. You may add characteristics such as ethnicity, location, occupation, disability, marital status, to those listed.

Write a scene for each one, with the character as first-person narrator. See how specific you can make each voice to the character and setting as well as how different you can make each voice from the other. This exercise can be repeated as you mix and match the elements or add items to the lists. Redo each scene in third person to see how that changes the voice.

SITUATION	CHARACTER	SETTING
Finding a body	*Age and gender*	*Period*
Accused of a crime	25-year-old man	Present day
Confronting a villain	25-year-old woman	19th century
Injured, seeking help	60-year-old man	Middle Ages
Kidnapped or abducted	60-year-old woman	B.C.
Rescuing someone	13-year-old boy	Regency England
Interviewing a suspect	13-year-old girl	Future
Preventing a disaster	*Class, education, status*	*Location*
Declaring love	Rich	Big city
Home after long absence	Poor	Small town
Waking up with amnesia	Middle-class	Rural
Arriving in the wrong place	Working-class	Wilderness
Saying good-bye	Homeless	At sea
Keeping a secret		Closed community

KATHERINE HALL PAGE

Point of View: An Exercise in Observation

KATHERINE HALL PAGE is the award-winning author of the series featuring amateur sleuth and caterer Faith Fairchild. In addition to the series, published by William Morrow and Avon Books in the United States, she has written short stories, mysteries for younger readers, and a cookbook, *Have Faith in Your Kitchen*. She lives in New England.

In *Why I Write*, George Orwell wrote, "Good prose is like a window pane." This one sentence distills the act of writing for me—creating words that will in turn permit the reader to fully view another world, entering it for a moment as an observer. And it is in this process that point of view plays such a crucial role.

There is nothing so disturbing to the reader as the sudden introduction of another viewpoint. We are stopped abruptly: *Wait a minute—who is this? What happened to the other voice I was hearing so consistently?* Or worse: *How did he or she know that?*

It's a particularly hard trap to avoid in the mystery novel as we struggle to play fair with the reader, providing information while strewing red herrings. The temptation to drop a hint by adding another POV in the midst of a narrative is great. "This will keep them guessing," we chortle to ourselves. And yes, it does keep them guessing—wondering what on earth is going on as they shut the book to pick up another, one less confusing.

Of course it is possible to write from multiple points of view, and I enjoyed doing this recently in *The Body in the Sleigh*. I wrote from the POVs of my series character, Faith Fairchild; Mary Bethany, a spinster who keeps goats on a Maine island farm; Miriam Carpenter, a troubled college student; and one of the island's teenagers, Jake Whittaker.

It was a challenge to make the POVs distinct, which I accomplished by keeping them well apart, so that I wasn't jumping from Miriam in one sentence to Faith in the following. POV is inextricably tied to voice, and adopting each of these voices was one of the most pleasurable writing experiences I've had.

It is very different from adopting a voice in dialogue, and combining voice and POV will be the point of the exercise below. In *The Body in the Attic*, I achieved this by including a diary from the 1940s that Faith Fairchild finds in an old house in Cambridge, Massachusetts, during her husband, the Reverend Thomas Fairchild's, sabbatical. Excerpts from the first-person diary were introduced as separate, italicized sections throughout the book, and provided POV—as well as the details of the crime that had occurred in the house—for Faith Fairchild and the reader at the same time.

I used a similar POV technique in *The Body in the Ivy*, an homage to Agatha Christie's *And Then There Were None*. I was telling eight women's stories, college friends, moving from the late 1960s to the present. What made sense again was to separate them. For each character, I wrote chapters about each of the four years she spent at the fictitious Pelham College and spread these out against the backdrop of the friends' present, lethal reunion—stranded on an island with a murderer on the loose, a murderer who was one of them.

Since I write in the third person, it would seem that multiple POVs would be the norm. In first person, we always know the POV source; in an ongoing series, the POV is also going to be the series character. I write as Faith Fairchild (no, not channeling her and no, not one of those lucky writers whose characters tell them what to do). Her voice is the main one readers hear and it is through her eyes that they gaze upon the world I have fashioned for them. The following exercise may give some idea of how I go about all this.

EXERCISE

The intent here is to adopt another persona and, having done so, to describe a place from that point of view. Look through Orwell's pane of glass at your surroundings. You may be inside or outside. Pay particular attention to small details. Be aware of all your senses. This is especially true if you are in a place you know well—the place you write, for example.

Now, select one of the following and write a short description from the chosen POV. It need not be a polished piece of writing. What's important is to get the words down on paper. You may also do this with another person or a group. Read aloud what each of you has written and ask for guesses as to the identity of the observer.

An anxious mother or father with a toddler	An architect
	A director scouting a location
An elderly person	A recluse
A reporter	An entrepreneur
An alien	A time traveler from the past
A murderer	An ant
A time traveler from the future	A four-year-old
	A teenager
A ghost	A divorcée
A chef	Someone from another country who has never been to the United States before
A detective	

You get the idea. Try as many as possible and try to make them as different as possible. You can also add a corpse on the floor for variation and write the description again. As you are writing, your character may grab you. See if this leads to a story idea and pursue it.

Above all, write. Write every day, even if it's only a few sentences in a journal or a daybook. And always remember Mary Roberts Rinehart's words, and the title of her lovely little book on the subject, *"Writing is work."*

JON P. BLOCH

Creating Believable Dialogue

JON P. BLOCH is the author of the Rick Domino series, as well as other tales of depravity. In his spare time, he is chair of the sociology department at Southern Connecticut State University.

F iction asks the reader to suspend disbelief. Although the reader knows that this is a story and not real life, on a certain level the distinction is blurred. Suspension of disbelief is especially important in the reading of a murder mystery. The reader is willing to accept plot contrivances and conventions of the genre, provided that the story is engaging and suspenseful.

Since most murder mysteries essentially consist of the crime-solver talking to one person after another, dialogue is especially important in holding the reader's interest. It must (a) move the plot forward, (b) reveal or reflect the character's personality, and (c) provide the reader with possible clues. And somehow, the whole thing must seem like it really could happen.

There are a number of strategies to make your dialogue believable. At the most basic level, there is what is sometimes called *mystification*. This means that you present the material in such a way that nobody wants to disbelieve it. In other words, the story—which again is largely carried by the dialogue—simply is much too interesting not to believe. The reader wants it to be true.

It is not possible to create believable dialogue if your characters are not fully realized. And dialogue is one of the main tools used to flesh out characters. Consider two examples:

A. *"Did you kill him?" asked the cop.*

"No, I swear I didn't. I'm innocent."

B. *"Did you kill him?" asked the cop.*

"Yeah, right. In five minutes' time, I stopped at the store for smokes, drove back in the opposite direction to stab my SOB of a brother-in-law fifty times, and then without even stopping to buy a Handi-Wipe, went directly to my kid's second-grade play. She played a carrot, by the way."

The reply given in example A could be said by anyone. It does not reveal anything unique about the character, nor does it provide the reader with clues or move the plot forward. By contrast, example B does all of these things.

In real life, murder is far from entertaining. Yet when it's a story, there's something enjoyable about it. The reader likes the suspense; I almost want to say that murder mysteries are cuddly. They are fun to read on a rainy night. One even accepts the creepier aspects if they are presented correctly. If you entertain readers with your dialogue, they are mystified and they do not question the credibility of the story.

One proven method is to be hard-boiled. Your characters have seen it all, and so it doesn't ruffle their feathers if someone has been murdered. This helps the reader not feel bad about enjoying the story of a murder:

"They found her body hacked into little pieces," said the detective.

Mary shrugged. "Well, that's life."

Another common tool is *humor*. Sometimes extremely scary or suspenseful stories are on some level funny:

> *"They found her body hacked into little pieces," said the detective.*
>
> *"Well, people weren't exactly standing in line to say how much they loved her," Mary replied. "Only a total masochist could be sorry she's dead. That reminds me—I have to call my ex-husband."*

Humor can also be found in *snappy dialogue* that moves the plot along quickly and keeps the reader turning pages. Rather than something flat like "Let's drive to Mary's house and talk to her," try something more like this:

> *"Guess it's back to Mary's. Gee, lucky me."*
>
> *"Well, since you haven't used foul language all day, I'll come with you."*
>
> *"Something tells me I'll be using plenty before we get to Mary's."*
>
> *"In that case, my darling, fuck you."*

Also, confessions or speeches made by characters who seem to be disturbed or obsessed can seem particularly dramatic:

> *She turned away from me and stared out the window. "Snow—it's odd, isn't it? Homey and childlike and yet so . . . well, so dead. I think my husband should be buried in the snow. It's really the least I can do. After—you know, what happened. It was the first time I used a power saw. Frank would've been proud of me. He was always trying to get me over my fear of power tools. Though I suppose death makes pride impossible."*

Juxtaposition is also effective—taking two things that don't usually go together: "That reminds me—on the way to the morgue I have to pick up my daughter's Girl Scout cookies."

Also consider the *narrative* surrounding the dialogue. A quick example:

A. *"I hated him," she shouted.*

B. *"I hated him," she said with a yawn.*

There's nothing particularly compelling about someone shouting that she hated someone—anyone might shout such a statement. But to say such a thing with a yawn? *Say, who is this woman, and who was this man?*

Finally, trim the fat off your dialogue to make it move more quickly and thus be more entertaining. If words do not develop character or move the plot forward, you may be better without them. For example, consider A versus B:

A. *"I told my wife I was going to the hardware store to buy some nails. Instead, I went straight to Mary's apartment. I was frightened, so I took a deep breath before ringing her doorbell to go inside."*

B. *"I told my wife I was going to the hardware store. I drove straight to Mary's. I took a deep breath and rang her doorbell."*

B is more interesting, because it moves along more quickly. Also, we get to figure out for ourselves that he took a deep breath out of fear, rather than having it all spelled out.

EXERCISE

1. Give each of your characters a confession speech. If they are distinct characters, these speeches will not be interchangeable.

2. Try taking the same statement and make it hard-boiled, then humorous, then dramatic, and then try making it part of a snappy conversation.

3. Go through all of your dialogue at the time of day you are most objective and critical (for me it's early in the morning). See if you can make the dialogue shorter in ways that add to its interest rather than detracts from it.

STANLEY TROLLIP

Writing a Non-English-Speaking Character

STANLEY TROLLIP is a retired professor of educational psychology. He spent his professional life in the United States and now splits his time between Minneapolis and South Africa, where he was born. He is one half of the writing team known as Michael Stanley. He and writing partner Michael Sears wrote several mystery short stories and three novels set in southern Africa. Their latest novel is *Death of the Mantis*.

The Detective Kubu series is set in a southern African country, Botswana. Kubu is a detective in the Criminal Investigation Department of the Botswana police. His home tongue is Setswana, but he is a good English speaker; he was schooled in English, the official language of Botswana.

Kubu interacts with his colleagues as well as other Batswana (citizens of Botswana) in Setswana. In the line of duty he talks to people whose mother tongues include English, German, Afrikaans, and other languages. He makes a weekly visit to his parents, who are quite old and formal. So how does one capture these differences in the way characters speak?

It makes no sense to have two people speaking in Setswana for English-speaking readers. Obviously readers wouldn't understand anything. So when a conversation is in Setswana, we do one of two things. The first is to say that the person is speaking Setswana:

"When is the ambulance going to arrive?" he asked in Setswana.

This is effective, but not colorful. So we also use:

"Dumela, rra. *When is the ambulance going to arrive?"* he asked.

Dumela is the Setswana word for "hello," and *rra* is Setswana for "sir." Even though their meaning is usually obvious from the context, we put words like these in a glossary at the back of our books, so we don't have to explain them in the text.

After we have introduced the fact that the conversation is in Setswana, we write the rest in the normal conversational English of the area. The way an American would say something, for example, may well be different from the way an Australian would say it. Or an Englishman. In southern Africa, English speakers often use words derived from Afrikaans or one of the indigenous languages, so it makes sense to have our characters use them as well.

For example, in southern Africa, a pickup is almost always referred to as a *bakkie*, which is actually an Afrikaans word. So we use that word in conversation. Similarly, instead of enjoying a barbecue, people enjoy a *braaivleis* or *braai*. Translated literally, *braaivleis* means "cooked meat" in Afrikaans. Wherever possible, without detracting from the flow of the story, we incorporate these words to ensure that readers know they are reading about a foreign country. For example:

> "Get onto the back of the bakkie," *Andries instructed the five boys.* "Oom Piet is having a braai *this afternoon. Make sure you leave some meat for the grown ups.*"

Here, the words *bakkie* and *braai* give the piece local flavor. The word *oom* (literally "uncle" in Afrikaans) has a more generic meaning. It is the way Afrikaners refer to people they respect. In this example, Oom Piet is probably just a neighboring farmer, not an uncle of the boys. In real life, if I meet an Afrikaans-speaking man older than I, I may well call him *Oom* as a mark of respect, even if I'd never met him before.

The comment about the meat helps to give context to the word *braai*. This piece also captures one other cultural aspect of life in southern Africa. Everywhere you go, on farms, in the countryside, and in cities, people are transported in the back of pickups (*bakkies*). It is part of the culture, even though it is illegal.

One can use the same device of incorporating specific words to differentiate characters, which helps readers to know who is talking without having too many *he said*s. For example, the forensic pathologist in our books, Ian MacGregor, is an immigrant from Scotland. Here is an excerpt from *A Carrion Death*:

> As Kubu was leaving, the pathologist walked in, obviously recently showered.
> "Did you just get back?" Kubu asked.
> "About half an hour ago. I had to have a wee Scotch to calm my nerves. You are a rascal leaving me with that maniac driver, Andries. He insisted on driving the police Land Rover!" His accent had thickened noticeably. "He was verra upset with you, bossing him around like that. And he took it out on me and the rangers."

It is obvious from the words he uses that the pathologist is Scottish.

If speakers who are not good at a language speak in that language, we try to show this by having their sentences broken and ungrammatical. In the following extract from our third novel, *Death of the Mantis*, Ndoli is a Setswana speaker and the Bushman knows only a smattering of Setswana.

> Ndoli turned to the Bushman. "When you find?" he asked slowly in Setswana.
> "Soon." The man shrugged.
> "Move him?"
> The man shook his head. "Give water."

We reveal the formality of Kubu's elderly parents through their language and actions. This is how Wilmon, Kubu's father, greets them every time Kubu and his wife come to visit.

> Kubu walked up to his parents and greeted them, "Dumela, rra. Dumela, mma." He then extended his right arm to his father, touching it with his left hand as a mark of respect.
> Wilmon responded solemnly: "Dumela, my son."

*"I have arrived," Kubu said formally. "And I apologize for being
late."*
"You are welcome in my house. How are you, my son?"
"I am well, Father. How are you and Mother?"
"We are also fine, my son." Wilmon's voice was strong, but quiet.

Touching your right arm with your left hand as you shake hands
or give or take an object is a mark of respect among the Batswana.
Wilmon's words are also formal and a little stiff, and we show this
formality by never using contractions in his speech.

The final area of conversation that you need to pay attention to
relates to the normal places and things people talk about, such as food,
politics, religion, and sport. Ensure that you don't have your characters talking about things that people in that area wouldn't be discussing. Obvious examples would be having a Frenchman talking about
baseball (unless he had spent a lot of time in the USA), or someone
from Mexico discussing cricket, or a Norwegian eating curries. These
anomalies may happen in real life, but always remember you are trying to make your readers believe in the characters.

EXERCISE

1. Choose a culture different from your own. It can be from another
   country or from within your own, such as the Navajo culture or
   Latin culture if you live in the United States. Spend half an hour
   or so researching that culture on the Internet: language, beliefs,
   traditions, location, and so forth.

   Then write a conversation between two native speakers from
   that culture in such a way that readers would be able to differentiate
   the conversation from dialogue between two native English speakers. You want your readers to feel they are experiencing the culture.

2. Invent a character who is a white English-speaking American.
   Have him or her briefly describe a car accident.

Now have a Mexican immigrant describe it—in reality the conversation would be in Spanish, but your book is written in English.

Finally, have a European tourist (English, French, Italian, or German) describe it—here they would be speaking their version of English. Try not to make your characters into caricatures.

CHRIS KNOPF

What Madison Avenue Can Teach You
About Writing Better Dialogue

CHRIS KNOPF writes two Hamptons mystery series starring Sam Acquillo and Jackie Swaitkowski. He also wrote *Elysiana*, about which *Publishers Weekly* said, "Smart dialogue and sharp social observations distinguish this stand-alone thriller from Knopf."

I'd already spent about thirty years in ad agencies writing copy before my first novel was published. I'm often asked if copywriting benefited my fiction, and I always say, "Yes, in every way possible." This is particularly true as it relates to dialogue. And this is even truer for writing mysteries and thrillers, inhabited as they usually are by tough guys, crackpots, and regular Joes. It's hard to convince your reader of gritty realism when your characters talk like nineteenth-century elocutionists.

Writing to a fixed increment of time is another important discipline copywriters have to master. A TV commercial (we call them spots) is usually thirty seconds. Radio usually sixty. Of the two forms, I think radio is the best exercise for fiction writers. TV spots are little movies, fictions for sure, but as in the big-movie business, the visual elements often dominate. In radio, words matter, and, as with a book, there're usually no visual aids. Radio, like fiction, relies on manipulating the theater of the mind, using language to engage and seduce the audience into buying an artificial reality. Unlike fiction, however, you need to tell your whole message in sixty seconds, or less. This teaches you how to prune, condense, and telegraph your story, which almost always makes for a more energetic mystery or thriller.

We're taught in advertising to keep our copy conversational, to write the way people speak. Which is usually in sentence fragments. Sometimes only one word. Honestly.

Grammatically iffy. But highly readable.

Speech is far more economical than written exposition. Even the most voluble blowhard will tend to drop unnecessary verbiage, frequently skipping things like pronouns to get right to the action verbs.

"Watcha' doing there, Joe?"

"Catchin' fish. You?"

This example also points to another reality of spoken English. We often drop the *g*'s off gerunds and other "ing" words. Even the well educated and erudite will do this, only more sparingly (e.g., Barack Obama). Also, we nearly always use contractions whenever available. Few things will mess up conversational speech more than using "do not" or "cannot" when "don't" or "can't" will do. Just don't overdo it. Informality can't sound ignorant.

There's a place for monologue in advertising and fiction, but when two or more people are speaking, there's little in the way of long dissertation. Rather, they tend to pass phrases back and forth like a pair of tennis players. Especially in great crime fiction (e.g., Elmore Leonard).

When writing radio and TV commercials, not only are you drafting copy, you're casting potential talent, framing out the type of people you'll need to fulfill the spot's objectives. So you need to hear your characters' voices in your head.

EXERCISE

Write a sixty-second radio commercial using only dialogue to sell a product that probably doesn't exist. Like woven nose-hair ribbons or an ion-powered composter. Make it a conversation between two people of distinctly different characters. Concoct a story line wherein these two people could be realistically discussing your new product. Before writing your commercial, describe the characters and the story line (the creative concept). What screenwriters call a treatment.

For general guidance and inspiration, you can hear lots of great spots on YouTube, or go to the Radio Mercury Awards website.

Keep in mind the conventions of normal conversation described above, but go one better. Knowing that you have to tell a story, define one or more characters, and convincingly sell a strange new product in sixty seconds, apply the rules of haiku to your copy: no extra words, every word must add meaning.

This lies at the heart of great dialogue, especially the hard-boiled variety. If you can say it in three words instead of five, it's almost always more powerful. And it's really not that hard to do if you're willing to cut until the life goes out, and then carefully add back.

Then, write another spot that is strictly monologue. As before, write your treatment and describe your character.

Then let somebody who doesn't care about your feelings read the spot and give you feedback about what you were trying to achieve. See if you made a convincing argument, not just a well-wrought conversation. Compare their comments with your treatment, and either glory in your success, or go back and try it again.

JACK FREDRICKSON

Murder with Giggles:
Humorous Voice in Crime Fiction

JACK FREDRICKSON is the author of three novels in the Dek Elstrom series: *A Safe Place for Dying*; *Honestly Dearest, You're Dead*; and *Hunting Sweetie Rose*, all from Thomas Dunne/St. Martin's. Some of his short stories appear, as often as the editor can stand it, in *Ellery Queen's Mystery Magazine*. Others have been anthologized in *The Blue Religion*, edited by Michael Connelly; *Chicago Blues*, edited by Libby Hellmann; and *Crimes by Moonlight*, edited by Charlaine Harris.

To show I know what I'm writing about, I'll open with quotes that won't at first make sense. They come from two works of varied literary regard.

"If you really want to hear about it, the first thing you'll probably want to know is where I was born, and what my lousy childhood was like, and how my parents were occupied and all before they had me, and all that David Copperfield kind of crap, but I don't feel like going into it, if you want to know the truth." Holden Caulfield, *The Catcher in the Rye*, J. D. Salinger.

And: "Eat my shorts." Bart Simpson, *The Simpsons*, various writers.

Each has a strong voice that successfully frames how each character sees his world. But now imagine how Salinger and *The Simpsons* writers might have continued these snippets, say, if they'd been improperly medicated.

For example, Holden Caulfield might go on, "Now I must leave. I have just enough time to stop by Walgreens for Gummi Bears—the pinks are my favorite—before the Miley Cyrus retrospective starts down at the Bijou."

And for Bart: "Eat my shorts?" Professor Simpson repeated. Fingering his bow tie, he smiled wryly at his seminar of doctoral candidates. "Of course I'm merely being rhetorical. Certainly, no one would look to such square-legged garments, under- or over-wise, for sustenance. They lack nutritive value, and . . ."

Is either of these funny? Nah. But preposterous? You bet. And that's the objective I'm lounging toward: Humor comes from contrast, from the unexpected.

As do good mysteries and thrillers. Done right, humor can add dimension to characters, primary or minor, as well as provide the means to lull readers into a temporary state of well-being before whacking them upside the head with something truly frightening.

Humor is good. Humor can be evil.

I tumbled onto this while writing my first crime novel. My wife and I were vacationing in California. Always an optimistic adventurer, though for this trip too trusting, she'd booked us into what we discovered was a New Age place, north of San Francisco.

Our door had a sign asking guests to remove their shoes, so as not to disturb the karma in the room. Judging by the filthy carpet, not many guests had complied. No doubt, our karma was disturbed.

Besides the karma, our package included a breakfast of two flattened granola cakes and raspberry. (You read that right: one lone red berry riding atop two depressed cakes. They'd never get away with that where I live, just west of Chicago.)

Because there were no heaping platters to look at while waiting for our own breakfasts, I naturally took to eavesdropping on the foursome at the next table. They wore beads, braids, and flowered print dresses . . . well, not the man. I can't report on everything he was wearing because my wife absolutely forbade my crawling under their table to confirm my suspicion that he was sporting bell-bottom jeans and Earth shoes, duds kept from the sixties, that decade of love.

All four wore something else: exceptionally ruddy complexions. And they laughed, oh they laughed, even though it was very early in the morning. (They wouldn't get away with that either, out here, west of Chicago. Routinely, we awake in sour moods, braced for news of our governors being arrested.)

From their boisterousness, I learned the four were New Age therapists—proud practitioners, apparently, of therapies they performed with their hands. (Without leaning over more closely, I couldn't be sure what they were talking about. Nonetheless, I do allow that things of that sort might go on here, in some sections west of Chicago.)

What really piqued my imagination about them was the frequency at which one, and then another, would get up and cross the room for a refill of cranberry juice. I'd already helped myself to the coffee and orange juice, but from a table much nearer to ours. Being new to the land north of the Bay, I wondered if keeping the cranberry juice separate from the orange juice was a cultural thing particular to that area, like karma and carpets, and raspberries riding solo atop granola cakes.

I questioned our teenaged waitress, who was quite ruddy herself from budding youth and pure thoughts. "Why do you keep the cranberry juice so far from the orange juice?"

She smiled indulgently, as though my Chia head was suffering disabling dryness, and said, "Oh no, sir. That's not cranberry juice. It's sherry. We keep it out all day."

The boisterous therapists had gotten ruddy getting ripped on sherry.

It was wonderful. I scuttled home, and set to use our stay in my novel.

I began writing the whole of it. Observing the karma sign, dirty carpet, and the sherry-sippers would allow my protagonist to crack wise, offering another view of the tilted way he looks at the world. Inserting it as a light chapter into a string of darker ones would change up the pace, and get about that business of lulling the reader.

One thing nagged, though. As I wrote, and rewrote, and rewrote, I began to realize I was facing one of the grand questions of the cosmos: How can a writer tell if his work is funny?

It set me to sputtering like something with too much voltage. What if what I was writing wasn't funny at all?

As good fortune had it, Richard Russo, the Pulitzer Prize–winning author of *Empire Falls* and no mean humorist himself, was speaking to an undergraduate literature class at a nearby university. I slunk in, sat my gray-headed self low in the front, hoping no one would notice I was a few decades too old for the group. When he took questions, I asked, "How does a writer know when his stuff is funny?"

He smiled indulgently, as though my graying Chia head . . . well, you know, and said, "If it makes you laugh."

There it was. There it all was, the cosmos opened up with five syllables: "If it makes you laugh."

Fans congratulated me on my creativity when the book came out. In particular, both cited the scene in Northern California.

Did that business with the therapists and the cranberry juice really happen? A lot of it, sure. Did I embellish, and make it preposterous? You bet. But the guts of it I observed, and then polished with my imagination.

And even after I obsessed through several rewrites, it still left me cackling, crazed as a jaybird, down in the dark of the basement where I write.

EXERCISE

The exercise? You already know. Observe—a conversation, a dance class, a bowling tournament, a piano recital, a television commercial, a bunch of wise heads pontificating on a Sunday morning news show, or absolutely anything and everything else that occurs around you, real or imagined.

How would your character see what's unfolding? Can humor usefully amplify that, by showing us the absurdities she sees in her world?

With modification? Great! Take over, imagine, veer off. Be preposterous.

Will this also lull your reader, make her happy, encourage her to settle back and beam at her place in a wonderful world?

Yes? Even better!

Are you laughing? Wonderful! You've done it.

SETTING AND MOOD
Your Story's Backdrop

WILLIAM KENT KRUEGER

Setting and a Sense of Place in Mysteries

WILLIAM KENT KRUEGER is the award-winning author of the *New York Times*–bestselling Cork O'Connor mystery series. He has taught genre writing at the Loft Literary Center, the University of Minnesota, the University of Wisconsin, and Ball State University. He lives in Saint Paul, Minnesota, and does all his creative work in a small coffee shop near his home.

Ask any biologist what's most important in shaping an organism and the answer will probably be the environment. Any sociologist will tell you that to understand a human being you have to look first at the environment in which that person was raised. In a piece of fiction, environment translates into setting. Simply said, this means that stories rise out of and are inexorably shaped by the unique elements of the place in which they occur.

My favorite authors in the mystery genre tend to be those whose work is suffused with a profound sense of place: James Lee Burke, Dennis Lehane, Craig Johnson, Libby Fischer Hellmann, Louise Penny, Deborah Crombie. These are authors in whose work action is so tied to place that the two are nearly inseparable. In these stories, the events and the way in which characters react is predicated largely on the geography and culture of the setting. After I've read a book by one of these authors, I feel as if I've taken a journey, but not just a literary one. I generally feel as if I've been transported sensually to a different place. And, man, do I love that. No wonder, then, that this is, in large measure, the kind of experience I try to offer readers of my own work.

What do I mean when I talk about setting?

Globally speaking, *setting is the locale of the story.* This would be Los Angeles for Michael Connelly's Harry Bosch, south Boston for Dennis

Lehane, Wyoming for Craig Johnson, or, in my case, the great North-woods of Minnesota.

At another level, setting is where each scene in a story takes place: a deserted beach, a diner, a busy office, a living room. At the most basic level, setting is what grounds a reader physically in every exchange that takes place: the sound of a semi gearing away from a truck stop, a waiter pouring wine at a table in a posh restaurant, the way a shadow falls across a room. First and foremost, setting is place.

Setting is also character. Setting ought to be looked at in the same way we look at any important character in a story. Characters have voices, smells, physical traits, cultural biases; settings are no different.

The voice of New York City is very different from the voice of rural Ohio. The one may growl and rumble and speak hurriedly, while the other is laconic and punctuated by the sound of meadowlarks and the distant thrum of a tractor. The smell of Seattle is very different from the smell of Omaha. Though they both belong to large cities, the face of Chicago would never be confused with the face of Miami. And the whole cultural milieu of, say, Boston, is a universe away from that of New Orleans.

Setting is atmosphere. It helps create the mood of the story. What would the stories of Carl Hiassen be without the bizarre, surreal Florida backdrop? And how suspenseful would the stories of Raymond Chandler be without the mean, shadowy streets of L.A. ratcheting up the tension? Think about Tony Hillerman and the emptiness of the southwest desert country, which adds such a marvelous feel of isolation and aloneness and introspection to his Chee and Leaphorn stories.

Finally, setting is motivation. What happens in a story, the why of it, should be largely because of where the story takes place. The event that kicks off and drives a Hillerman story, more often than not, rises directly out of some element specific to the Navajo people and the Four Corners area. The unique culture and mores of southern Louisiana provide wonderfully convoluted rationale for the events that occur in James Lee Burke's work. And for me, the dynamics of racial tension, prejudice, and misunderstanding in northern Minnesota often give rise to the particular actions in my stories.

How do you create a profound sense of place? My biggest piece of advice here is that you don't offer a travelogue. Don't give a litany of detail. In the same way that character is best established gradually and through pointed, well-chosen observations, setting is evoked by capturing succinctly the essence of a place. Here's an example of how effectively Chandler paints the nature of Marlowe's office with a few wry observations:

> The pebbled glass door panel is lettered in flaked black paint: "Philip Marlowe. . . . Investigations." It is a reasonably shabby door at the end of a reasonably shabby corridor in the sort of building that was new about the year the all-tile bathroom became the basis for civilization.

Imagine sensually when establishing setting. What's the look, smell, sound, feel, even taste of a place? (Think the dirty rice of Burke's New Iberia or the fry bread of Margaret Coel's Wind River country.)

In summary, place plays such a multiple role in a story that it is, in my own thinking, among the most important elements any writer considers when sitting down to create a piece of fiction. A profound sense of place grounds a reader not only in the work as a whole, but also in every moment of the action. Without this solid grounding, a writer risks leaving his reader adrift on a great anonymous sea.

EXERCISE

Here's one of my favorite setting exercises when I teach creative writing. It's very simple. Below is a list of several locales. In a few sentences, using well-chosen details, give a description of each locale that would make the place come alive in a reader's imagination. Remember to combine the elements a reader might expect with some that will surprise.

- A diner
- The living room of an expensive home

- The exterior of a rat trap hotel
- A city street
- The main street of a small town
- The midway of a county fair
- An alley by daylight
- An alley by night
- The office of a P.I.
- A stretch of lonely highway

BRUCE DESILVA

Scene of the Crime

BRUCE DESILVA worked as a journalist for forty years, most recently as a writing coach for the Associated Press, before retiring to write novels full-time. His reviews of crime novels have appeared in *The New York Times Book Review*. His first crime novel, *Rogue Island*, was a *Publishers Weekly* "first fiction" selection and won the Edgar Award for Best First Novel of 2010. He and his wife, Patricia Smith, an award-winning poet, live in New Jersey.

The most memorable mysteries, thrillers, and crime novels transport you to interesting places and let you see, hear, touch, and smell them. Dennis Lehane's books, for example, take you on a hellish journey through the working-class neighborhoods of Boston. Daniel Woodrell's best novels drag you through the underbelly of his native Ozarks. Read James Lee Burke's Dave Robicheaux novels and you have been to New Iberia, Louisiana, even if you've never left your house.

Choosing the right setting is essential. As a great crime novelist named Thomas H. Cook once said, "If you want to understand the importance of place, imagine *Heart of Darkness* without the river."

One of the places I know best is Providence, Rhode Island, the setting for my first crime novel, *Rogue Island*. When the main character is forced to flee the city, he takes a few words to tell readers why he misses it, providing one of the book's establishing shots:

> *I missed the scent of salt, spilled petroleum, and decaying shellfish that rose like Lazarus from the bay. I missed the bellowing of the parti-colored tugs that bulled rusting barges up the river. I missed*

the way the setting sun turned the marble dome of the statehouse the
color of an antique gold coin.

When he pays a visit to the city's arson squad, the description
moves in closer:

From the outside, the drab government building looked like randomly
stacked cardboard boxes. Inside, the halls were grimy and shit green.
The johns, when they weren't padlocked to save civil servants from
drowning, were fragrant and toxic. The elevators rattled and wheezed
like a geezer chasing a taxi.

You probably noticed that these descriptive passages are short.
Yours should be, too. Crime fiction readers crave action and dialogue.
They get bored by long, descriptive passages, no matter how well written. You can keep your details short simply by not telling readers
things that they already know.

If you read novels written in the eighteenth and nineteenth centuries, you can't help being struck by the length of the descriptive
passages. Sometimes they go on for pages. For example, when a writer
like Herman Melville wanted to take his readers to a village on Nan-
tucket, he felt that he needed to describe everything—the architecture
of the stores, churches, and dwellings; the rigging on the ships in the
harbor; the cries of the swooping gulls; the stench of smoke and blub-
ber rising from the whalers; what was hung in the shop windows; what
the men and women on the streets were wearing; the bridles on the
horses; and even how the streets were paved. Those details were end-
lessly fascinating to the readers of his day because it was all new to
them. Few had ever been more than fifty miles from their homes, and
there was no mass media to bring the outside world to them.

Today's readers are different. They have millions of images stored
in their heads from movies, TV, photographs, and their own real-life
experiences. Now just a word or two is enough, sometimes, to convey
an image that would have required Melville to go on for pages. For example, he would have needed a lot of words to describe the 1,063-foot-
high, iron lattice tower erected on the Champ de Mars in 1889. Today,

all I have to write is "Eiffel Tower," and I'm done. Even if you've never been there, you've seen pictures and video of it. You already know what it looks like.

Suppose, then, you've decided to set a scene in a dentist's office. You don't need to describe the dental chair, the tray of gleaming steel instruments, or the dentist's white smock. Just write the words "dentist's office," and today's readers will picture all of that in their heads. What you should describe, however, are the things that make this particular dentist's office different from the typical one. For example, if the out-of-date magazines in the waiting room are *Guns & Ammo* and *Soldier of Fortune* instead of the usual *Newsweek* and *Sports Illustrated*, you will want to mention that.

In *Rogue Island*, part of the action occurs at Providence's old city hall. Since most readers can conjure an image of a traditional city hall without my help, all I had to do was add a bit of detail about how Providence's city hall differs from the norm. What I wrote was this:

> *City Hall, a Beaux-Arts atrocity at the southern end of Kennedy Plaza, looked as if a madman had sculpted it from a mound of seagull shit.*

And that, I think, was enough.

When you write your descriptions, don't limit yourself to visual details. Smells, sounds, and touch are often more powerful than visual descriptions.

Go back to that dentist's office for a moment and picture only what you see.

That wasn't so bad, was it?

Now listen to the whine of the drill. Didn't it immediately get scarier?

Now fill your nostrils with that burning-tooth smell as the drill does its work. Still scarier, right? And I don't even want to think about how it feels.

Physical descriptions are important, but they are not sufficient to create an effective setting for your book. In fact, they are the smallest part of the job. You must also understand your setting's history, its culture, and its people—how they talk, what they value, and what it is like for them to live and work there.

Unlike big, anonymous cities such as New York and Los Angeles, where many fine crime novels are set, Providence is so small that it's claustrophobic. Almost everybody you see on the street knows your name, and it's almost impossible to keep a secret. Yet the city is big enough to be both cosmopolitan and rife with urban problems. Like some small people, the little city has both an inferiority complex and a chip on its shoulder. And Providence has an enduring legacy of organized crime and political corruption that goes all the way back to a colonial governor dining with Captain Kidd.

This is the milieu in which the plot of *Rogue Island* unfolds, and it influences the way every character thinks and acts. For example, my protagonist is an investigative reporter. It's his job to expose corruption. But he also grew up in this place; it's a part of him. So he sees nothing wrong with placing a bet with a bookie or paying a small bribe to keep his decrepit Ford Bronco on the road. As he sees it, graft comes in good and bad varieties, just like cholesterol. The bad graft enriches greedy politicians and their rich friends. The good graft supplements the wages of low-paid state workers, making it possible for them to start college funds and put braces on their kids' teeth. Without it, the protagonist says, not much would get done in Rhode Island, and nothing at all would happen on time. It is unlikely the character would have held such views if he had grown up in, say, Portland, Maine, or Portland, Oregon.

EXERCISE

Pick a place you know well, because, first of all, you are going to have to describe it; and you will have to do this in more ways than one. You will need what movie directors call an "establishing shot" that shows what your city or town looks, sounds, and smells like from a distance. You will also need to move in closer to put your readers on the streets and in the buildings where the action unfolds.

1. Write an establishing shot of the city or town where your mystery, thriller, or crime novel is set. Don't just describe what you see. Use all of your senses. When you finish, it will be too long. Cut it in half. Then cut it in half again.

2. Visit a location—a street, a bar, or maybe a house—where one of the scenes in your book will take place. Take notes on everything you see, hear, smell, and touch.

   If it is a bar, for example, does it serve draft or bottle beer? Shots of whiskey and rye or fancy mixed drinks? Is it dark or well lighted? Are the bar stools new or old and battered? Do you see polished brass rails and ferns in ceramic pots, or is the main decoration a ten-year-old girlie calendar hanging from a nail? Is there a jukebox? What kind of music is on it? Does the bathroom smell of pine, disinfectant, or urine?

   Does the bartender wear a jacket and tie, or does he have a white apron over a T-shirt and jeans? Is that an iPhone or a .45 clipped to his belt? Is this a pickup spot, a place where young professionals socialize, or a hangout for serious drinkers? Is the floor freshly washed and polished, or can you feel the grit under your shoes?

   Using your notes, write a vivid description of the place. When you are done, cut it in half, eliminating unnecessary details. Then cut it in half again, leaving only those details absolutely necessary to give readers a good feel for the place.

3. Write a thousand words about how the history and culture of your setting affect the values and attitudes of your characters. If you don't know enough about the place to do that, read a book on local history and then sit down with a local historian to discuss what you've learned. This thousand-word passage will not appear in your story, but it will inform much of what your characters think and do.

PHILIP CIOFFARI

Creating Mood in Crime Fiction

PHILIP CIOFFARI has published a story collection, *A History of Things Lost or Broken*, which won the Tartt First Fiction prize and a D. H. Lawrence Fellowship award; and a mystery/thriller, *Catholic Boys*. His latest novel, *Jesusville*, was published in 2011.

One of the first flat periods I reached as a writer occurred after several years of writing. I felt that I'd hit a wall, that I'd traveled a certain distance but I'd stalled out. I couldn't get beyond where I was. My prose seemed competent enough, yet I felt it was uninspired. Something was missing: some element of passion or intensity or texture.

In an effort to determine precisely what that missing ingredient was, I revisited those novels and stories that had most captivated me in my teenage years, works that included William Faulkner's *The Sound and the Fury*, Graham Greene's *The Heart of the Matter* and *The End of the Affair*, Carson McCullers's *The Heart Is a Lonely Hunter*, Truman Capote's *Other Voices, Other Rooms*, and virtually all of Edgar Allan Poe's short stories.

What they all have in common is a highly developed sense of mood that permeates every aspect of the story: the place, the characters, and what those characters say and do. Every one of those novels and stories, each in its own way, created for me a world complete in itself, a world with its own distinct colors and sights and sounds, its own emotional resonance—a world, at least for the time it took to finish the book, more interesting and compelling than the mundane, real world I lived in.

I realized that in my own writing I'd managed to get the facts as well as the basic story structure onto the page, but that coloring those facts so that they resonated deeply with the reader would be a more challenging task.

So I began to think about all the ways I might enhance my fiction by paying closer attention to mood and atmosphere, which touches upon every aspect of the writing process: setting, character, dialogue. I have come to think of it as a necessary part of each and every scene in a story.

Setting is perhaps the most tried and true vehicle for establishing mood. Take, for example, Poe's effort to make us feel the doom and gloom of the house in "The Fall of the House of Usher":

> *The room in which I found myself was very large and lofty. The windows were long, narrow and pointed, and at so vast a distance from the black oaken floor as to be altogether inaccessible from within. Feeble gleams of encrimsoned light made their way through the trellised panes, and served to render sufficiently distinct the more prominent objects around; the eye, however, struggled in vain to reach the remoter angles of the chamber, or the recesses of the vaulted and fretted ceiling. Dark draperies hung upon the walls. . . .*

He uses the room's accessories and limited light to convey an overwhelming sense of dread and trepidation.

Equally important is establishing the mood or condition of our investigator's mind, as Martin Cruz Smith does with his detective, Arkady Renko, in the opening scene of *Gorky Park*. In addition to the physical details of setting, a glimpse into Arkady's mind-set brings us more fully into the moment: "A chief investigator should have smoked a fine brand of cigarette; Arkady lit a cheap Prima and filled his mouth with the taste of it—his habit whenever he dealt with the dead."

Engaging us in the inner life of the detective brings us more intimately into the story. Not only are we reading to find out if and how the crime will be solved, but we are reading to learn more about who the detective is, what he or she feels about life—which is, in effect, another puzzle to be solved, another mystery to be unraveled.

Albert Camus creates his murderer's mind-set—one of alienation and detachment—quite simply in a courtroom scene in *The Stranger* when he has Meursault paying more attention to the room's excessive heat and to an annoying fly buzzing about than he does to his being indicted for taking a life.

Dialogue also plays a part in creating mood. Each section of dialogue within a scene should have a specific tone—comic, thoughtful, menacing, or whatever. We can manipulate that tone with both diction and syntax, and as much by what is unsaid as what is said.

In developing mood through setting, character, and dialogue, I would suggest the use of motifs. These repeated patterns of imagery are a reliable way to reinforce atmosphere within a scene or throughout an entire story or novel. If it's a hot day or a cold day, a fall day or a spring evening, repeated images and details—of heat, cold, things withering or blooming, light and shadow, to name just a few choices—can engage the reader in a sensual way and add immeasurably to the world you're creating.

EXERCISE

Once you have a draft of a scene, work on enhancing the mood and atmosphere. You can begin with any of the aforementioned elements but let's, for example's sake, begin here with your setting. Use the physical details of the place—its colors, its quality of light, its sounds and smells—to reinforce the action of the scene. Consider using details typical of the place, as well as details not so typical to such a place. In other words, go beyond the generic details to those details that make this particular motel room unique, that make it somewhat different from all other motel rooms in its class. Then add at least one motif related to the setting, an image (something visual, auditory, tactile, or olfactory—something related to the quality or feel of the place) that you can weave through the scene and, if applicable, through successive scenes.

Then add details to create the inner mood and mind-set of your characters, especially your hero and your villain. It's not only what a character does, but what he feels or thinks as he does it. In other words, what's the climate inside his head and heart? What mood is he in? Is this typical of how he feels, or is this something new or unusual for him? And so on. Again, if possible, employ a motif to illustrate his inner climate.

Look, too, at your dialogue. Is each speaker's voice distinct, reflective of his personality, social class, educational level? Does it reflect the speaker's inner life? Motifs can be useful here, as well. Are there expressions, turns of phrase, word choices you can repeat that will help the reader get a better feel for the speaker?

Each successive scene you write can build upon the foundation you've laid.

REED FARREL COLEMAN

Let's Get Engaged

REED FARREL COLEMAN, called a "hard-boiled poet" by NPR's Maureen Corrigan, has published twelve novels in three series and one stand-alone. He is the three-time winner of the Shamus Award and has been twice nominated for the Edgar. Reed has also won the Macavity, Barry, and Anthony awards. He is an adjunct professor of English at Hofstra University.

I may define myself as a writer, but I was a reader long before I ever put pen to paper or tapped out my first words on an ancient manual typewriter. Although my experience of reading has necessarily changed as a result of aging and my choice of career, I still get an incredible thrill at being transported beyond the bounds of my physical being by a collection of words printed in black ink on off-white pages. That ability of the printed word to transport us, to pull us out of our own lives and limited experiences into different universes—some very much like our own, some vastly different—is as close to real magic as we're ever likely to get. But it isn't magic, is it?

One of the first points I make to my students is that as genre writers—crime/thriller writers, in our case—we have an added burden when we sit down to write a novel or short story. Above all else, our job is to entertain the reader. By entertain, I don't mean to simply amuse or distract. Here I am using a broader definition of the word, a definition that obliges the writer to engage his or her readers on several levels.

If we can't do that, none of the rest of what we do matters. All the beautiful, poetic, and succinct prose you can muster won't count if you can't get the reader to keep turning the pages in one direction. Weighty and significant themes, fully developed characters, a wonderfully constructed plot—none of it will matter if our words go unread. You can't engage and entertain an audience that isn't paying attention.

For my students' sake, I do this gesture where I reach up, grab my own shirt collar, and pull my face into the pages of an open book. It's kind of goofy, I know, but it makes the point. Pull the reader in early or risk losing the reader completely. Too often in the crime/thriller genre, nascent writers take this admonition about engaging the reader to mean they should supply a corpse on page one, preferably in line one of the first paragraph. While that can work and has worked and will probably continue to work, it's dreadfully unoriginal and not really a formula for long-term success. Besides, the success of any ploy is at least somewhat dependent upon the writer's talent and skill. Clichés can work, but to make them engaging sometimes requires more effort than it's worth. What I'm saying is that in this genre there are a hundred, a thousand different ways to engage readers that don't involve a corpse or a guy walking into a bar waving a gun.

I found that poignancy works for me. I don't go for the throat, I go for the heart and I go for it right away. I like to set the tone, to reach right up to the reader in the first few lines. Here are some first and second lines from my novels:

Nothing is so sad as an empty amusement park. And no amusement park is so sad as Coney Island. (*from* Soul Patch)

Katy's blood was no longer fresh on my hands and after 9/11 people seemed to stop taking notice. (*from* Innocent Monster)

We walked through the cemetery, Mr. Roth's arm looped through mine. The cane in his left hand tapped out a mournful meter on the ice-slicked gravel paths that wound their way through the endless rows of gravestones. (*from* Empty Ever After)

Poignancy is what I'm comfortable with, but I use other ways to lure the reader in when the book I'm working on calls for it. For instance, when I was writing *The Fourth Victim* under my pen name Tony Spinosa, poignancy was definitely not the way to go. So I went with this: "At his best, Rusty Monaco was a miserable, self-absorbed prick and tonight he was paying even less attention than usual to the world outside his head."

New York Times–bestselling author Lee Child engages the reader by getting the reader to see through his protagonist's eyes. Lee is very skilled at putting you, the reader, inside Jack Reacher's head. Readers can't help being pulled into a book if they are inside the protagonist's head. But no matter how you pull the reader in, no matter your method of engaging the reader, get to it early. Here are some examples of how different authors pulled me into their books from the get-go.

Ree Dolly stood at break of day on her cold front steps and smelled coming flurries and saw meat. Meat hung from trees across the creek. The carcasses hung pale of flesh with a fatty gleam from low limbs of saplings in the side yards. (from Winter's Bone *by Daniel Woodrell)*

Thrill parties every night over on Hussel Street. That tiny house, why, it's 600 square feet of percolating, Wurlitzering sin. Those girls with their young skin, tight and glamorous, their rimy lungs and scratchy voices, one cheek flush and c'mon boys and the other, so accommodating, even with lil' wrists and ankles stripped to pearly bone by sickness. (from Bury Me Deep *by Megan Abbott)*

When I finally caught up with Abraham Trahearne, he was drinking beer with an alcoholic bulldog named Fireball Roberts in a ramshackle joint just outside of Sonoma, California, drinking the heart right out of a fine spring afternoon. (from The Last Good Kiss *by James Crumley)*

It's almost impossible to be thrown out of the Garda Síochána. You have to really put your mind to it. Unless you become a public disgrace, they'll tolerate most anything.
    I'd been to the wire. Numerous
    Cautions
    Warnings

Last chances
Reprieves
And still I didn't shape up. (*from* The Guards *by Ken Bruen*)

Suicide bombers are easy to spot. They give out all kinds of telltale signs. Mostly because they're nervous. By definition they're all first-timers. (*from* Gone Tomorrow *by Lee Child*)

If I'd blinked, I would have missed it. (*from* Learning to Swim *by Sara J. Henry*)

Remember, engage the readers early. Grab them by the collar and don't let go. Keep them turning the pages in one direction. Appeal to the readers' hearts, their minds, their senses. Don't limit yourself to clichés. If you lose readers' attention, you lose them. If they're engaged, if you're entertaining them, not only do you have them where you want them, you have them where they want to be.

EXERCISE

1. Write the first line or two of a novel appealing to one or more of the reader's senses.

     For example: *When Joe Mulligan rapped on the perp's door, there was an odd mix of scents in the air. Burnt bacon and death, he thought, burnt bacon and death.*

2. Write the first line or two of a novel appealing to a reader's sense of place.

     For example: *There was always more to the weather at Coney Island than the temperature. The wind howled through the abandoned rides, their rusting superstructures creaking like old bones.*

3. Write the first line or two of a novel appealing to a reader's sense of fear.

     For example: *The coffin lid collapsed in on her as the dirt poured over it. The pressure of it squeezing the breath out of her lungs. She clawed at the raw pine, her nails snapping off, splinters burying themselves in her bloody fingers as she was buried alive.*

4. Reveal a character's major flaw in the first line or two of a novel.

    For example: *As usual Misha was disappointed and nothing disappointed her more than the self-doubt that twisted the image looking back at her from the mirror.*

LOU ALLIN

Layering the Landscape

LOU ALLIN is the author of the Belle Palmer mysteries set in Northern Ontario, ending with *Memories Are Murder*. Now living on Vancouver Island where the rain forest meets the sea, she completed and published the first two novels in a new Vancouver Island series: *And on the Surface Die* and *She Felt No Pain*. In 2010, Lou debuted *That Dog Won't Hunt*, a novella for adults with literacy issues.

There are a thousand and one ways to write fiction. I agree with Ortega y Gasset, who said, "Tell me the landscape in which you live, and I will tell you who you are." Setting is critical to me. In the diverse environments where I have lived since I left Ohio, ignoring nature can easily kill a person. I seek to traverse, transpose, and then transport the reader to my world: once the wilderness of Northern Ontario and now Vancouver Island.

In my first visit, I write only the bare essentials. Who's there and what they are doing. Conversation is at a minimum because later the scene may whisper more and increase my options. At this point, I may complete only one or two pages.

The next time, I add sensory details, starting with sight. I'm not the kind of a person who painstakingly writes a scene inch by inch, savoring everything in my path, perfecting one sentence before moving to the next. Some sensations I don't think about. Others don't occur to me until the fifth or sixth draft. Adding hearing, touch, smell, and even perhaps taste, I visit and revisit and revisit until I am satisfied. Layer upon layer, the painting emerges. Each time, another ten percent on average is added to the text.

Both of my literary homes have had four distinct seasons. And as each season emerges, it offers different opportunities. Northern Ontario has very severe winters, but only during the winter does the land open for travel by snowshoe, skis, or snowmobile. Summer is humid and frantic with high temperatures and murderous bug invasions. It's hard to imagine -40 degrees Fahrenheit in *Northern Winters Are Murder* when it's 104 degrees in *Blackflies Are Murder*. Solid walls of rain during Vancouver Island's winters stand far apart from the droughts and forest fires of summer. The seasons change as I go through my drafts, and at a leisurely pace of a book a year, usually I come full circle. I always live where I write. The one exception was my stand-alone novel, *Man Corn Murders*, which took place in the red-rock desert of Utah. For that I depended on a month-long trip to the canyons.

My reference library includes books on birds, animals, plants, fungi, geology, history, astronomy, fossils, everything important about my landscape. I've bought topographic maps to guide me. I'd rather not construct a road where there isn't one, or stick a river in the middle of a bog. Once I did make an old brewery into a grow-op near an abandoned rail line designed to carry shipments of marijuana. I got a big laugh out of the aptly named Budd car (a single coach with engine on board used in the far north).

My clintonias don't bloom in early September when the yellow flower has become a purple fruit. April is the time for skunk cabbage. Salmonberries ripen before blackberries. Wherever I have lived, I keep a monthly diary of emerging plants. Nor do I want to make a mistake about local animals. There are no foxes on Vancouver Island, nor are there moose, but you may see an elk. There are plenty of black bears, but very few grizzlies.

Instead of the devil, the angel is in the details. By the time I reach the final version of the scene, the reader knows whether sweat is evaporating on skin, what the wind is like, what's on the path, what's singing in the stillness, what trees are in leaf in what order, and, if bare, how the snow on branches is behaving in the thaw. How does the frosty air feel in the nose and are the hairs prickling? Is the rock face granite or sandstone? When the sensory experience is complete, the final process begins. That's when I add subtleties like an analogy between nature and the individual. Some may call this the pathetic fallacy, but nature often reflects the way I feel.

EXERCISE

Here's a bare-bones page where I begin the scene with only the rough-est idea of the setting. It's northern Ontario in the dead of winter. Belle Palmer and her new friend Jack MacDonald have taken a walk to clear their heads and plan how they might help Jack's wife, who has been accused of murder. The complete scene is about ten times this original:

> *They climbed into the woods on their snowshoes. Finally they sat down. Jack threw a pine cone for the dog to chase. He began telling Belle about his marriage to Miriam (Mimsy). He lit a cigarette. Noises and images from the forest surrounded them. A bird. A moving tree branch. Melting snow. She pointed out favorite landmarks. Finally they rose and reached the top of a hill overlooking the gigantic lake.*

What kind of specific sensory details could you use in this scene?

LOUISE PENNY

Setting as Character

LOUISE PENNY is the author of the Armand Gamache mysteries. Her books have made bestseller lists internationally, including the *New York Times* list, and have won the British Dagger, the Canadian Arthur Ellis, and the American Anthony, Agatha, and Barry awards. Like her characters, Penny lives in a small village in Quebec.

There is no Frigate like a Book
To take us Lands away.

—EMILY DICKINSON

I suspect that Emily Dickinson was talking about both interior and exterior landscapes. But at some stage the two meet and meld, and that's what I'd like to talk with you about. You want your book to be a ticket onto that frigate. You want to construct a whole world for these literary tourists, filled with sights and sounds and sensations.

When you set about writing that first book you almost certainly consider the characters. The detective, the victim, the suspects. But there's another character. One as real and as powerfully alive as any of the rest. And that's your setting.

Like any of your characters, describing how they look is important, but describing how they feel is vital. The same is true for a setting.

Where will your novel be set? In the countryside or a city? In a fictional place? In your hometown, or an exotic locale? Paris? Tahiti? Venice? Kansas City?

There's no right or wrong answer or choice. Anyplace can be made riveting, if the writer feels strongly enough about it. But a good piece of advice I was given is to choose a place you're already familiar with.

There are thousands of people trying to convince an editor to buy their books, so what will distinguish yours? To convince an editor or agent, you need to use every tool at your disposal. And one tool often overlooked is a keen sense of place. Readers love being transported. And you have a chance to offer them just that.

Think of Donna Leon's Venice, Ian Rankin's Edinburgh, Tony Hillerman's American Southwest and the Navajo. Others have set crime novels in these locations, and will again. So what distinguishes these authors? Why are they so associated with that territory? Because of their passion for it; because they breathe life into the setting.

Because when you read their books you feel as though you're there.

So, how do you bring your setting alive? Not with endless description, that's for sure. We've all suffered through that, and skipped and skimmed and groaned. No, it's done simply, elegantly. With a well-placed word, the telling detail.

Here's what I try to do. I try to make my books, set mostly in a village in Quebec, sensual. Not sexual, but the classical definition of sensual. Using all the senses. How else would you construct a world? It's more than buildings. It's sensations.

If my books are frigates then I want there to be no mistaking the destination. When people read my novels, I want them to taste the flaky croissants, smell the rich cafés au lait, feel the bone-chilling cold that burrows into the marrow, and I want them to see what I see. The beauty of the Quebec countryside, and the peace it promises.

And then I shatter that peace with a crime. How much worse is a murder in paradise than in a place already marred?

I struggle in each book to refine the picture and breathe life into the setting.

But how to get that subtle, telling detail?

Do you know what I do? I way overwrite my first draft. Throw everything at it. I don't worry about going on and on ad nauseam about a cabin or a tree or a croissant. I once spent two pages describing a rose. I knew it wouldn't make it into the final draft, and it didn't, but it was fun and freeing.

There's no right or wrong approach to a first draft. Many terrifically successful and creative writers edit as they go. Others, like me, prefer to just toss everything at the page and not worry about it until the book is finished. I know the book is in there somewhere. It helps keep my critic at bay and to allow myself to take risks.

It also makes space for inspiration—things unplanned. For me, the internal critic leads to fear, and fear leads to playing it safe, and that leads to the book I didn't really want to write, and a book most people would feel they've read a hundred times before. It wouldn't be fresh and alive, and mine.

So my advice is to not worry about that first draft. Really go to town. Indulge yourself. Have fun describing every feeling, every smell, every touch, every building. The back alleys of Paris, the lavender fields of Provence, a sandwich in Boise, a spring morning in New Haven.

And then in the second draft get out the knife, and take most of that out. Carve away and shape. Like a sculptor.

And in the third draft whittle away some more.

And in the fourth draft change this word for that. Fine-tune.

And in the fifth draft you polish.

It is thrilling, to create a world. But it doesn't just happen. It takes hard work, dedication, a vision. And it takes joy. The genuine pleasure of inviting people to join you on this voyage, to visit what you've created. But you have to make the trip worthwhile, and make the passengers feel precious and valued.

And finally, a tip. When I'm planning a new novel, I start a notebook and in it I have a section on "Description." As I walk around I write down small details that I can sprinkle through the book. Smells, tastes, sights. Things that might bring a book alive. Grace notes for the voyage.

EXERCISE

1. Write down where your novel is set. And when. What season. What era. That's crucial. Close your eyes, and see it, and feel it. And hear

it. Write down headings for the five senses, then a series of adjectives under each, describing the sensations of your setting and season.

2. If your setting really was a character, what would be its "character"? Describe it as though it was human. What it looks like, how it feels. Is it happy, drab, peaceful?

DAVID FULMER

The Reality Show Called Settings

As the author of seven critically acclaimed mysteries, DAVID FULMER has been nominated for a Falcon Award, a Barry Award, a *Los Angeles Times* Book Prize, and the Shamus Award for Best Novel, and he has won a Benjamin Franklin Award and the Shamus Award for Best First Novel. A native of central Pennsylvania, he lives in Atlanta with his daughter, Italia.

L ike every other lesson that I've learned on my path to creating fiction, the importance of setting came the hard way. For years, I regarded setting as a bit of a bore, just a static backdrop or window dressing for the fun stuff like action and dialogue. I've found that more fledgling authors than I can count suffer under this curse.

It happened early on, during my prepublished career. As I worked through my stories and novels, I sensed something missing but couldn't put my finger on it. Then I began deconstructing the work of authors I admired and found that they all gave setting its due.

I had not been paying enough attention to the settings of my narratives and it was costing me.

Once I began working hard on creating strong settings, I discovered that it paid off in ways I hadn't considered—mostly deeper in the book, where so many authors get hung up and sometimes stuck for good. It's a desert out there where the bones of once-promising writing careers lay bleaching in the sun. Speaking of settings.

It's not that settings aren't considered as part of the original idea for a book or story. It's no accident that when the curtain goes up on a play, or a movie begins, we're either immediately or very directly fixed in time and space. It's the frame of reference and viewers—and readers—need to enjoy what comes next. So the problem is not that we don't recognize setting as an essential element. The issue is that we tend not to give it enough importance in our narratives. How I wish I had figured this out sooner.

I can condense what I learned and now apply it to two basic principles. One is my belief that setting and character are the two essential foundations of great stories. The second is that a great setting functions as a character in a great story.

As to the first principle, I know that an evocative, vibrant setting is necessary if I want to draw my readers into the world I'm creating or conjuring. Those readers will be there, with all the sights and sounds and smells, immersed in a total sensory experience that comes from the page and takes hold in their minds. And since this is all about evoking, if there was ever a time to employ "Show, don't tell," this is it.

So I've got my setting. Now, when I introduce characters whom I've worked to develop into interesting, dimensional, and nuanced creatures, the amount of heavy lifting they'll do is remarkable. Think of it as great actors being placed on a fabulous set and told to improvise. They'll nail it every time.

The second principle—that a setting functions as a character—is a bit harder for some writers to grasp. Put most simply, settings that are treated as static backdrops lie there, without providing support to drive the story. Think of your day and you'll realize that you've been reacting to your environment throughout. We all interact with our surroundings as we walk through history. So should our fictional characters. The goal with settings is to evoke surroundings that are in flux and so are all the more interesting. In short, powerful settings are essential to sustaining the grand illusion of a fictional narrative.

Doing that is a process of immersion, of becoming so familiar with your fictional setting that you can close your eyes and be there in the midst of it all and know what's around every corner. The way to gain this immersion is research—backstory, if you will—which means first of all absorbing everything written or broadcast about the place. For historical media, this means not just the book learning, but perusing the newspapers of the day. It's the only way to get down in the muck and noise of daily life in that time and place.

Once the writer has it, the next step is to get it on the page, and to do that we work the craft and study the masters. There are too many authors to mention who flat-out nail settings. A few that have caught my fancy are Joyce; O'Connor; Steinbeck; and more currently, E. L. Doctorow; James Lee Burke; Tony Hillerman; Martin Cruz Smith; and most of the fine Latin American authors. The way to find authors who excel is to read the very first description of setting in one of their books. If time stops and space disappears and you find yourself there, that's mastery of this component of the craft.

Notice that these authors don't belabor the point or try to overwhelm you with details and verbiage. They give just enough to make the sale and then they're out of there. That said, you know these authors understand their settings in their bones.

They understand that they need to provide just enough to get the reader oriented and involved and then get on with the narrative. And that's all. Novels don't work as travelogues. Like every other component of fiction writing, the setting serves to drive the story, and not the other way around.

Just as dialogue is a skill that's based on having a good ear, setting involves concentration of the senses; seeing rather than just looking, in other words. Since we're a very sight-oriented culture, the visual aspects are foremost in our descriptions. Next come the aural cues like traffic, nature sounds, music, and the like. Followed by smells, which are a tough sell but have incredible power of memory. Then possibly touch and taste, which won't get a lot of practice in mystery writing. But all five senses are in the author's tool belt and available to use in creating settings that evoke.

By the way, those who write about their hometowns don't get a pass. Remember that ninety-nine-plus percent of your readers don't live there and will need to be introduced and seduced into your setting, with the understanding that they're strangers. This requires the same editorial discipline that you would bring to writing a story in first person. It's not a place to indulge yourself. Read it—no, see it— through your readers' eyes.

Just a few more points. Writers of speculative fiction need to heed these same lessons as they create, rather than re-create, the worlds where their stories take place. I make a habit of finding a good street map of the setting at the time the tale takes place. Then I get it blown up to perhaps three feet by four feet and tack it to a wall. That way I can move through the world the way my characters do. I'll also dredge up whatever evocative photographs I can find, print copies, and tape them on the walls of my office.

I'm always looking for other little tricks; anything to help me better create the scene. That's the importance I give to settings in my fiction.

EXERCISE

1. Write a location, such as a park, a store, a house, or some other setting, on each of five index cards.

    Then write one sound on each of five cards.

    Do the same for one smell and one touch.

    Taste is tough, so you can let that pass.

    Then pick one from each pile and write a paragraph or two describing the place, remembering always to show and not tell.

2. Select a local news story from the newspaper or radio. Write out a description of the scene where it takes place, concentrating on the sights, sounds, and smells. Share it—and see if your reader gets it.

G. M. MALLIET

Stormy Weather

G. M. MALLIET's *Death of a Cozy Writer* won the Agatha Award in 2009 for Best First Novel, an IPPY Silver Medal, and was nominated for four other awards. The second St. Just book, *Death and the Lit Chick*, was a 2010 Anthony nominee; the third is *Death at the Alma Mater*. Malliet is currently writing a new series for Thomas Dunne/Minotaur Books. The first book in that series is *Wicked Autumn*.

ovelist and screenwriter Elmore Leonard advised writers to "leave out the parts that people skip." You'd think weather would definitely fall into that category. After all, weather is the kind of thing people talk about when they don't know what to say. It's conversation filler for those awkward moments, like when you're trapped with a stranger in a slow elevator ("Hot enough for ya?"). It's the default topic when you're scrabbling to find common ground with someone new ("I hear they're calling for snow").

Boring, but somehow necessary, right?

Elmore also said, "Never open a book with weather."

Clearly, Elmore has a thing about weather. But is he right?

Your unspoken contract with your readers is not to bore them, and incessant talking about the weather is bound to do that. So is using a long description on page one that serves as a warm-up exercise while the author gathers courage to launch himself into the narrative.

Those descriptions belong either in the wastebasket, or in an abbreviated form at a later point in your story when pacing becomes important—the movement from action to reflection and back to action. The quiet, in other words, before the storm—no pun intended. The still moments that can be used to lull your unsuspecting reader into complacency, just before you launch your next surprise at him or her.

Try to imagine a book without weather. *Wuthering Heights*, or *Rebecca*, or any book grounded in a menacing atmosphere. It would feel a bit thin, wouldn't it? Unmoored, so to speak, and vacant. Weather often presages events, or acts as a contrast—the sunny sky that mocks the protagonist's feelings of doom and despair.

So weather is crucial to orienting the reader, but as with anything in writing, there are ways and ways.

You can come right out and say, "It was raining." There's nothing wrong with that. But the gentle, unobtrusive reminder of the rain later in the chapter doesn't hurt, and can even be used as a small window into the nature of your character. Example: "St. Just deposited his sodden umbrella in the stand set aside for that purpose at the entrance to the private club. The stand appeared to be an elephant's foot, and he sincerely hoped, not a real one."

Especially when writing a series, I find it necessary to change the seasons from book to book, if only so each book offers a new challenge and stands out in my mind from the last. What will the sky look like this time? How will I dress my characters? What are they eating or drinking—piña coladas or hot coffee? The weather influences all these decisions.

For even in Florida, the seasons change: it's not sunshine every day. The same challenges apply—perhaps more so—in a climate that doesn't have the dramatic shifts enjoyed in Great Britain, the setting for all my books to date.

The weather can play a part in solving the crime in a crime novel. In my first book, the police detectives arrived on the scene of an old English mansion on a winter's day. The grounds were covered in snow. Undisturbed snow. This was the first clue they and the reader had that the murder had been committed by one of the inmates of the house. Especially when you're writing a traditional mystery, you need to limit the possible number of suspects and eliminate the passing stranger as a potential suspect. Footsteps leading to and from the house would, after all, indicate a break-in. If you indicate that the murder was com-

mitted by an outsider—there were footsteps in the snow—you may be
writing a thriller or a forensic crime novel instead.

Either way: No weather, no clue that can help narrow the field of
suspects.

No weather, no setting that readers can sink into.

No weather, no sensory experience that draws the reader into your
world.

And that is what you're doing in writing a mystery novel: creating
a world, sunny or stormy, to which your reader can escape.

EXERCISE

1. Think of your favorite season. Now write down any of the smells
   you associate with that season. Example: "Summer—suntan lo-
   tion." "Fall—burning leaves." Choose evocative smells that have
   immediacy for you, and that will pull your reader out of, say, his
   winter and into your summer.

2. Describe an incident in your life that you connect with the season you have chosen as your favorite. Now try doing this without
   any reference to the weather or its manifestations. (Difficult to do,
   isn't it?)

3. Look out the window wherever you happen to be right now, or
   take a walk outside with your pen and notebook. Describe the
   clouds and their color, and the movement, if any, of the trees. Are
   the trees bare? What color and pattern is the bark? Is there snow
   on the ground? A bright sun in the sky? Are the birds singing, or
   have they followed the warm weather south? If there are people
   walking by, what are they wearing? Warm woolen coats, or shorts
   and T-shirts?

   What sounds do you hear—is that a leaf-blower in the distance?
   More important, how does this scene make you feel? Excited, optimistic, peaceful, sad? What memories does it call to mind?

4. Decide: In what season do you want to set your novel? What aspects of that season might become a clue for the sleuth in your

novel? Example: Say you've chosen to set your novel in the winter. When the body is found, might a clue be the fireplace—the length of time a fire has gone untended or has been allowed to burn out?

How will this affect the time of death, as calculated by the police coroner? (There are vast resources online that can help you with this. Minute forensic detail isn't necessary, but you don't want to get it completely wrong, either.)

5. Carry a notebook with you, always. Put a date by your observations, and see how often they tie into the seasonal changes. I can almost guarantee that something you've observed will end up in your book, transformed into the telling detail that adds a touch of magic and realism to your story.

RHYS BOWEN

The Importance of Setting—
Grounding Your Story in Time and Place

RHYS BOWEN's books have been nominated for all the major mystery awards. She currently writes the Agatha- and Anthony-winning Molly Murphy books, featuring an Irish immigrant in turn-of-the-century New York City, and the bestselling Royal Spyness series, about a penniless minor royal in the 1930s. Rhys is a transplanted Brit who now divides her time between California and Arizona.

I remember the first time I went to India. I arrived after an overnight flight, and went straight to sleep at my elegant hotel. I awoke to the rhythmic clang of a bell, went out on my balcony, and there was an elephant walking past. I still remember the surprise and delight, realizing I was in another, very different place.

That trip left many indelible memories—in Delhi the sweet herby smell of the dung fires of the poor; life happening on the streets—people being shaved, children being bathed. Cows and donkeys pushing their way past street vendors, and the early morning boat ride down the Ganges, seeing the riverbank full of pilgrims as they came to bathe. The sparkle and swish of silk saris, the enticing colors and tastes of a big curry dinner.

You will see from this anecdote that my memories are of all five senses. This is how we perceive our world. So when we want to bring a setting to life in our books it is obvious that the description should not just be a visual one.

I came to writing mysteries through a sense of place. I had long enjoyed the classic English mysteries, and then I discovered Tony Hillerman. Here, for the first time, was a writer who took me to a place and made me believe that I was there. When I read his books I was in the Southwest, and even though I had never been there in person, I was able to act as guide the first time my husband and I drove through Hillerman country.

So when I decided to write mysteries, I knew what I wanted to achieve: I wanted to write books that would take people to another time and place. Not tell them about another time and place—make them feel as if they were there experiencing it for themselves.

I started with the Constable Evans books and re-created my childhood memories of Wales in those stories. Then when I switched to Molly Murphy, I tried to emulate Hillerman and bring the world of New York in 1900 vividly to life. I wanted my readers to feel that they were there with Molly.

I was lucky because my heroine was a newcomer to the place, and the easiest way to bring a place to life is to see it through the eyes of a character. Coming from the lonely west coast of Ireland, Molly is overwhelmed by the sights, sounds, smells of the crowded streets of the Lower East Side. I could evoke those streets, because I had walked them myself. I had heard how sound echoes back from the tall tenements, and I pictured how it would have been when hawkers shouted their wares, children played, babies cried, and teeming life went on day and night.

It's hard to bring to life a place where you have never been. You can't really give the feel of London, unless you've been there. Obviously we can't go back to the fourteenth century, we can't all go to Prague or to Antarctica. But we have to have been somewhere similar to Prague or Antarctica, if we wish to create the feelings of those places.

So I do my homework and make it accurate. I go to New York and walk the streets that Molly walked. I also have a huge collection of photographs taken at the time. So that if I'm writing about a certain street, I can see what the name of the tailor shop was and what was on the billboards. Remember, if you make one slip, everybody will tell you about it.

I reckon that I use about a tenth of the information I know, but the fact that I know the other nine-tenths makes it a better story. It's those one or two telling details rather than every historical fact or every geographic fact that bring a place to life. The cry of a hawk on a bleak hillside can evoke a sense of loneliness more vividly than saying how remote the hillside was. Our sense of smell is the most evocative as far as memories are concerned, so evoking a particular scent can take your readers to a time or place, by bringing to life their own memories. . . .

EXERCISE

Close your eyes. You are in a forest. How do you know that you are in a forest? Bring it to life with all of your senses except sight. Repeat with an airport, a medieval castle. (And remember that secondary characters and their senses are very useful in creating time and place.)

Good luck and happy writing.

MICHAEL WILEY

Writing in Place

MICHAEL WILEY has written the award-winning Joe Kozmarski mysteries *The Last Striptease, The Bad Kitty Lounge,* and *A Bad Night's Sleep.* He is a member of the Mystery Writers of America, where he serves on the Board of Directors, and the Private Eye Writers of America. He is a professor of English at the University of North Florida in Jacksonville, but sets his books in Chicago, where he grew up.

The best mysteries offer more than suspenseful plots and intriguing characters. They offer well-rendered places: places that we inhabit while reading and that inhabit us when we are done. Who can forget the Sternwood mansion with the big "stained-glass panel showing a knight in dark armor rescuing a lady who was tied to a tree and didn't have any clothes on but some very long and convenient hair" in Raymond Chandler's *The Big Sleep*? Who can forget the one gin joint out of "all the gin joints in all the towns in all the world" in CASABLANCA?

Place matters. The opening lines of my mystery *The Last Striptease* describe the area surrounding Chicago's North Dearborn Street as "a high-priced neighborhood full of forty-year-old guys fresh out of divorces from suburban wives . . . guys with good money from good jobs or okay money from okay jobs and dreams of an easy life interrupted only by vigorous sex after years of cutting the backyard grass every summer weekend."

Early in *The Bad Kitty Lounge,* my detective enters Holy Trinity Church on Chicago's northwest side:

> *The chapel was bright and painted as fancy as a twelve-year-old in mascara. A painter had climbed a scaffold and covered the vaulted*

ceiling with fat, rosy-skinned angels frolicking in heavenly blue skies. A portrait showed Jesus and Mary wearing crowns, Jesus dressed like a little prince, Mary in a red and gold getup that made her look like a model from an old Imperial margarine commercial. Still, the place took your breath away—all the color and light in the middle of the graying neighborhood.

The opening of *A Bad Night's Sleep* describes a razed "seven-block chunk on the south side of Chicago." If developers had "let it sit for twenty years, it would have turned back into the prairie that had stood there a couple of centuries ago. Thirty years and you could've put on a coonskin hat and gone deer hunting."

These descriptions aren't as memorable as those in *The Big Sleep* or CASABLANCA. But they establish tone, attitude, and atmosphere, and they reveal character, enabling the plot to play. My detective knows the North Dearborn neighborhood because he hunted for an apartment there himself after his own divorce. As a lapsed Catholic, he has mixed feelings about being in the Holy Trinity Chapel. A lifelong Chicagoan, he knows what the streets and neighborhoods have been and what they could become. The descriptions carry the books in the directions they need to go.

That is as it should be. Setting should offer more than the place where events occur. It should enable events—never overtly (plot-changing lightning strikes and the appearance of deus ex machina went out of style with the ancient Greeks), but by telling readers about the world available to the characters and about the characters' attitudes in and toward this world.

Two suggestions:

1. Robert Graves used to advise writers to adopt the perspective of "readers over their own shoulders" when making revisions. In observing a familiar place, you need to defamiliarize yourself; try to watch yourself in the act of looking and notice both what you see and what you miss.

2. Most published novels include disclaimers saying that any resemblance between places in them and actual places is "entirely coincidental." Don't take these disclaimers overly seriously. Make your places real.

EXERCISE

Try the following:

1. Visit a place that you think should appear in a mystery or thriller. Go in person. Spend time there even if you've been there before; get to know the place anew. Bring a laptop or a pen and paper. Make notes. Write sketches.

2. Regard the place through the eyes, ears, and nose of a thief.
    Regard it as a murderer.
    Regard it as a detective.
    What matters for each of them? How does each experience the place differently?

3. In each of these roles, notice the place in its totality, and also notice the odd and sallent details. Who or what inhabits this place? What are the colors, sounds, and smells? What metaphors suggest themselves? What is the history of the place?

4. Decide on an action that should occur in this place: a theft? a murder? the apprehension of a thief or murderer? What do your characters see or make use of? What obstacles or thrills does the place present to each of them?

MOTIVE AND EVIDENCE

Key Ingredients of Mystery

KEN KUHLKEN

Crime Fiction—What For?

KEN KUHLKEN's stories have earned a National Endowment for the Arts fellowship. His novels are *Midheaven*, a finalist for the Ernest Hemingway Foundation Award for Best First Novel; *The Loud Adios* (Private Eye Writers of America Best First Mystery Novel, 1989); *The Venus Deal*; *The Angel Gang*; *The Do-Re-Mi* (a finalist for the Shamus Award for Best P.I. Novel); *The Vagabond Virgins*; and *The Biggest Liar in Los Angeles*. In *Writing and the Spirit*, he offers a wealth of advice to writers and everyone looking for inspiration.

I mean, why do we write this unsavory stuff?

I suppose it's because we try to write the kind of stories we find most engaging. Why waste our efforts on anything else?

In college I majored in literature and became familiar with many great poets, dramatists, novelists, and short story writers. Though I admired and learned from writers of many stripes, the ones I returned to wrote about crimes.

It wasn't so much the crimes that intrigued me, but the characters involved in the crimes.

Knowledge usually reaches me best through stories, especially knowledge about human nature, what I and all those other strange people care about beneath our masks, and what we are capable of.

Perhaps no truer lines have been written than these Noah Cross speaks in the film CHINATOWN: "You see, Mr. Gittes, most people never have to face the fact that at the right time and right place, they're capable of anything."

The summer after high school I read Dostoyevsky's *Crime and Punishment*. Raskolnikov, a young man tormented by poverty and his own cynicism, becomes obsessed with what nineteenth-century thinkers called "a fixed idea." The idea and its implications compelled him to murder a pawnbroker.

While reading I felt as obsessed by the story as Raskolnikov was by his idea. The experience somehow deepened my spirit, my intellect, and my passions.

In a college English class we read Flannery O'Connor's short stories. The violence in them disturbed me. She made brutality so real, some years would pass before I could reflect and recognize that when the Misfit, a serial killer in "A Good Man Is Hard to Find," says about the grandmother, "She would of been a good woman if it had been somebody there to shoot her every minute of her life," he might've said the same about any of us.

We humans are deep and mysterious creatures, capable of great good and even greater evil. And we are masters of self-deception, not only capable of anything, but also capable of rationalizing anything. Stories about crime, about people in circumstances that send them to extremes of all kinds, are simply the best place to learn about us.

EXERCISE

Good crime novels feature characters whose motives we can grasp. As each of us writes a novel, if we are doing justice to our characters, we will allow them to grow. But they can't just grow every which way.

The most compelling characters begin, in the writer's mind and often on the page, with a trait that can be described in a single word that describes an emotional state. Lonely, haunted, loving, vengeful, bitter, desperate, soft-hearted, and lost come to mind.

Of course this one-word description is only the beginning. It gives the character direction and requires that he or she act in consistent accord with this trait.

Pick out a few of your characters and describe each of them with a one-word emotional trait.

Then write a few scenes in which the traits become exposed. In one scene, try to blatantly expose, while in at least one other, subtly expose.

VALERIE STOREY

Deep Motivation: Characters Have Feelings, Too

VALERIE STOREY is the author of seven books, including *The Great Scarab Scam*, an Egyptian mystery for young readers, and *The Essential Guide for New Writers: From Idea to Finished Manuscript*, a how-to book based on her series of writers' workshops.

The other day I read a great quote about how when we want something, we don't really want the actual thing as much as we want the feeling attached to the object or desired goal. The idea intrigued me because for a long time I've been curious to know what it is exactly I want from my writing.

Years ago when I was working on my first book, I shared the same fervent desire all new writers hold: *I want to be published!* The desire carried me through multiple drafts, dozens of query letters, synopses, outlines, and trips to the post office. I was so focused on my goal, it never occurred to me to ask, "Why? Why do I want publication?"

It was only after my first signed contracts that I realized a published book was certainly a lot of fun, but it didn't make me feel any different from how I used to feel before I was published. If anything, publishing probably made me feel a little more nervous and insecure: *What if I can't do it again?* In some ways it took more courage to continue writing once I'd sold my first book than it did when I was a newbie, blissfully unaware of the added stress that came with publication.

The feelings we—and our characters—pursue can sometimes be so basic we don't even know we want them. Until I sat down and examined why I wanted to write, I had no idea the answer would be that I wanted to feel part of a community, one made up of writers, readers, publishers, and people devoted to the written word. In other words, I was seeking family. Once I knew that, I also felt the pressure to be perfect slip away. Writing was just talking, conversing, and hanging out with an amazing group of people who continue to inspire me on a daily basis. Writing was fun. It made me feel happy and connected.

It's much the same for our characters. By exploring the feelings lurking beneath characters' desired goals, we can bring to life stories that are much deeper and richer—and more honest—than we could have first imagined. For instance, we often spend hours inventing a character from birth date to first childhood memory to current political association. We then try to put that character into some kind of action, usually based upon the pursuit of some difficult-to-achieve goal.

But once we've decided that Lucy Three Trees is thirty-two years old and wants nothing more than to stop a serial killer targeting blondes who all went to the same prep school, we need to know *why*. And to make Lucy's story one that readers will never forget, the why has to go way beyond: "It's Lucy's job. She's the only homicide detective within two hundred miles of her isolated post on the Canadian border, where she was raised by reclusive nuns."

What readers want and need to know is: Why on earth is Lucy living so cut off from the rest of civilization, and what is the emotional payoff that keeps her there? In other words, what is the feeling Lucy is attached to that both motivates her to catch the killer and keeps her from venturing beyond her tiny town of Moosebonnet, population 746½?

Sometimes when we're justifying a character's reasons for doing (or not doing) a required story action, it's very easy to fall back on that parental catch-all, "Just because." But because can be a good tool if it makes you dig a little deeper.

Let's say Lucy Three Trees wants to catch the killer because her younger sister, a blonde, was killed when their mother was in the hospital having throat surgery. A child herself at the time, Lucy felt powerless to stop either her sister's murder or her mother's illness, and she has blamed herself ever since.

Taking things a step further, we can then start uncovering Lucy's feelings through various aspects of her life, such as her appearance, her relationships with others, her specific interests and knowledge, or her dreams and hopes for the future.

Suppose Lucy is single; this makes her feel in control of her life and answerable to no one. She doesn't have to rely on anyone to rescue her and thereby make her feel helpless. She has a degree in French literature. This helps her to feel more worldly and sophisticated despite her isolated rural surroundings. The degree also makes her feel connected to her mother's grandfather, a famous French novelist of his day. Caring for the nuns who raised her after her mother's death brings out Lucy's nurturing side; she can overcome her feelings of depression that resulted from the loss of her mother and sister. By making sure the nuns have firewood and warm coats, Lucy can feel important to them. Dreaming of a trip to France ensures that Lucy feels hopeful: one day she will leave Moosebonnet, maybe for good. Lucy is six feet, two inches tall. This makes her feel both powerful and freakish. The tallest woman in Moosebonnet, she feels larger than life, and she knows she can be intimidating when she needs to be. Her height also makes her feel she will never find a life partner, which adds to her depression. Lucy has a strong French Canadian accent that makes her feel she'll never be accepted or understood by anyone if she does go to France, and it's what's kept her from making that trip abroad. Her accent has also prevented her from applying for a job in the big city; job interviews make her feel like a hick.

Knowing and exploiting Lucy's deepest feelings of depression, inferiority, and self-doubt is what will make her a real, live person on the page; one who will be consistent in her choices and actions, and one who will also be a good opponent and target for the story villain.

Story sleuths, villains, and potential victims often mirror each other's deepest feelings. Goals such as "the pursuit of justice" may be shared by all three, but the desired feelings will be very different: sleuths like Lucy Three Trees may take a stranger's murder personally, while the killer may feel very justified in his (or her) actions as he seeks to right a past wrong, real or imagined. And his poor victim may have unwittingly put herself in harm's way by wanting to feel loved by or helpful to the killer when he came to her school with his sad story of the headmaster destroying his university entrance exams ten years ago and thereby ruining his life.

EXERCISE

1. Make three lists: one for your main character or sleuth, one for your story villain, and one for your primary victim.

2. Identify your main story goal for each of these three characters.

3. What will achieving that goal make the character feel?

4. Why isn't the character feeling that way now?

5. Has the character ever had that desired feeling before?

6. If so, how many times? When was the first time?

7. Why does he or she want that particular feeling? What is the importance of it?

8. When and how was that feeling taken away?

9. What bad feeling does the character want to avoid?

10. In conclusion, brainstorm a list of people, places, things, or desires the character might want in addition to the main story goal. Isolate the feelings that go with each of these wants.

A particularly interesting outcome to your story can occur when your characters end up with feelings—good or bad—that were not the ones they set out to have. Character reactions to these new and unexpected feelings will greatly aid your ability to "show, don't tell." And the more you let your characters act on those feelings, the more interesting they will be for you to write about, and for your fans to enjoy reading.

EMILY ARSENAULT

Characters and Their Secrets

EMILY ARSENAULT's *The Broken Teaglass*, a mystery that takes place at a dictionary company, was a 2009 *New York Times* Notable Crime Novel. Her second novel, *In Search of the Rose Notes*, is about two eleven-year-old girls who try to find their missing babysitter using a set of Time-Life books about the paranormal as their guide.

I'm a reader, in part, because I'm a nosy person.

And I was a nosy kid, too. That's how it started. When I was around ten, I loved secrets. But I didn't have all that many, and neither did my friends. Fortunately, there were plenty of juicy secrets promised in the blurbs on the backs of the books I'd buy at the mall:

The old house is haunted by a ghost who has kept a terrible secret for two centuries . . . As their friendship develops, Karen starts to suspect that Amy is hiding something from her . . . In the attic, Dana finds a clue to a family secret.

Paperbacks promised more secrets than real life.

Sometimes I was disappointed with the revelations. *What? This whole time Amy was hiding that she was afraid of dogs?! Because a dog bit her last year? Who cares?* But I almost always loved the experience of tearing through the book to get to them.

I suppose I write suspense because it offers me a similar experience. As a suspense writer, I get to control the secrets. It's like a nosy ten-year-old's dream, knowing everybody's business and getting to withhold and dole out bits of it at my discretion. In adult life, we sometimes encounter people who are curious, but whose stories (and secrets) we'll never know. So one method I use for creating characters is to take someone I've encountered—someone whose idiosyncrasies interest me, but whom I know only superficially—and create a fictional backstory for them. This includes assigning them a few secrets.

Whether or not you choose to form your characters this way, it's always useful to ask yourself what baggage they carry—whether it's something to be revealed explicitly or not, whether it is the crux of your mystery or not.

But with the license to be nosy comes responsibility. You must always ask yourself—is it realistic for this person to withhold this information here? If so, why? Is he shy, devious, frightened, or perhaps protective of someone else? Is this behavior consistent with previous behavior? Is it fair to the reader? Would someone with a secret like that really say this? Is this piece of information going to be satisfying in this particular spot in the story? Should it be earlier or later? Is it worthy of the reader's time? Is the nosy ten-year-old in your reader going to feel betrayed, bored, or condescended to?

A suspense writer must balance the revelation of information as an element of plot with realism and consistency of character, i.e., *This is the perfect spot in the story for the reader to learn this—but wait, does it really make sense for the character to have withheld this till now? I'd love for this character to blurt this out here, but does he realistically have sufficient motivation to do so?* And it's quite easy to write yourself into a corner that forces you to have to choose between pacing and character realism.

It's a tricky dilemma—one that I struggle with more often than I'd like. But one way to minimize it is to know your characters well before you put them in a difficult situation. Know their baggage. Know how they carry their baggage. Always keep in mind that it's not just the secret driving the plot, but the person who carries it.

EXERCISE

Create a character with a secret—or less sensationally, a piece of information he or she has good reason to withhold from other characters.

Then, write two dialogues:

In one dialogue, your character is speaking to someone who

knows the same information. In the other, your character speaks with someone who does not. The dialogues should not be about this information—but peripherally related to it. You may not use either dialogue in your story, but it's worth exploring how the character carries this information.

After you've written both dialogues, study the differences between them. How has the character changed between the first and the second? Did his or her speech change? Did the behavior change? Is the speech and behavior here consistent with the character's personality—or does it seem forced for your convenience? Did your character have to lie (either overtly or subtly) in order to keep the secret hidden? If so, how well does he or she do it?

JULIET BLACKWELL

Driven 'Round the Bend: What Drives Characters?

JULIET BLACKWELL is the nationally bestselling author of the Witchcraft Mystery series. Her new Haunted Home Renovation series began with the release of *If Walls Could Talk*, also a national bestseller. Under the pseudonym Hailey Lind, Juliet penned the Art Lover's Mystery series with her sister Carolyn, which includes the Agatha-nominated *Feint of Art*. *Arsenic and Old Paint*, the fourth in the series, was released in 2010. A two-term president of Sisters in Crime Northern California, she is also a former board member of both SinC/NorCal and Mystery Writers of America.

I have a background in cultural anthropology, which, once you get past the jargon endemic to any academic subdiscipline, basically analyzes what it is that makes us human. Humans act on emotions as well as instinct, and by and large they remember—and are altered by—their past. Humans pursue revenge, and experience romantic love. Humans might desire knowledge, wealth, fame, lust, success . . . the list goes on.

Other animals have flashes of some of the above—and not all humans desire the same things—but it is our humanity that drives us to want more than to eat, sleep, and procreate. Our drives are powerful . . . and they run deep. They color every action, deed, and thought. What drives us is not always easy to define, much less to tease out how it affects us, and what it might influence us to do.

But this is where we writers have the advantage. We know what drives our fictional character, and we can use it to propel their story. And if we don't know and understand that drive, we need to sit down and figure it out.

To one character, an insult directed against one's mother is met with a shrug. To another character, it's reason enough to lash out with violence, and even to kill.

What makes the difference? Backstory. Our characters' backstories are critical when considering what drives them to do what they do.

I love coming up with intricate backstories for my characters. Even though readers rarely find out more than a small slice of that history, in order to drive my characters—to make them dynamic, fallible, and complex—I need to find whatever it is that stokes the flames of their action.

We see this not only in the critical decisions and action scenes that shape the novel, but also in the character arc over the entire course of the book. What drives this person? This is a crucial question in crime fiction when the protagonist is not a professional, and thus derives no career impetus to solve a crime, pursue a villain, or prevent a bad guy from committing a crime. Why would an amateur get involved in solving a murder? Does she need the money? Is her reputation at stake? Could a friend be threatened? Is she determined to cover up a secret from her past?

In thrillers, protagonists are further driven by the clock, by the need to save someone (or the entire world) by a certain point in time.

In series novels, authors must pursue multiple drives: the immediate motivation to solve a mystery or resolve a conflict, and the overarching, multinovel ambition to avenge a father's death, or redeem oneself in the eyes of one's spouse.

There are immediate versus enduring drives. Most of us can imagine taking a human life under very specific circumstances: in self-defense or to protect a loved one. But to go on killing for years involves a different kind of drive. A deep-seated psychological illness, in the case of serial killers. Or the external drive of being in the military, where one must carry out orders. Or working in a prison as an executioner.

All of those scenarios rely upon the characters being driven to do what they do.

It's no fun to read about Clarence Smith, who works an everyday job in retail and then comes home to eat dinner in front of the TV set before going on to bed, night after night. Unless, of course, the writer can convince us that Clarence has a rich, fascinating inner life. Perhaps

Clarence's mild façade is covering some deep childhood anger at his brother, a rage that will fester until he blows. Or could there be a wonderful imagination at work, stifled by fear of failure but soon to blossom? Maybe Clarence is suffering under a family curse that causes him to be a couch potato until the unexpected arrival of a neighbor with a magical talisman she gives him in exchange for one seemingly inconsequential act of kindness he committed that very morning. . . . The possibilities are endless, because human motivation is endless.

As a writer, you are the ruler of your written universe, all-knowing and all-powerful. Your character might well think she's driven by altruism, while you know (and let the reader know by subtle references and clues) that she's actually driven by a desire to be thought of as the good sister. Another character might believe himself to be driven for justice, while he is actually out to exact revenge.

So play with our human desires and needs to drive your characters to the brink, and even beyond. And never forget to ask your protagonist: *What drives you to do what you do?*

EXERCISE

Flip through the newspaper. Find an article about a compelling crime or mystery. Journalists aren't supposed to reflect upon emotion or motivation, so fill in those details yourself.

Say the story is about a mother killing her child. What could have driven her to do such a thing? Remember, there are always multiple sides to every story, even in a horrific crime like infanticide.

Write a scene leading up to the crime. Does the child remind the mother of her own traumatic past? Is the mother all alone, young and inexperienced, with no support and no one to give her a break? Is she angry at the child's father? Does the child represent someone or something in her life so feared that she kills it? Could there have been, anywhere, a sense of altruism?

And keep the story going. What happens in the moments and days following the crime? How about ten years from now? Does this crime drive the mother to alcoholism or drug abuse? To cherish and overprotect her current family, but to do something horrific to cover up her earlier crime? Could someone be blackmailing her? Or has her ability to deal with the crime made her a magnanimous, open person who is still eaten up by guilt, driven to be altruistic and to help other young mothers?

Write a scene wherein your protagonist can't let go of the past. How does her crime affect everyone else in her life: her family, friends, neighbors?

Try this exercise with more than one person writing about the same article, say, in a writing group. The different ways each writer chooses to explain the crime (and its aftermath) will demonstrate how varied a character's drives and motivations can be, even when given the same basic outline or facts.

STEPHEN D. ROGERS

Tell the Truth and Lie

STEPHEN D. ROGERS is the author of *Shot to Death* and more than six hundred shorter pieces. His website includes a list of new and upcoming titles as well as other timely information. And that's no lie.

I must have been somewhere between preverbal and kindergarten age when I answered my mother with a lie.

While I no longer remember the question or the falsehood, I certainly remember the result of my experiment. My mother immediately marched me to the upstairs bathroom where she washed out my mouth with soap.

The soap was white, and the taste was terrible.

I won't repeat what my mother said to me that day, but only because I can't remember the exact words and to get them wrong would be to lie. Lying is bad. I know that now.

A mouthful of soap will do that.

The years go by. Somewhere along the way, I decide I'm a writer, and in second grade, I put together a book of logic puzzles and codes. Nonfiction. Truth.

Fast forward to fourth grade. For some reason, our house has horrible television reception, and we can't get any of the UHF channels, which means that I can't watch *Creature Double Feature* on Saturday afternoons.

I decide that if I can't watch monster movies, I'll write one, and so I begin a novel where a man is returning from Kmart when he hears on the radio that giant dinosaurs have been sighted. He rushes home to warn his family and finds them relaxing in the living room with its dark wooden paneling and pea-green carpet.

That's as far as the story went. I hit the pea-green carpet and I stopped. I think it was the truth of that detail that emphasized how much everything else was a lie.

Even then, I realized that successful fiction did not lie but told the truth. I understood that I did not have enough life experience to tell the truth about dinosaurs or the feelings of a father trying to protect his family from said dinosaurs, and so I let the project die.

Fast forward to sixth grade, when I develop the theory that life experience can be figurative as well as literal, and thus start a novel featuring a hit man for the Mafia.

While I'd never killed anybody, I knew the challenge of completing a difficult mission that was frowned upon by society. After all, I was inside writing stories instead of going outside to play ball.

A strange thing about that hit man. No matter how many people he beat up and killed, he never lied about what he did. In fact, he never lied at all.

Nor did my next main character. Nor did the next, or any of the dozens that followed. I wrote about men and women, the young and the old, the good and the bad, and none of them lied.

Fast forward to high school, when I start writing more mysteries. One of the first things I come to understand is that mysteries involve secrets, and secrets are protected by lies.

The killer, obviously, lies in an attempt to get away with murder, but others must lie for a variety of reasons. They lie to hide embarrassments. They lie to impress the investigators. They lie to cover up what they don't remember. They lie and—as the author finds helpful to complicate the story—they provide red herrings.

The investigators, too, lie. They lie to suspects in order to provoke a confession. They lie to cover up their mistakes. They lie to protect their coworkers and their jobs.

Even the victim lies, once we include lies by omission.

I grit my teeth and train myself to be more forgiving of my characters and their need to be less than perfectly honest. The fault lies not in my characters but in myself.

My perspective changes as I continue to write. Even though my characters may lie, they are honestly motivated to do so, and my stories tell the truth, as all stories should.

I continue to write and then eventually to sell what I write.

The fact that I'm selling changes the value of my opinions. I begin to critique and to teach, and discover that either my mother had traveled from house to house with her bar of soap or that the honest-character problem was more common than I originally believed.

Why it's a problem becomes more evident.

Characters who never lie aren't realistic. Characters who never lie fail to produce as much conflict as possible. Characters who never lie remain flat.

The idea that characters can and should always tell the truth is in fact a lie that can render a story unpublishable.

That's when I polished and codified the following exercise.

EXERCISE

Beginning with your main characters and continuing with others of any import, write the following short scenes in order to determine how each character lies.

1. The character tells a white lie to protect another character's feelings.

2. The character lies to another character about something trivial.

3. The character lies to another character about a task that should have been done but wasn't.

4. The character lies to another character in order to hide an embarrassing truth.

5. The character lies to another character to get away with a crime.

Details to consider and reflect upon:

Does the character's manner of speech change when lying? Does the character's voice change? Does the character talk less or talk more?

Does the character become defensive, aggressive, evasive?

Does the character lie boldly, lie using half-truths, or lie by omission?

How does the character's body language change when lying? Think face, hands, and whole body, either in concert or separately.

How are these details affected by the size of the lie, by the probable consequences if the lie is discovered?

How much of the truth does the character manage to include?

How effective a liar is the character?

How good at recognizing lies is the character being lied to? How does that person respond: verbally, emotionally, and physically?

Now think about your characters as a group. Compare and contrast the answers you generated in order to ensure that your characters aren't all the same. If one character reveals a lie by change in tone, another should do so by looking away, and another by a change in stance.

Be true to your characters and their individual stories.

Tell the truth and lie.

GERARD BIANCO

Planting a Seed

GERARD BIANCO is an award-winning author of the mystery/thriller *The Deal Master*. The marketing techniques he developed to promote his novel were featured in Carol Hoenig's book *The Author's Guide to Planning Book Events*. Bianco's lectures on the art of mystery writing are popular among writers and readers alike. He is writing his second book, *Poor Choices*—a group of short stories, poetry, and two plays.

Reading a great mystery novel is a lot like horseback riding. Sometimes, you're cautiously slow-walking on unfamiliar turf. Other times, you're head-bobbling-wobbling trotting. Then there are those times when you're whooshing along on a take-your-breath-away gallop. This variety of pace is one of the key elements contributing to the thrill and excitement of the ride. Another is fear. (What if I fall off the damn horse?)

In keeping with this metaphor, mystery writing then becomes somewhat like laying out a course for the rider. The author must include an assortment of terrains to make the ride interesting and somewhat challenging. There have to be grassy hills to climb and soft, sloping landscapes to descend. There must be twists and turns, tree-laden paths, and long, smooth straightaways for those blazing gallops.

To accomplish this, writers use an assortment of subtle and not-so-subtle techniques to enhance their storytelling and add the necessary oomph required for a successful mystery/suspense yarn. From the many techniques available, consider the following.

Planting a Seed. How do you write a page-turning mystery—one in which people say, "I couldn't put the book down"? How did authors like Raymond Chandler, Erle Stanley Gardner, and Agatha Christie create stories that keep us glued to the page? One technique they used is called Planting a Seed. These authors sprinkled their mystery stories with several small, subtle mysteries that forecast evil—ruthless, merciless, cruel, and unscrupulous events that will take place later on in the novel. These little mysteries, many times placed at the end of a chapter, add breadth to the story, carrying the interest of the reader from the beginning of the novel to its successful conclusion. Tied together with the larger whodunit, they keep the reader turning pages faster than you can say, "221B Baker Street."

In my lecture series "Subtle Writing Techniques Used to Create a Successful Mystery Novel," I stress the importance of taking the extra steps necessary to bypass the competition you'll come up against in today's highly aggressive marketplace. Incorporating the technique of Planting a Seed will place you well ahead of your fellow authors. Both the TV and film industries understand the importance of Planting a Seed to capture the viewer's attention. Commercials, film clips, and trailers are filled with nerve-tingling uncertainties that leave the viewer panting for more.

Let's take a look at a few examples of mystery seed-planting from some of the authors I mentioned earlier.

Raymond Chandler in his last sentence of chapter 4 in Farewell, My Lovely *wrote: "I went out of the Hotel Sans Souci and crossed the street to my car. It looked too easy. It looked much too easy." It doesn't take a brain surgeon to figure out that later on in the story, "it ain't gonna be so easy." By planting those two little sentences, Chandler keeps us wondering what will happen next.*

In The Case of the Musical Cow, *Erle Stanley Gardner wrote at the end of chapter 13: "The co-ordinates had located the position of car seven within two hundred feet. The trap was ready to be set." Can't you just hear the eerie music being played after those lines?*

Agatha Christie proved she is the "Queen of Crime" when, in her short story "The Double Clue," she introduced the diabolical character Countess Rossakoff and Poirot's suggested love interest, and then prophesized, through Poirot, that the countess and the detective will, one day, reconvene. In his final words of this story, Poirot sighs and says to Hastings: "A remarkable woman. I have a feeling, my friend—a very decided feeling—I shall meet her again. Where, I wonder?" The seed Christie planted kept her readers on the edge of their seats, waiting for her next story.

Once you begin to recognize how authors use these subtle mysteries to keep the reader racing through the story, you'll begin to understand their importance and use them in your own mysteries. It's essential to remember, as with most techniques of writing, not to overplay your hand with too many of these keenly placed accents, otherwise your story will become burdensome and taxing. Keep your dialogue crisp and your descriptions sparse. Say no more than is required to get your point across. Your terseness will create a sense of urgency that will have your reader yearning for more of what you're dishing out.

Here's an example of the seed I planted, along with the brevity that I used in my book *The Deal Master*. At the end of chapter 11, I wrote:

With his shoulders up around his ears, he quickly walked away from the action without once looking back. When he reached the corner, he turned left. Then, when he was certain no one was looking, he sprinted as fast as his legs would take him towards what he thought was freedom, but on the contrary, was nothing of the kind.

EXERCISE

Reread one of your favorite mysteries, searching for those places where the author interspersed subtle mysteries to keep you wondering what will happen next.

Then practice writing ten different endings of a chapter, making certain to plant seeds that will induce readers to miss a night's sleep because they couldn't put your book down.

PEGGY EHRHART

Clues Are All Around You

PEGGY EHRHART is a former college English professor who now devotes
her time to writing mysteries and playing blues guitar. As Margaret J.
Ehrhart, she has published widely in the field of her academic specialty,
medieval literature, and has also won awards for her short fiction. She is
a longtime member of Mystery Writers of America and Sisters in Crime.
She is the author of the Maxx Maxwell blues mysteries, *Sweet Man Is
Gone* and *Got No Friend Anyhow*.

Clues are the backbone of the traditional mystery. The mystery
genre has expanded over the years to include many subgenres,
but we trace the classic form to Edgar Allan Poe's "The Murders in the Rue Morgue" (1841). That form was elaborated on by Arthur
Conan Doyle; celebrated by British writers during the "Golden Age"
of the mystery (about 1913 to World War II); and is still being written
by writers like G. M. Malliet, Julia Spencer-Fleming, and many others.

Think of "The Murders in the Rue Morgue" or one of Sherlock
Holmes's cases. We have an initial setup, often a crime scene, with a
bewildering assortment of inscrutable details. "The Murders in the
Rue Morgue" presents us with, among other things, "a razor, be-
smeared with blood," "two or three long and thick tresses of gray
human hair . . . seeming to have been pulled out by the roots," and
"two bags, containing nearly four thousand francs in gold."

The sleuth analyzes those details, or clues, and unearths more in
the course of his sleuthing. He eventually pieces all his evidence together, explains what actually happened, and fingers the killer.

If you aspire to write mysteries in the traditional style, you would
do well to make a study of clues.

A clue is anything in a mystery that points or seems to point to the solution. A clue can be a smile, a sound, a smell—even, in the case of Conan Doyle's "Silver Blaze," an absence. The fact that the dog didn't bark helps Holmes finger the villain. But for the purposes of this exercise, we'll be dealing with physical objects as clues.

Clues are everywhere. As you go about your daily routines, keep your eyes open for details you can incorporate into your mysteries. As I was sitting in my car one day in Manhattan, waiting for my parking space to become legal at six p.m., I watched a street person going through the bags of trash piled along the curb. He was collecting recyclable bottles that he could return for the deposits. I watched as he added several bottles to his shopping cart. In some cases, though, he looked inside a bag, even one that obviously contained bottles, and rejected the contents.

Why doesn't he like those bottles? I wondered. Well, they probably weren't ones that he could redeem for money. Maybe they were wine bottles, instead of beer bottles or soda bottles. But I let my imagination take over. What if my sleuth was watching a street person go through bags of trash? What if this scene played out in front of the apartment of a person whose untimely death she was curious about?

My sleuth solves music-related crimes. There's a style of blues guitar called bottleneck—because the guitarist uses the neck of a bottle, cut off and smoothed along the cut edge, to stroke the strings, instead of pressing the strings against the frets with his fingertips. The resulting sound is unearthly in its beauty.

I decided to write a scene in which my sleuth asks the street person why he doesn't like the bottles in a particular bag. "No necks," he says. "Can't take 'em back." This makes her realize that the dead man had been preparing for an upcoming guitar competition that would showcase his bottleneck guitar skills. And she's one step closer to a solution—lots of motive for murder in the competitive world of bottleneck guitar enthusiasts.

EXERCISE

Take a walk in your neighborhood, letting your imagination wander as you observe your surroundings. Look for things that raise questions in your mind.

For several weeks last year, every time I took a walk in my sleepy suburban town, I would see playing cards scattered in the gutter, on the sidewalk, and on people's lawns.

Find your own similar mystery and pretend that it's a clue in a recent murder case. Invent a victim, a murderer, and a motive, and figure out how your clue takes your sleuth one step closer to a solution.

DOUGLAS CORLEONE

Forensics: The Cutting Edge

DOUGLAS CORLEONE is the author of the Kevin Corvelli crime series published by St. Martin's Minotaur. His debut novel, *One Man's Paradise*, won the 2009 Minotaur Books/Mystery Writers of America First Crime Novel Award. His other novels include *Night on Fire* (2011) and *Choice of Evils* (2012). A former New York City criminal defense attorney, Corleone now lives in the Hawaiian Islands, where he writes fiction full-time.

There is no escaping technology. Seasoned writers of crime fiction know this as well as anyone. Today, law enforcement personnel utilize state-of-the-art techniques to solve everything from hit-and-runs to homicides. If your crime story is set in the present (or the future), chances are it is going to include some aspect of forensic science.

In crafting crime fiction, the writer must remember that forensics is used not only in the investigation of criminal activity, but also in the analysis and presentation of evidence before the court. Consider the classic film 12 ANGRY MEN. Fifty years ago, a jury could deliberate on a murder case where the only evidence was a questionable eyewitness and a history of bad blood. Today, even the angriest of the twelve angry men would have to vote "not guilty" from the start, given the evidence in that case. Of course, a case lacking such physical evidence wouldn't even be tried in the twenty-first century. Today, those twelve angry men would be discussing such things as trace evidence, including hair and fiber analysis; DNA; and the like.

The challenge in using forensics in crafting your crime story is threefold. First, your science must be authentic and your conclusions must be correct. This involves research. While developing my second novel, *Night on Fire*, I used no less than a half-dozen sources to familiarize myself with arson investigation. I learned how investigators determined a fire's point of origin, how they ruled out accidents, and what steps they took to discover the identity of the arsonist. In addition to book research, I contacted experts in the field and inquired about their techniques. Much of what I learned never made it into the story, but simply knowing the behind-the-scenes stuff gave me the confidence to write my novel with authority.

The bulk of my research didn't make it into the book, because much of it was boring. Which leads me to our next challenge—keeping your story dramatic. Science isn't always sexy, and you must be careful not to bog your readers down with lengthy scientific explanations. Use only enough science to get your point across. One way to do this is to limit your scientific explanations to dialogue. Lengthy exposition may cause your readers to fall asleep. But sharp dialogue keeps the story moving. A fast-paced Q&A between one who knows forensics and one who doesn't can actually enhance the story while getting your scientific points across.

The third (and probably the toughest) challenge in using forensics in crime fiction is to keep it fresh. I've lost count of the *CSI* spin-offs on television, which is to say nothing of the dozens of *CSI* knockoffs. If you watch these shows, it may seem impossible to come up with anything fresh in the field of forensics. But that's precisely where your creativity comes into play. The science itself doesn't need to be entirely new, but the way in which you use it should be. For example, in my novel *One Man's Paradise*, I used lip-print identification (technically termed *cheiloscopy*) not only as evidence of the suspect's presence at the crime scene, but also to create a dramatic courtroom hearing to determine whether such evidence should be admissible at trial.

The use of forensics will help you remain on the cutting edge of crime fiction. The following exercise helps me decide whether an area of forensic science can be used dramatically in my story, and whether or not I can present it in a fresh or novel way. See if it helps you employ forensics in your story.

EXERCISE

1. Select an area of forensic science, e.g., fingerprint identification; bloodstain patterns; impression evidence (such as shoes and tires); trace evidence (such as hair and fibers); firearms testing; arson investigation; or autopsy findings (such as identifying wounds and toxicology reports).

2. Research that issue using at least two separate sources. Plenty of information can be found on the Internet, but be certain the sources are reliable. There are also a number of books written specifically for crime writers. You can generally find them in the writers' reference section of your local bookstore. Also, don't be afraid to approach a local law enforcement agency or criminal defense attorney. Experts are typically gracious and more than willing to help writers. You can thank them later in the acknowledgments when your book is published.

3. Decide how this area of forensics can be used in a fresh way in your story. Think outside the box. First write down how this sort of forensic science is usually used to solve crimes. For example, impression evidence such as shoe prints is generally used to show that a suspect was present at a crime scene. How can a smart criminal manipulate law enforcement using this knowledge?

4. Finally, stage a scene in which this forensic evidence and its implications are discussed. Do this primarily through the use of dialogue. Try to refrain from using too many technical terms, but don't condescend to the reader, either. How would two professionals (maybe a forensic scientist and a homicide detective) discuss this evidence? How would they use it to determine the identity of their suspect?

SCENE OF THE CRIME
Creating Scenes

JAMES THOMPSON

Conflict and Scene Design

JAMES THOMPSON's first internationally published novel, *Snow Angels*, is a representative of Nordic noir. A murder mystery set against the endless night of the Arctic winter, *Snow Angels* was selected as one of *Booklist*'s Best Crime Novel Debuts of the Year (2010) and nominated by the American Mystery Association for an Edgar Award in the category of Best First Novel.

Before we begin, ask yourself two basic questions about your work in progress.

First: Is your story compelling enough that we care about its outcome? To answer this question, ask yourself if you've told us something we don't know, if you have exposed the world to us in a way in which we have never before perceived it. A daunting task.

Second: Do we empathize with your protagonist enough to give a damn about his or her success or failure? Your success or failure in these areas will depend on your treatment of conflict, scene by scene.

Your story will be composed of building blocks. From largest to smallest, these are the story as a whole (ending in a story climax); acts (in the vast majority of stories, there are three); scene sequences; scenes—the subject at hand; and beats, turning points within a scene.

Our responsibility, as storytellers, is to tell the truth. Not the ultimate, unknowable truth, but the dramatic truth of the stories we choose to relate. We create characters and attempt to expose the cores of their inner beings. We can accomplish this only through conflict. What people say means nothing. Our actions define us.

The more pressure placed upon us, the tougher the choices life confronts us with, the more we learn about who we truly are. Conflict reveals character. Because of this, your antagonist is of paramount importance. If your protagonist doesn't have an opponent whose powers equal or exceed those of the protagonist, you can't test his or her ultimate limits, you will fail to fully exploit conflict, and your story won't reach its full potential.

Through conflict, significant changes occur. Every beat should be designed to create change through conflict.

EXERCISE

I would like you to write a scene every day for a month. *Every* day. If you don't have access to a computer on a particular day, stick a piece of paper and the stub of a pencil in your pocket.

The length of the scene doesn't matter; it can be five beats or fifty. All that matters is that in each scene, through conflict, a change occurs that drives the story forward.

Given my reputation for dark and graphic storytelling, the stricture I'm going to place upon you may surprise you. The characters in each of these scenes you will write must remain relatively calm. No one may raise a hand in violence or a voice in anger.

There are two points to this exercise. The first is to help you build the habit of writing every day.

The second point is to ensure that you learn to never confuse mayhem and conflict. After a month, I think the golden rule will be instilled in you: Every scene must turn the story in a new direction.

KATE M. GEORGE

Using Everyday Activities to Create Conflicting Emotions and Increase Tension

KATE M. GEORGE is the author of *Moonlighting in Vermont*, winner of the 2009 Daphne du Maurier Award of Excellence in Mystery, mainstream division, and its sequel *California Schemin'*. She currently lives in central Vermont with her husband, four children, three dogs, and two cats.

Details. They can make or break any project. Details are the elements that create realistic settings in fiction, and factual or not, they give us the framework our characters live within. The details of my life make up the rhythm of my days, and are pertinent only to me. The details of my protagonist's life draw us in to her reality, making them vital to anyone who reads her story. Without them we are moving through a vacuum.

So ask yourself: What are your hands doing when you fold a towel? What does the fabric feel like? What are you thinking when you make a salad? Are you feeling, smelling, seeing the peppers and tomatoes? Or is your mind elsewhere, while your hands go about their tasks automatically? Recalling these moments will bring life to your writing.

I once worked in an exclusive inn where ironed, hundred-percent cotton sheets were the norm. A huge ironing machine took up a chunk of the floor space in the laundry. I say ironing machine and not iron because it looked like no iron I'd ever seen. Ten feet long at least and six feet tall, with a metal chimney protruding from the top, it sported roller upon roller, every one so hot that your fingers would blister if you accidentally touched them.

It was hot standing at the iron, lovely in the winter when we were cold from running in and out of cottages, but miserable in the summer when the air-conditioning couldn't keep up. The smell of hot cotton was everywhere. Despite the cushioned floor mats, our backs ached and our feet hurt from bending over to snatch the pillowcases from the bottom of the laundry carts.

It took two people to iron a sheet. The first step was to stretch the top of a damp sheet between us and feed it into the rollers. The trick was not to get our fingers caught or to burn them. Then we'd take a quick step back to grab the sheet midway down its length and hold it taut, while feeding it through the machine. If we didn't hold it just right, letting the fabric run through our fingers, it would wrinkle. Wrinkled sheets had to be rewetted and sent through again. The sheets were hot and burnt our fingers as we folded them, but if we left them to cool, the cotton could wrinkle and need to be—you guessed it—ironed again.

Sometimes the linens or bedding we were ironing would get wrapped around the rollers and jam the iron. We were supposed to keep an eye out and push the emergency off button if that happened, and if we weren't paying attention and the iron jammed, the whole operation was halted. Since everything from sheets to tablecloths needed ironing, it could be a big problem. One evening I was so focused on breaking my record for most napkins ironed, and beating out the women who were working with me, that I failed to notice that the napkins I fed the machine weren't emerging. I managed to jam the iron so badly that we couldn't even extract them with our secret weapon— a metal hanger. Maintenance had to come take the iron apart. Not a happy evening for any of us in housekeeping, and especially bad for me. My boss was not pleased.

Towels didn't need to be ironed, but like everything else they had to be folded a particular way. Spa towels were folded in thirds along the length—with the tag in, but the cotton label out, and then rolled. Hand towels were folded differently from bath towels, which were different from the bath sheets. It was one of the first things a house-keeper learned. You could get your ear chewed off by any number of people if you made a mistake, so we tended to be quick learners or moved on to other employment.

Scenes like the one above have become part of Bree MacGowan's life as well as my own. The details gleaned from my experience flesh out the lives of my characters. I use the exercise below to sink myself into memory, and I combine memory and imagination to write scenes that draw my readers into Bree's world. I rely on the details gained from writing exercises to flesh out my characters and my novels.

EXERCISE

What happens after the breakup? The fire? The murder? Life goes on as usual, but your protagonist is irrevocably changed. Dishes must be washed, clothes laundered, dinner cooked. Your assignment is to put your protagonist into an everyday situation in the aftermath of a life-altering event. Combine the routine activity with the thoughts and memories of the abnormal. Mix the mundane with the unexpected. How does your protagonist synthesize the difference between what he or she is doing now and the adrenaline-inducing experience just survived?

Each character will have different styles of coping and various degrees of success in maintaining normalcy after a crisis. Discover how your characters behave in the aftermath of disaster by writing them into everyday life and observing how they cope.

Is your heroine considering an outfit to wear to a funeral, or just getting dressed for the day? What thoughts are going through her head? What memories and feelings do the smell, colors, and textures of the clothes invoke? Can she even choose an outfit? Is it easy? Difficult? Why? What is she, or he, thinking?

Is your hero making himself dinner after narrowly escaping death? What is he feeling? Do the smells and textures of the foods comfort him? Upset his stomach? Remind him of a person in his life? What thoughts are going through his head?

Is your protagonist at his day job trying to function normally while having to keep wayward thoughts in check? Does his body continue to function, to maintain the usual standard of work while the mind is elsewhere? Or does the system break down? How does the character react? What is the protagonist thinking? What is he feeling?

You get to choose the catastrophic event for your character, and here are more situations that might help you decide on an everyday activity: folding laundry, writing an e-mail, washing dishes, bathing, brushing teeth, driving the car, talking with mother, reading a book, surfing the Web, filling the car's gas tank, washing the car, shopping for groceries, shopping for a present, shopping for clothes. Also use your protagonist's occupation to discover more daily activities that you can use to contrast the extraordinary with the mundane.

So here you go: Set your timer and write for a full ten minutes, even if you think you're done before the timer goes off. Take advantage of the moments you have and *write*.

JOHN LUTZ

Action and Reaction

JOHN LUTZ is the author of more than forty novels and 250 articles and short stories, including virtually every mystery subgenre. His awards include the Edgar, the Shamus, the Trophee 813, and the Golden Derringer. He is a past president of both Mystery Writers of America and Private Eye Writers of America. His latest book is the suspense novel *Serial*. His novel *SWF Seeks Same* was made into the hit movie SINGLE WHITE FEMALE, and his novel *The Ex* was made into an HBO movie, for which he coauthored the screenplay.

Action. That is largely what drives the modern thriller novel. What lends it velocity?

In this genre, things happen, and they happen fast. Or they are about to happen. Or they have just happened.

There is danger here for the author as well as for the characters.

What sinks so many thrillers is that the action scenes are too obviously planted in an attempt to set a frenetic pace. Which makes the book . . . a book, and not an exercise in the combined active imaginations of writer and reader. The puppeteer's hand shows. The compact is broken. The reader no longer trusts the writer; the real world, lurking just beyond the pages, intrudes. If one element of the novel is unconvincing, so is the rest of it.

So how do we make the action more an integral part of the story, a plus instead of a minus? There are some obvious methods, such as minimizing adjectives and adverbs to quicken the pace. Or using sentence fragments (as in the opening paragraphs above). Or introducing the ticking clock, so the character is fighting time as well as whoever or whatever else constitutes the main problem.

An effective technique, too often ignored or not used to full effect, is to involve most or all of the senses. Weapons glint in the sun or look dangerous in the shadows; blood has an unpleasant taste; the flesh of the combatants is sweaty and slippery; perspiration has an odor; bone makes a distinctive sound when broken; there might be ragged breathing, cries and moans of pain, soles scuffling on grass or dirt or gravel. So there we have sight, taste, feel, smell, and sound, all easy enough to use in even a brief action scene. All five senses. Makes my pulse quicken just reading about them.

However, when it comes to violence in fiction, there can be too much of a bad thing. It strains credulity if every dozen or so pages your main character enters a room and he or she gets involved in a slugfest or a shootout. The trick here is to alternate various types of action. A knife fight on page 100 is less convincing if there has already been a dandy such scene on page 90.

One thing you can do to make it easier to alternate (and therefore make more plausible) action scenes is to categorize them. There are fistfights, knife fights, gunfights, poisonings, strangulations; not to mention miscellaneous methods of introducing violence, such as drowning, falls from high places, being run over by vehicles, devoured by animals, crushed by falling objects, to name just a few.

On to chase scenes. There are footraces, vehicle chases, chases in interesting places such as subways or construction sites, injured characters dragging themselves to reach lifesaving weapons before their opponents do, water pursuits in boats or swimming . . . And we've touched only on types of races against time itself. Getting far enough away or finding shelter while the timers on explosives tick relentlessly on, obtaining the antidotes of poisons before doses become fatal, getting balky cars started, or coaxing other mechanical or technological devices to work, before it's too late.

Plenty of opportunity for the thriller writer.

Also effective is the aftermath of violence. Descriptions of broken furniture and shattered bones, of bruises and fatal stab wounds, of mayhem created by bullets or shotgun pellets. The book's violent episodes can be relived in the characters' (and readers') minds, and are also disturbing. And a disturbed reader is an involved reader.

A good, safe scare is what the thriller writer strives to create. And what the thriller reader is looking for. Remember when you were a kid and the roller coaster scared you silly and then finally leveled out and rolled to a gentle stop? What a relief! And the first thing you wanted to do was buy another ticket so you could go around again. The danger that wasn't real danger was intoxicating.

Same way with a good thriller. The reader wants to go around again. Wants to read the author's next novel, or catch up with a backlist, if one exists.

So if you are writing a thriller—a novel containing action and velocity as well as suspense—there are plenty of techniques calculated to keep the reader squeezing the pages. Among the most effective are to vary your types of action scenes, and when writing them to make good use of all or most of the senses.

Diversification works, and not only in the stock market. When you read what you've written, make sure you've applied these techniques and included different types of action. They help make it possible for the reader to believe, which is why the reader opened the book in the first place. Readers really do want to suspend disbelief. Avoid writing two or three gunfights or knife fights or car chases or dark-room bonks on the head in a row.

That kind of thing happens only in real life.

EXERCISE

In the last ten years, the thriller has become one of the most popular types of fiction. Understanding why can be helpful.

Read some of the most successful thrillers and mark the pages where there are action scenes (or aftermath scenes) and note how the author has alternated types of violence to avoid the monotony of repetition.

Notice how the senses are employed to involve the reader. Also how the aftermath scenes, such as homicide sites or other types of violent crime settings, are described so that what has happened already comes alive in the characters' and readers' minds.

When you've read a good thriller—or any kind of novel—take the time to analyze it. What made it work? What kept it from making your top ten list? For that matter, when you've read a bad novel, try to figure out why it didn't work.

Like it or not, every book you read is a lesson learned or ignored.

WAYNE D. DUNDEE

Convincing Threats for Your Protagonist

WAYNE D. DUNDEE lives in west central Nebraska and is the author of seven novels, three novellas, and more than two dozen short stories. Most of his writing has featured his P.I. protagonist Joe Hannibal, although he recently also began writing in the western genre. His work has been translated into several languages and has been nominated, in various categories, for an Edgar, an Anthony, and six Shamus awards. He is the founder and original editor of *Hardboiled* magazine.

It has long been recognized that one of the best ways to create suspense in a good mystery/thriller is to place in jeopardy a character the reader empathizes with. This character could be a likable innocent, a love interest, or comrade of the main protagonist . . . or, obviously, the protagonist himself (or herself).

And yet while it may be obvious that suspense can be generated this way—by putting your protagonist in danger— effectively writing such a situation can be quite challenging. Especially if your protagonist is a series character, and even more so if you write (as I do) in the first person. In cases like this, the reader clearly knows that, no matter how dire the threat, the narrator/protagonist is going to somehow survive. . . . And particularly when you use first-person narrative, things surely aren't going to conclude with: "And then they killed me."

So how, then, might you jeopardize your protagonist to a degree that will cause the reader to squirm at least a little bit and actually fear for the worst?

Let's start with the source of the threat against your protagonist. You need either a dangerous circumstance (a raging fire or fierce storm could be examples) or a convincing bad guy.

We'll take the bad guy first, the nemesis pitted against our hero. Either a villain who is capable of inflicting death or serious harm; or one who has at his or her disposal forces who can deliver same. Or both. Nothing brings out the best in a hero/protagonist or amps the suspense and anxiety in a reader like a villain who's been shown to be dangerous and totally ruthless, capable of the most heinous deeds.

A good example of this might be the James Bond series (either book or movie), which everyone is likely familiar with to some degree. Bond is at his best when up against the worst of the villains he has faced—Blofeld, or Goldfinger and his henchman Oddjob come to mind. Once again, we know that Bond is somehow going to come out on top, yet when his adversary has been sufficiently painted as being a worthy opponent, then suspense and a sense of jeopardy for the hero can nevertheless be created. Yes, we accept that ol' James is going to make it through. But when the threat against him is effectively staged, the question then becomes "How?" . . . and thus suspense is still generated.

Jeopardy from a more indirect source, such as the aforementioned fire or storm, can be handled in much the same way. Every reader immediately knows the devastation that can be wreaked by such forces, so the threat part is quickly established. The task then becomes to stage a convincing sequence of events whereby the protagonist/hero is placed in the path of this threat in some manner that leaves him or her trapped or otherwise vulnerable to said devastation. Effectively presenting this comes down to pacing and capturing with words the scene/situation in a way that will make it come alive for readers, make them feel as if they are right there experiencing what your protagonist is going through.

As an example of this, I present the climactic scene from my novel *And Flesh and Blood So Cheap*, in which Joe Hannibal, my P.I. protagonist, finds himself caught in the path of a tornado. A thunderstorm is already raging around him and he has just endured a savage beating when:

> *I struggled to my hands and knees. I thought again of the pistol Sei-Mu had dropped. Desperately, I swept my gaze over the ground,*

twisting this way and that. If I could just spot the weapon, somehow drag myself to it before . . .

My rubbery right arm had given way, spilling me nose down into a muddy, cigar-shaped depression—a culvert track, I guessed, from some long forgotten driveway—when I first sensed it. The whole pitch of the storm shifted. I felt my ears pop as if experiencing a sudden altitude change. The rush of the wind started to pick up volume, like a draft being forced through a narrowing gap. A fusillade of hail raked my back and legs. The wind rush became the clamoring roar of an approaching train, then a dozen trains, then a hundred, all racing wide open side by side.

Lifting my face from the muck, squinting due to the rain and flying debris, I saw it then. Moving across the meadow straight for us. Dramatically, breathtakingly backlit by lightning. A fat, squirming tube of grayish black connecting earth and sky, fed on high by thunder and lightning and at ground level by dirt and grass and rocks and trees and anything else unlucky enough to get caught in its path. A tornado—one of the most ferocious natural forces conjurable on the planet, the terror that lurks behind every Midwest summer. I'd seen the aftermath of their devastation many times, but I'd never before looked down the gullet of one. . . .

If I've accomplished what I set out to do, I have allowed the reader to take what they already know about tornadoes and couple that with what Hannibal is seeing and feeling firsthand as the destructive force bears down on him. The result, hopefully, is that the sense of jeopardy is amped-up for maximum impact.

Always remember, paint your scenes and characters vividly, but at the same time don't be afraid to let the reader bring something to the experience as well. In other words, there are times when it's better not to *tell* your readers everything but rather to *show* them certain things and then let them draw some conclusions on their own.

To emphasize this point, let's go back one more time to the villain. The last thing you want to do is to introduce such a character as "the nasty, evil, highly dangerous Dr. Killcrazy." This gives the reader nothing, implants no genuine sense of dread because you've given no basis for *why* Dr. Killcrazy should be feared and considered dangerous. The only way such an introduction might work is to have someone, in an exchange of dialogue perhaps, provide such a description. Nevertheless, the most effective way to handle it is to layer in key scenes showing the villain committing nasty deeds. This allows readers to reach their own conclusion that here is a dangerous individual, while at the same time clearly demonstrating why through your story's events. Subsequently, when your protagonist becomes pitted against this villain, you have already laid the groundwork to create that sense of jeopardy for our hero.

For stand-alone thrillers featuring a nonseries protagonist, all of the foregoing is made somewhat easier because the suspense may be heightened, as there is no guarantee that the hero will come out alive. But that part—not knowing for sure who will win out in the end—is mostly in the reader's mind. The mechanics of writing scenes and creating characters that will create a proper sense of danger and/or threat remain basically the same.

Bottom line: Placing your protagonist in jeopardy can be done for greatest effect by creating a convincingly threatening villain or circumstance. Write your scenes and descriptions vividly for ultimate impact, layer in your plot elements at the proper pace, and wherever possible show—don't tell—your readers what you want them to experience.

EXERCISE

This exercise is quick, easy, and can be applied to any genre and almost any situation. Best of all, it empowers you the writer to go back and judge for yourself the effectiveness of what you have written.

For starters, you need to select a passage or scene from a book or movie that has made a lasting impact on you. It can be a dramatic scene, a love scene, an action sequence, even something humorous . . . whatever you like. It would be best if the source for this scene is available (in your book or DVD library) for reference after the exercise is completed.

Once you have made your choice, try not to reread or view the sequence again ahead of doing the exercise. The goal here is not to re-create the sequence exactly as you first experienced it, particularly if it is a written passage. The idea is to try to capture, in your own words, the essence of the scene or passage—why it spoke to you, why it made a lasting impact—and to see if your writing skills can convey that same feeling.

Once you've written the sequence to your satisfaction in your own words, go back and review the original. Then compare. Exact dialogue—or names, or hair color, or clothing style—doesn't matter. In fact, putting your own creative spin on these things could be a good thing. What matters is: Did you capture a satisfactory measure of the same drama, emotion, excitement, or humor that initially made the sequence memorable to you?

And does your presentation of the same sequence stand the test of possibly evoking that same reaction in another reader? If you can truthfully answer yes to these questions then you have accomplished a step toward making your own original writing speak to—and stick in the minds of—future readers.

This exercise can be repeated with different selections until the ability to capture the desired effect is achieved.

An old adage says that writers with genuine talent, even if they set out to purposely mimic the styles of others, will, in the end, have their own talent and style shine through. I believe that to be true. Writing is all about conveying images, words, and events and putting them together in a way that tells a story and hopefully leaves a lasting impact. Whatever catalyst one uses to hone the skills to be able to do this is acceptable, as long as the ultimate goal is to develop your own voice in the end.

MEG GARDINER

Ratcheting Up the Suspense: How to Keep Readers Guessing, Worrying, and Turning the Pages by Structuring Scenes to Have at Least Half a Dozen Mini–Turning Points

MEG GARDINER writes two series of internationally bestselling thrillers. *China Lake* won the 2009 Edgar Award for Best Paperback Original. *The Dirty Secrets Club* was one of Amazon's Top Ten Mysteries and Thrillers of 2008 and received the *RT Book Reviews* Reviewers' Choice Award. *The Liar's Lullaby* was chosen by Stephen King as one of his hits of 2010. Originally from Oklahoma, Gardiner practiced law in Los Angeles and taught writing at University of California, Santa Barbara. She now lives near London.

A scene isn't a scene unless it has a turning point. Without some shift in the fortunes of at least one character—for good or ill—a batch of prose is just exposition, or conversation, or description. It becomes a scene only when something changes. Boom.

The turning point should occur near the end of the scene, and that change, that shift in circumstances, drives the book forward. When drafting a scene, you might initially design the turning point to come as a surprise. The scene toddles along, and then the hero announces he's secretly married. Or the couple riding the scooter go around a corner and pitch headfirst off a cliff.

That moment of surprise, of being taken unaware, will stop readers in their tracks and then, you hope, get them rushing to turn the page to the next scene, or chapter, all the way to the end of the book.

Surprises can delight readers. But if everything that comes before the surprise is mundane, then, as an author, you've blown it. To really grip readers, you need to have mini–turning points during any big scene, points where the trail switches back and forth unexpectedly, moving the characters' expectations and emotions up and down. This turns fluff into grit. This draws out the suspense, and increases tension. It tightens the screws. It's how you ratchet up the suspense.

Life doesn't run smoothly. Life on the page, especially in crime novels and thrillers, runs ragged. But that's what readers love. That's the thrill and appeal of crime fiction: sharing vicariously in the characters' struggles—physical, emotional, and moral—at the moments of greatest pressure and crisis in their lives. So create sympathetic characters and put them in jeopardy. Readers will go along for the ride.

I learned about tightening the screws in a scene through trial and error. When I wrote the first draft of my novel *China Lake*, one scene was informational (okay, expository) though in a Grand Guignol way. The heroine, Evan Delaney, attends a church service run by an extremist pastor. Evan's sister-in-law has joined his flock, and during the fiery sermon, Evan realizes that the sect is pining for the Apocalypse.

Then a man bursts in screaming. He raves incoherently at the pastor and runs out. The service ends in a shambles.

Dramatic ending. And, so what? Evan was a bystander. She wasn't involved in the action. There was no action, no back-and-forth, no nothing.

In the second draft, I tossed obstacles in Evan's path. She's not merely watching the service; she's hiding at the back of the storefront church because she knows she's unwelcome. Then she's exposed as an outsider by one of the fanatical worshippers. The crowd turns ugly. Evan calls to her sister-in-law for help. But the pastor puts the sis-in-law on the spot: Reject Satan . . . and Evan. Evan begs her: Please back me up. Show me you're still my friend; that we're still family. Instead, the sister-in-law sics the crowd on Evan. Security goons grab her and haul her down the aisle—she hopes to the street, but perhaps to a beating. The crowd closes on her.

Then the raving man bursts in.

His intrusion stops the scene dead. But it doesn't rescue Evan. The intruder is disheveled, threatening, possibly drunk, and definitely ill. Perhaps with an infectious disease. A scary guy. Woo.

That was draft two. I knew the scene still needed more. Draft three: As he raves, the intruder is grabbed by the security guards. He breaks away. And runs out.

Bzz. Not enough.

Rewrite. He continues raving. The guards collar him and try to drag him off. He grabs Evan to anchor himself.

Caught in his grip, Evan sees that he's fevered, coughing, and likely deranged. And they stumble toward the storefront's plate-glass window, then straight on through.

That made me happy. And kept readers turning the pages.

And did you notice? By building in mini–turning points, the characters came to life, their relationships took on edge, and I came up with a better ending to the scene. That's why I value this exercise.

EXERCISE

Start with an idea for a scene. Think of a basic idea, with a turning point: a scene that goes from A to B. Broad strokes.

Now go back and build in obstacles and the unexpected. Put twists in the road. Block the protagonist's path. Throw down impediments that are by turns physical and psychological, accidental and deliberate. Breakdowns. A monkey wrench. A landslide—verbal, literal, or emotional.

Here's an example. A to B: The heroine learns a killer has broken into her best friend's house. She races there and prevents her friend's murder.

In the first draft, the heroine may rush straight to her friend's home, burst in, and save the would-be victim.

Now fill that in. By applying pressure throughout, thwarting the heroine's desires, you can increase the suspense and tension.

The heroine finds out the murderer is at her friend's house. She tries to call and warn the victim, but the phone is dead. She must go herself. But her motorcycle won't start. She hot-wires it and races down the road.

She sees the house ahead—but a truck is jackknifed across the road, blocking her. She abandons the motorcycle and runs, cutting through traffic. She phones the police—they will send help. But they're also blocked by the wreck.

Now it's up to her. She gets there and the door is wide open. Is she too late? She runs inside. The murderer has beaten her there. She must find a weapon. She grabs an electric drill—but the power is out. She finds a baseball bat and runs up the stairs. The door is closed. And then . . .

The rest is up to you.

VICKI HENDRICKS

Exposing the Sex Scene

VICKI HENDRICKS is the author of the noir novels *Miami Purity*, *Iguana Love*, *Voluntary Madness*, *Sky Blues*, and *Cruel Poetry*, the latter a finalist for an Edgar Award in 2008. Her collection *Florida Gothic Stories* was published in 2010. Hendricks lives in Hollywood, Florida, and teaches writing at Broward College. Her plots and settings reflect participation in adventure sports like skydiving and scuba, and knowledge of the Florida environment.

I hope not to disappoint, but writing a sex scene is not as much fun as participating in one. You'd probably already guessed! A sex scene, whether in the crime genre or a mainstream novel, is basically the same as any scene, but generally with less dialogue. It requires specialized vocabulary, ranging from gutter to romantic to clinical, but must perform normal scene functions: developing character, moving plot, and cementing theme. There are usually just two characters, although your imagination is the only limit. (Warning: Same-sex partners wreak hell for pronoun usage.) The action can range from normal to eccentric, and the coitus doesn't always have to be successful, and/or beautiful.

One of the most highly acclaimed sex scenes in the past twenty years can be found in Harry Crews's novel *Body*, where an obese young virgin is seduced in her bathtub by an obsessive bodybuilder who claims to be a "skin technician." I originally set out to mention this scene as an example of less than beautiful sex, but Crews's ingenious humor and descriptive technique create a scene that, in the eye of this beholder, renders uncanny sexuality.

Developing character (see Jason Starr's masturbation scene in *Twisted City* for a hilarious, character-revealing scene) and cementing theme probably come naturally into the sex scene when you're in the midst of a novel or story, but in order to move plot, there must be an arc and a climax—maybe two climaxes! (but not necessarily)—that cause a change. Since there is often a lack of pithy dialogue, the subtext—underlying emotions, beliefs, motivations, and unspoken thoughts—becomes extremely important in building conflict to create the arc of the scene. Even if the conflict is mainly internal on the part of the protagonist, it should spill over into action.

Although writing a sex scene is no different from writing any scene, and a sex scene in a crime novel is similar to a sex scene in any mainstream novel, sometimes motives can relate to the crime or perhaps motives might develop that set up a crime. Think of James M. Cain's sliver of a sex scene in *The Postman Always Rings Twice*, when Frank and Cora first meet. In Cain's day, he couldn't write much beyond a kiss—in this case a bite—but he creates enough passion in a few details to have us believe that these characters will be satisfied only by murdering Cora's husband.

In another possible case, perhaps the protagonist wishes to manipulate the other character or to give up his or her own control. If the writer is particularly clever, the conflict can go so far as to be between the protagonist and an antagonist of the novel. An interesting sex scene that demonstrates this deliciously is in James W. Hall's first novel, *Under Cover of Daylight*, where longtime adversaries overcome their motivations long enough to have believable, wonderful sex. Since connection and disconnection are an intricate part of any plot structure, a literal coupling of bodies can supply the dramatic action for change or development.

In my novel *Miami Purity*, the main character is a stripper obsessed with sex, so the many sex scenes bring out her character, as well as blind her to manipulation. In *Cruel Poetry*, the main character is a freelance prostitute, and her enticing sexuality in multiple scenes binds the other two narrators to her decadent and dangerous lifestyle.

It is especially important when creating a sex scene to build up enough subtext in advance, so that the reader can interpret the actions for full intrigue and emotional power. Once the clothes are off, there's no time for explanation. My exercise will require you to put the emphasis on subtext, so that the scene has legitimate purpose and no one will label it gratuitous. For the best results, use two characters that you already know well.

EXERCISE

PART ONE

In column A, list the motivations, fears, hopes, beliefs, regrets, and emotions that you want to come into play in order for the protagonist to undergo a change or development that will move the plot. If you are in the midst of a story or novel, you'll already know what is important. This could be a change in the relationship or a self-realization. It could go so far as to be a reversal, for a climactic scene. In column B, list bits of dialogue and actions of a sexual nature that would dramatize the items in column A.

PART TWO

Now put your columns away and go into your dream state. Imagine the scene: the location, the atmosphere, the surface, the bodies. Write it. Make your protagonist act and the other character react. Do not look back at the columns unless you get stuck.

LORENZO CARCATERRA

Ready, Set, Action

LORENZO CARCATERRA has written eight books: *A Safe Place, Sleepers, Apaches, Gangster, Street Boys, Paradise City, Chasers,* and *Midnight Angels.* He was a writer and producer for *Law & Order* and was the managing editor for the CBS series *Top Cops* for three years. He has written feature scripts for movie producers and TV pilots for several networks. He is at work on his next novel, as well as a feature script for Olive Productions and a pilot for Barry Levinson.

I love action scenes, whether they're in movies, on television, or in the pages of a book. I especially love *Great* action sequences—from Ken Follett's *Eye of the Needle* to Michael Mann's bank heist gone wrong in HEAT to Kiefer Sutherland taking out one more target in *24*.

I imagine such love of action comes to me naturally. I was raised in Hell's Kitchen, a New York City neighborhood populated by tough men, many of whom had done hard prison time, my father included. They were physical men, living in the moment, and their first response to any incident or threat was to lash out and to do so quickly. The stories they would tell usually centered on criminals caught in a bad spot—from "Two-Gun" Crawley and his shoot-out with a squadron of heavily armed cops in a warehouse on West 96th Street (the inspiration for the James Cagney movie ANGELS WITH DIRTY FACES) to the machine-gun daytime murder of Vincent "Mad Dog" Coll in a drugstore phone booth on Eighth Avenue near Twenty-third Street.

The movies of my childhood starred urban action tough guys—from Cagney to Humphrey Bogart to Edward G. Robinson up to the then current Kings of Cool: Steve McQueen, Charles Bronson, and Clint Eastwood. The television in our railroad apartment (when the set wasn't at the pawn shop) was usually tuned to the action of *The Untouchables* and the heroics of Lee Marvin in *M Squad*.

This taste for action also inspired the books I was drawn to: all the works of Alexandre Dumas, especially *The Count of Monte Cristo* (to this day, still my favorite novel), Victor Hugo, Jack London, Rafael Sabatini, Sir Arthur Conan Doyle, and, as I grew older, the books of George V. Higgins, Elmore Leonard, and Ed McBain.

There is no doubt that the stories told to me by my father and the men of my neighborhood, along with the books, programs, and movies those tales led me to, have influenced the books I've written. My novel *Gangster* is an outgrowth of those criminal tales told to me over many a hot summer night, the fire hydrants open wide, cold water bringing welcome relief from the oppressive heat. Another book, *Street Boys*, a novel set in Italy during the last years of World War II, was inspired by my mother's experiences surviving those horrible months of daily bombings, losing a husband, a brother, and an infant in that turbulent time.

I have always tried to do justice to the action scenes I write. I have not always succeeded. It is easy to have them veer off toward a cartoon type of violence, straying from the danger and pain those scenes need to deliver, and I have been guilty of such an infraction far too many more times than I care to admit. The best action sequences move at warp speed and are not as clean and clear-cut as we'd like them to be—action is often sloppy and almost always bloody and more often there are a number of bodies left in its wake. It is essential when dealing with life and death on the page that the words and the images they convey be as deeply mired in truth as possible.

This is my goal, and while I don't always achieve it, it is what I strive for. I owe it to those men who shared their stories with me so many years ago. It is what they would have expected—that their tales reflect their reality.

They may not have been saints.

In truth, most of them were in fact sinners.

But they were all great storytellers.

EXERCISE

Let's set it up. We're going to take out a gangster. But not just any run-of-the-mill street thug. A tough man who was raised pretty much on his own on the streets of New York City and who, through violence and savvy, rose through the ranks to a position of criminal authority. He's avoided prison, killed more than his share of enemies, and has managed to survive into his late fifties, when most in his profession are toe-tagged before they see thirty.

He's slower now, not as mentally and physically sharp as he once was. His instincts are still there—those never leave a true gangster—but the read time is a click or two off. And in his line of work, that short amount of time can cost him his life.

He is driving to a meeting set up in an abandoned pier off the West Side Highway. It is early evening, just after dark. He is alone, behind the wheel of a late-model Cadillac. He has two guns on him—a .38 Special and a 9 millimeter. He is set to meet the leader of a rival crew, a younger, crueler version of what he once was, to see if together they can broker a peace and end the hostilities that have cost both gangs considerable sums of money and far too many members.

He pulls into the open doors of the abandoned pier. Behind him, cars inch their way through congested West Side Highway traffic. He goes in with his lights low, engine running slow and easy, his two guns within reach. He smells a setup but isn't sure and can't afford to make a move, either too early or too late.

Here is the key to the scene: He needs to die as he has lived.

He needs to go out like a hard-core gangster.

That's what the reader expects.

And that's what the character you've created would demand.

Now go ahead and have some fun.

CHANGING YOUR STORY

Revision

JAN BROGAN

Between the Drafts

JAN BROGAN, a journalist, is the author of the critically acclaimed Hallie Ahern mystery series set in Providence, Rhode Island. Her first novel, *Final Copy*, won the *Drood Review of Mystery* Editor's Choice award. She has taught nonfiction, mystery writing, and screenwriting workshops.

Writers approach a new novel in many different ways. Some write extensive character biographies and outline every plot detail before they start. Others do no planning at all and talk about channeling characters who decide their own fates in the story. But no matter what kind of writer you are—a compulsive outliner or a by-the-seat-of-your-pants free spirit—you can benefit by taking an organized approach to revision.

I often encourage new writers to be as fast and loose as possible with a first draft. Lowering standards helps a writer be less self-critical and more creative. It's impossible to get into a flow of writing, losing yourself in the story, if you are anticipating judgment and worrying too much about perfect prose or punctuation.

In some ways, writing a first draft is like weaving cloth—creating the raw material. Once you've got enough material, you need a pattern or plan to cut it up and sew the pieces into the garment.

The input of a writers' group, or even self-critique, is difficult to assess when the writer is still in the midst of the first draft, working out decisions, playing with the many possibilities for plot and character development. There can be a tendency to undercorrect—reject needed input, as well as to overcorrect—change too much in a knee-jerk response.

So the question is: How do you get the necessary perspective to sort through the good and bad ideas of a first draft, as well as the good and bad criticism of chapters or scenes along the way? And what's the most effective way to organize decision making and keep track of the changes that need to be made?

In addition to developing a comprehensive review process, I've learned to impose a four-act system, adapted from screenwriting, to help identify slow stretches of story that need to be tightened and scenes that need to be bigger and more climactic.

The result is a mystery that knows where it's going and gets there at a pace that keeps the reader turning the pages. Just as every writer has a different method for writing a draft, there are many different ways to attack revision. But the system I've developed, which I call Between the Drafts, has worked miracles for me.

EXERCISE

Materials needed:

Four manila folders

A full pad of letter-size writing paper

Pens and/or pencils

1. Leave at least three days, but preferably two weeks after you finish the first draft, then print out the entire manuscript.

2. Label the tabs on the four manila folders: Act I, Act II, Act III, and Act IV.

3. Take the hard copy of the manuscript and all the materials to a comfortable chair in a quiet place to read—preferably away from wherever you wrote the first draft. (I like fireplaces in winter and screened porches or decks in summer.)

4. Divide the hard copy into four sections or acts according to the guidelines below. Each section should end at a turning point. (Don't

worry too much about exactly where to divide the manuscript; you may wind up changing it after this process is over.)

- The first act, typically twenty to thirty percent of the manuscript, is considered the setup that launches the story into motion.

- The second act, about thirty to forty percent of the manuscript, ends at the midpoint, a turning point that sends the story in a new direction.

- The third act, between thirty and forty percent of the manuscript (depending on the second act), builds the action from the reversal to the climax.

- The fourth act, ten percent or less of the manuscript, is the resolution. This section ties up loose ends, often explains how the clues add up, and what the protagonist may have learned or gained from this particular story.

5. Starting with the first chapter, read slowly and take detailed, hand-written notes on each chapter. These notes can address anything from a vague pronoun to problems with character development. Include new ideas that occur to you, for example: "X needs depth, hint at failed relationship with Z," or "Plant access to poison here." In the left-hand margin of the writing pad, keep track of the page number. Even if it's a general critique for the entire chapter, note the page number where this criticism first occurred to you. Staple multiple pages together by chapter. Place in the appropriate manila folder.

   The number of notes per chapter isn't important, taking the notes by hand is. Numerous research studies have shown that handwriting stimulates different parts of the brain, and for me, somewhere between half and three-quarters of the way through this note-taking process, a miracle occurs. Suddenly, I can see through the muddle of my mistakes. I know exactly what I'm trying to say with my mystery. Each character's role and journey becomes clear. I have new authority, a stronger voice, and I know whether to accept or discard any criticism I've gotten along the way.

6. Next, go back to the computer. Tell the story as if you were sitting on a bar stool or at a lunch counter, explaining it to a friend for the first time. Don't get bogged down in details. The point is to streamline your thinking. If there are holes in your plot, you will see them. If your book meanders, it will become clear to you. The story structure will crystallize.

7. You may now want to eliminate or add chapters or scenes, redivide your manuscript, or move chapters from one act to the next. From the synopsis and chapter notes, you will write a brief revision plan for the entire book.

   Address only structural changes, or big changes that involve adding or consolidating characters, rearranging clues, or addressing theme throughout. Don't reiterate changes already detailed in the chapter notes.

8. Between the revision plan, the synopsis, and the chapter notes, you now have a blueprint for how to rewrite your second draft. Before I start revising each act, I reread my overall revision plan. Then I pick up the chapter notes and start rewriting, checking off each note as I address the problem. Sometimes, when rewriting, I decide the note is wrong; I liked it better the original way. That's okay, too. The process isn't perfect.

This method may seem like a lot of work, but I've learned the hard way that it can save the time and heartache of endless, unsuccessful drafts.

BRIAN EVENSON

On Revision

BRIAN EVENSON is the author of ten books of fiction, most recently the
novel *Last Days*, which won the American Library Association's award for
Best Horror Novel of 2009, and the story collection *Fugue State*. His novel
The Open Curtain was a finalist for an Edgar Award. He lives and works
in Providence, Rhode Island, where he directs Brown University's Literary
Arts Program.

The thing that makes the difference between a good book and a
great book is revision: taking the time to get the details right so
that the dialogue is convincing, the development of the action consistent, the description crisp and accurate, the mood just right.
With mystery and crime fiction this is especially important. Moments
where the seams of the storytelling show or where the author tele-
graphs what's coming next can ruin the experience for readers. These
lapses can make readers distrust the author's authority and can cast
the fiction's authenticity into doubt.

At times, that distrust is a tool you can use—there are sometimes
reasons to make readers doubt the veracity of a situation or of what a
character is saying—but it's a tool that should be used very sparingly
and very carefully.

When I'm writing a novel or a story, I try in the first draft to get
the dynamics of the story and the plot in place. I try to create a basic
sense of the order of events and what is happening, a clear sense of
the conflict, a sense of the characters and their relationships to one
another. I find if I can do all of that, I end up with a firm and sturdy
narrative skeleton, which I can build flesh and skin around. If this
skeleton isn't in place early on, it's much harder to build the story or
novel (especially a novel) into a convincing living body.

In the ensuing drafts, I think a lot about the story's pacing, a lot about the specific words that characters are using, a lot about how small details function in relation to one another, about what is revealed when and by whom. I'm looking to build up the story in a way that gives it a natural texture, which makes for a good, intense reading experience, one the reader can get lost in—the kind of reading experience I want to have as a reader myself.

If you don't have that basic skeleton to begin with, revision is a very different matter, a much more desperate and demanding process where you often end up throwing large parts of the story away and shifting around big blocks of text. It usually takes more time than scrapping the project and starting over, and a lot of writers I know have stories about the novel they revised, seemingly without end, but could never get quite right, the novel that's waiting in a drawer somewhere and is still not ready to be published.

Intense revision takes a lot of work, but sometimes it's worth it. Some projects get their hooks into you and refuse to let go. When I was writing my novel *The Open Curtain*, I thought I knew where the book was going. I had an outline, knew what should happen when, felt like I had a good road map. And indeed I did know where I was going for the first two parts of the book. Then I got to the third and final part and realized that everything I'd planned for it just wasn't right. It was like I'd followed the road map to a place where a bridge was washed out.

Then I did a stupid thing. Rather than try to figure out where the story needed to go, I stuck to the outline and followed it anyway. Not surprisingly, I ended up with a body whose head and torso appeared human but whose legs looked like they belonged to some other creature entirely. So I threw the last part away and tried again, not quite willing to dispense with the outline, but letting go of parts of it. That version was terrible, too.

Then I spent a long time—weeks first and then months—putting the outline aside and thinking about what should happen, trying different ideas for the ending that fizzled out. I was left with more than a thousand pages of material that I threw away. I knew the idea was good, knew I had something, but I just couldn't make it work. Several times I almost gave the book up, but I kept coming back to it. And finally, suddenly, when I least expected it, I started that third part again and something clicked, and all at once I knew I had it. The book went on to be a finalist for the Edgar Award.

That's an important part of revising: knowing when not to give up. Be persistent; be willing to spend some time and serious effort getting the book where you want it to be. Try to make an okay book a good book, and then strive to make that good book a great book.

Writing a novel is like entering a relationship, and like any relationship it can demand a lot from you if you want it to work. But you also need to know when to let go and move on.

EXERCISE

Take a scene that you feel is stuck—not working—and revise it to be in a different voice: if it's in first person, write it in third person. If it's in third person, write it in first. If it's in the voice of the detective, rewrite it in the voice of the murderer, thinking about what he might notice that the detective would not.

Then sit back and take a close look at your rewrite. What do you notice about the scene that didn't strike you before? What cracks or flaws do you see that weren't apparent before? Is the problem the point of view? Even though you were initially writing from someone's first-person perspective, were you trying to convey information the person wouldn't know? Is the problem that the third-person voice wasn't as objective as you thought? This is a way of giving yourself distance from the scene, letting you take a step back so you can see it more objectively.

Now take the revised scene and return it to the voice it was formerly in, but without looking at the original version—just working with the revised version. Try to preserve what you like about the new version while making it genuine to the original voice.

Tip: At a certain point in the revision process, I often discover I'm not sure about a character's voice—something has changed between how she speaks or acts early in the book and how she speaks or acts later.

The easiest way to determine what's wrong is to cut out all the static. Take the first few instances of the character's speech, then a bit of dialogue chosen from the middle, then the last few bits of her dialogue. Copy it all in a separate document, without anything else, then read it straight through. What changes? What stays the same? Think back to the book: Is there a reason for her to change or not?

Often this step will reveal what you need to know. Other times you will need to go a step further. Take a few more bits from the middle of dialogue. But take a little more than just her speech; take lines just before and after to get a sense of whom she's speaking to. More often than not, the problem will make itself clear.

M. WILLIAM PHELPS

Hooking Your Reader from Page One

Crime expert, lecturer, television personality, and investigative journalist **M. WILLIAM PHELPS** is the nationally bestselling, award-winning author of seventeen nonfiction books with more than one million in print. Phelps has appeared on CBS's *Early Show*, ABC's *Good Morning America*, *Montel Williams*, *Investigative Discovery*, and *Geraldo at Large*; on Court TV, the Discovery Channel, Fox News Channel, the Learning Channel, Biography, the History Channel; and on USA Radio Network; Catholic Radio; ABC News Radio; and Radio America. He has also consulted on the Showtime series *Dexter*.

We cannot discuss true crime without mentioning *that* book (you know the one). So let me address this right now and, hopefully, while doing so, make a point about what makes us all, as readers, turn the page of a good book and continue reading.

First and foremost, engaging, entertaining, and informative nonfiction writing should focus on the one thing great fiction does: storytelling. If you cannot engage your reader on page one, forget it; you have not done your job (and likely have lost that reader forever). This is why, after some years of . . . let's call it . . . educated reflection, I changed the way I begin my books.

Truman Capote is the one to thank for the nauseating way many contemporary true-crime authors (an early manifestation of myself included), not to mention those brilliant crime journalists—Jerry Bledsoe, Jack Olsen, James B. Stewart, to name a few—throughout the genre's history, have started their books. I'm referring to the incredibly dry and boring descriptive paragraphs of a city, town, and/or landscape in or around the location where the crime takes place. The idea behind this strategy, I have always assumed, is to drop the reader into this place where evil resides, allowing her to get comfortable in the terrain before the dark and wicked things that are about to happen begin.

Screenwriters use this device. But a camera swooping down on a town is a far different instrument than that of a book author trying to describe the town in a narrative. You lose a bit of suspense when you open your book with highways, byways, bridges, weather, and trees. We get what the writer is trying to do by setting up some sort of idyllic location in quintessential suburbia, where nothing of any importance occurs out of the norm: *Here we are, readers, in a slice of American Pie, out on Route 66, where a monster is undoubtedly lurking around every corner—the least possible place in the world where you'd expect murder to come about.*

Have a look at the following example: "There are sections of landscape bordering the quaint New England town of Northampton, Massachusetts, as flat as a tabletop—acres of farmland that, from a bird's-eye view, might make one think this small section of the Northeast is no different from Indiana or Kansas. . . ."

Now, with a smidgen of humility, I should note the above is an exceptionally written literary-quality paragraph (ahem) from my first book. Seriously, though, do the words actually convey anything essential to the story? Do these wonderfully crafted sentences—maybe even magical!—move the story forward or draw the reader into what should be a suspenseful narrative, begging her to turn the page?

Keeping that in mind, here is the opening from that book, *In Cold Blood*. You know, the one I spoke of earlier (a book I am not entirely convinced Capote wrote himself, by the way, and a book I consider to be nothing more than "faction"—facts on top of fiction): "The village of Holcomb stands on the high wheat plains of Western Kansas, a lonesome area that other Kansans call 'out there.'"

Now, can you see where I lifted my early style from? Open several of Ann Rule's books and you'll see what I mean: carefully constructed paragraphs (or even a few pages) of the landscape (generally with the identification of the interstate and a few rolling hills tossed in for good measure), designed to place the reader in the middle of suburban bliss.

Throughout the years, as I morphed into what my editor now calls a "real-life thriller" author (exciting, eh?), I realized that by placing this information (the dreary geography lesson nonsense) anywhere else but the beginning of your book, you increase your odds of grabbing the reader by the collar and shaking some excitement into her reading experience. That first page is when you have your reader's full attention. You want to hook her, not scare her away with the overblown prose of Emerson or Thoreau.

Consider this example: "She was fighting for her life. That was about all patrolman Michael Firestone knew as he sat behind the wheel of his cruiser, flipped on the lights and siren, and sped off."

A few action-packed, suspense-filled sentences opening your book embed questions in the reader's mind: *Who is fighting for her life? Why? What happened?* You can milk this strategy (and all great writing involves milking and strategizing) for some time, as long as you give readers answers, and not lead them down a path that will bear no fruit by the end of the section or chapter. There has to be a payoff. Maybe not a resolution, but something to keep your reader's curiosity piqued.

One more tip about opening pages (we'll call this a bonus). At the beginning of any book, you need to set the (narrative) tone of the book's voice into play immediately. I tend to spend a lot of time (maybe too much) on tempo and rhythm. What I mean by this is syntax: the way your sentences ebb and flow within the structure of the paragraph.

In most instances, I try to maintain a simple rule. If I write a long sentence, I follow it up with a short sentence. Also, I try to pay attention to the number of words in each sentence, compared with those surrounding it. Example: *He walked into the room. Looked around. Sat down on the metal chair. Took a breath.*

Whether you (or your reader) consciously realize it, you are setting up a rhythmic pulse in your reader's mind by writing the sentences she reads; you're telling her mind how to flow: *five words / two words / six words / three words . . .*

That said, however, a bit of warning: If you begin with a tempo, you need to keep it going. Or guess what? You'll lose your reader.

There are so many narrative devices we can choose from when beginning a book or story. If we make the right choices, the reader feels an instant connection. If we don't, the reader angrily claps the book closed, snapping, "That sucked." Truly, in most cases, it's just a matter of realizing the mistakes we've made and following that golden rule every writing instructor has pounded into our heads: rewrite, rewrite, rewrite.

For a number of years I taught a "How to Get Published" course I designed for wannabe writers. "The most important part of writing," I must have told my students three or four times per class, is reading. "As new writers trying to break into the business, we must read more than we write!" I preached.

One has to understand, comprehend, and learn from what published authors have done in order to get their own work into print. We know the tricks. The angles. We've made the mistakes—and, most important, learned from them. I mean, if you are going to write true crime, read the genre, study those successful authors within the genre, and get a feel for how a true-crime book is structured. Same goes for romance, mystery, and so on.

As a habit, you should pay close attention to the opening pages of any true-crime book you read. Doing that, you'll see that most authors—at least the great ones—begin with an action-packed, suspenseful scene. Something significant happens immediately. This is another trick screenwriters like to use: they make something happen within the first forty-five seconds that will have an impact on the plot later in the film.

EXERCISE

Go to your writing and truly and objectively read those opening sentences and pages. Then ask yourself (honestly): Will this engage my reader? Go back to the questions I brought up earlier in my essay and ask them again:

Do the words actually convey anything essential to the story?

Do they move the story forward or draw the reader into what should be a suspenseful narrative, begging her to turn the page?

Look, one of the biggest mistakes all new writers make is to not read their work through the reader's eyes. You are not writing for yourself, your neighbor, your spouse, your brother or sister (people you should never show your work to, by the way); you are writing for the reader. Your reader wants to be totally absorbed in the book.

Finally, as a true litmus test, when you think you've got those opening sentences, paragraphs, and pages trimmed down and as suspenseful as you can get them, make a recording of yourself reading your work and play it back after a few days. You will hear where you have made mistakes and have put your reader to sleep.

TWIST PHELAN

Getting Your Story Off to a Fast Start

A Stanford graduate and former plaintiff's trial lawyer, TWIST PHELAN writes the critically acclaimed legal-themed Pinnacle Peak mystery series (Poisoned Pen Press). Her short stories appear in anthologies and mystery magazines and have won or been nominated for the Thriller, Ellis, and Derringer awards. Twist is currently at work on a suspense novel set in Santa Fe featuring a corporate spy.

When writing suspense, I want readers to be immediately caught up in the story. I do this by starting with a plot trigger, which initiates or precipitates action—it hooks the reader and gets the narrative going. It doesn't have to be an incident. It can also be the introduction of a character or situation. No matter what form it takes, I put the trigger as close to the first sentence as possible.

How do I know I've come up with the best way to present the plot trigger? After I draft an opening, I rewrite it up to a dozen ways. Yes, I really mean twelve. Sometimes I choose one of the alternative openings to begin my story. Other times, I keep my original form, enhanced and honed by the alternative structures. In both cases, going through the exercise bettered my chances of getting my narrative off to a quick start.

EXERCISE

Here are twelve ways to start a story. Rewrite your opening chapter using as many of the techniques as you think will work for your material, then decide which works best in terms of getting the story off to a fast start, hooking the reader, and finding the right storytelling modality, i.e., the style or voice for the story you are setting out to tell.

1. Use only dialogue, no narrative. The dialogue must contain the plot trigger.

2. Introduce the main character and include the plot trigger—something the character does, in this instance—in your description. For example, show your character's reaction to a newspaper article or have her engage in internal dialogue.

3. Start the story from a character other than the protagonist's viewpoint. For example, have the antagonist watching the protagonist or a secondary character describing the setting. Remember, the plot trigger must be included.

4. Begin with a brief prologue. In this case, the plot trigger must precede the main plot action. Present this as an action scene, not a telling scene. For example, there's a murder, with the killer's identity hidden; the detective in the main story figures out who he or she is.

5. Omit all backstory and flashbacks. Yes, there may be gaps of information in the chapter. But the reader doesn't have to know everything up front or in chronological order. Also, just because a reader has information about a character doesn't mean she has an emotional investment in that character. For the author, emotional investment means that the reader identifies with the character, invests his own feelings in the character, or is emotionally affected by the character. It is the present circumstances facing a character, not the telling of the character's history, that draws the reader into emotional involvement with that character.

6. Weave the past into the opening chapter in a limited way. Establish the plot trigger using only short snippets of the protagonist's memory, such as a color or a smell or a fragment of conversation. Make sure these snippets broaden the reader's sense of the character, and do not stop the action.

7. Characterize the opening chapter from the protagonist's viewpoint. Include three references to the past. For example, the protagonist could say a building reminded him of the one he used to smoke behind in high school or that the woman who walked into his office had the same wavy red hair as did his sister. One of the references should relate to the plot trigger.

8. Pick a significant event from later in the story and foreshadow it in the first chapter. For example, if a protagonist is going to use a knife to defend herself in an important scene later in the book, have the plot trigger be her using a knife in the opening.

9. Describe a significant event that occurred previously in the setting of your opening chapter, with the event the plot trigger. For example, the protagonist could visit a group home from which two girls disappeared ten years ago.

10. Write the opening chapter in a different style. If the original is humor, make it noir. If it's romantic suspense, make it hard-boiled.

11. Write the opening as an action scene, one that moves the story line. But movement doesn't always mean action. Lots of white space on the page usually means you are doing a good job; fewer words means a tighter story.

    Use action verbs (yelled, ran, shouted). Use short, simple sentences (change all clauses into stand-alone sentences). Paragraphs should be short, only one or two sentences. Include at least two of these senses—sound, smell, touch, taste—in addition to seeing. Describe two physical traits of the character that is the focus of the scene; the description cannot include hair color, eye color, height, or smile. Include internalization (how the character is feeling). Don't include any interesting thing you learned in the course of research.

12. End the chapter with a narrative hook that relates to the plot trigger. The point of a narrative hook is to make the reader want to turn the page instead of putting down the book. Some examples of narrative hooks include:

- foreshadowing
- unexpected behavior by a character
- anticipation by the main character (he or she doesn't know what is going to happen as a consequence of the preceding action)
- having a character pose a question (that isn't answered)
- disclosing startling new information
- creating a new crisis
- having a character behave in an unexpected manner
- revealing a sudden insight

Each of these opening gambits entails a different storytelling style, to a greater or lesser degree. By considering up to a dozen versions of your first chapter, you will find a voice for your book. If one version jumps out as the best way to start your story, you are off and running. If you have several favorites, incorporate them all in another rewrite of your opening chapter. Print it out and read it aloud, asking yourself whether each sentence furthers the momentum of the story. (If a sentence doesn't do this, cut it.) The result is your opening, at least for this draft.

THOMAS B. CAVANAGH

Keep the Pages Turning

THOMAS B. CAVANAGH's novels include *Murderland, Prodigal Son*, and *Head Games*, which, among other recognition, won the Florida Book Awards Gold Medal for Popular Fiction and was a Shamus Best P.I. Novel nominee. Thomas has also written award-winning children's television shows for Nickelodeon, the Walt Disney Company, and many others. He lives in central Florida with his family.

Some mystery novels are suited for a leisurely pace. Well-mannered English countryside and cozy American bed-and-breakfast whodunits lend themselves quite naturally to a story that builds slowly and gains momentum gradually as the narrative progresses.

However, there are many other genres of mystery—thrillers being the prime example—where the pace can and should be much faster. As an author, though, knowing that you want your story to be a page-turner and actually creating the conditions for a fast pace are two different things.

I once had a job where I traveled somewhere almost every week. In fact, most of my first novel was written on airplanes. I intentionally chose what I believed to be fast-moving novels to read on these flights so I could pass the time more quickly. When I began to think seriously about writing a novel of my own, I knew that I wanted to write the same sorts of stories that I had been reading.

Here are just a few of the techniques I've observed other authors using to create page-turners. I've done my best to emulate these while keeping the voice and story uniquely my own, and you can, too.

Forward Momentum. John Grisham typically avoids subplots and flash-backs in his legal thrillers. While I might not go so far as to say you should never, under any circumstances, use a flashback (there are many examples where they have been used brilliantly), these strategies seem to be working out pretty well for Mr. Grisham. The point, of course, is that you don't want anything to detract from your story's forward momentum. You want your plot to start rolling like a boulder down a steep hill. Once it picks up speed, there should be no stopping it. A clumsy flashback or some ill-placed exposition will derail all that momentum and kill the pace you worked so hard to create.

Relentless Urgency. For me, perhaps the most important element for creating a fast pace is a relentless sense of urgency. I mean this as an internal pressure on the writer more than on any character in the story itself. In filmmaking, screenwriters and editors must fashion stories out of scenes, maximizing economy to minimize overall screen time. Novelists do essentially the same thing.

When you start writing a scene, ask yourself two questions:

1. When is the very latest that I can possibly enter this scene?
2. When is the very earliest that I can exit it?

As an author, you want to spend only as much page time on a scene as is necessary to accomplish the point of the scene, whether the goal is to advance the plot, reveal character, plant a false clue, or otherwise. If the important part of a scene is a conversation between two characters at a laundromat, do you really need to describe the two entering the building, waiting for their washing machines, inserting quarters, and pouring in detergent?

Consider jumping into the conversation just before the critical information is revealed. Imagine a clock that starts ticking as soon as you begin writing a scene, imploring you to *hurry up, hurry up, get out. . . .* Many authors tend to overwrite, starting their scenes far too early and then not knowing when to end them.

Multiple POV. One way to facilitate this cutting into and out of scenes (to borrow a film term) is to jump between character points of view. By switching to another character's POV, you create a new scene for pacing purposes, even if the characters remain engaged within the same overall metascene.

This works best in stories told in third person, where you can jump into the head of a different character in each scene. However, the same effect can be created in a first-person story (common in private eye novels, for example) by using transitions in time and location, even if the character POV remains the same.

Cliffhangers. Finally, one of the most effective methods to create a page-turner is to make readers want to continue reading just at the point where they would naturally put your book down: at chapter breaks. By intentionally ending a chapter in the middle of a scene, without any resolution, you create the classic cliffhanger. Your goal is to tantalize readers so much that they cannot resist turning that page to see what happens next. You can conclude the interrupted scene at the beginning of the subsequent chapter, keeping in mind the still-ticking clock and the need to move on as quickly as possible.

An alternative strategy is to cut away at the start of the next chapter to another, unrelated scene. The idea being your audience will be motivated to read through the unrelated scene to find out how the previous chapter is resolved, turning pages all the while. Of course, if not handled well, the risk in this strategy is compromising forward momentum.

Once you persuade readers to turn that page, to see what happens next, to stay up just a little later than they had planned, then you've done it. You've created the type of novel where your readers will look up and realize in amazement how many hours have passed since they started reading and that the flight is now making its final approach for landing.

EXERCISE

Reread a scene you have recently written. Identify the main reason you included the scene in your story. Perhaps you are introducing a new character, offering important exposition, foreshadowing a future event, providing a clue, recapping a chronology, or any number of other reasons.

Once you have identified the purpose of the scene, literally underline it (it may be a sentence or a paragraph). If you can't identify the reason for the scene, then you should seriously reconsider whether to include it at all.

Next, examine how much you have written on either side of the scene's purpose to set it up and conclude it. Analyze it objectively and assess whether you really need as much setup to establish the scene or as much wrap-up to conclude it and transition to the next scene.

As an experiment, try simply cutting the beginning and ending of the scene (you decide where, but be drastic) and then see if it still stands. If it does not, then you know you have cut too deeply. But if the scene still works and accomplishes its goal, you'll know that you didn't really need all of that extra setup and conclusion weighing down your story and slowing the pace.

KILLER SERIALS
From Book to Series

SHARON WILDWIND

Keeping a Series Going

SHARON WILDWIND is a Canadian mystery writer, writing teacher, and journal-keeper. Her first mystery series featured two female Vietnam veterans, Elizabeth Pepperhawk and Avivah Rosen.

A gents and publishers ask, "Is it a series?" The most common answers are (a) "If the first book is well received, I might consider a series"; and (b) "I hope it will be a series that goes forever." Neither answer is what an agent or publisher wants to hear from an author. They want to know market potential: How many books, how often, over what period of time? The author wonders, *How many stories do my characters have to tell?*

When considering a series, ask yourself four questions:

1. How healthy am I?

2. What are my current commitments?

3. What are my potential commitments over the next five years?

4. What is my vision for devoting the next five to ten years of my life to this series?

If you are already heavily committed, or think you might be, you might choose a three-book series instead of five books, or anticipate more time between each book.

Writing a series is akin to raising children, with a new child coming along every twelve to fifteen months. You not only have to produce the new child, but also need to care for the previous children.

Keeping a series going involves writing new books and marketing and promoting the previous books.

An unending series of books, published year after year by the same house, is gone. Series have changed, become shorter. Sometimes there are different publishers or different formats for each book. A successful series now runs three to five books. Anything past five is gravy. Think of the first three to five books as your series starter kit. This gets you into the market and gives you a chance to figure out where you want to go next.

Every series needs a time arc. How far apart will your books take place in character time? Some readers find characters discovering a body (mystery) or saving the world (thriller) every two weeks tiresome. Some don't care. They just want good stories. At the other end of the scale, if a long time passes between books, how will you handle your characters aging?

Some characters don't age. Between 1956 and 2005, Ed McBain kept the 87th Precinct series going for fifty-six books, as well as through numerous movie, TV, and comic book spin-offs. The squad room changed around them; the wars the detectives had fought in changed, but they remained pretty much the same age through the entire series.

For my own series, I wanted to do five books. I picked the date for the first one—July 1971—for a personal reason. That was the date I returned from Vietnam. I knew that the last one would be immediately after the fall of Saigon. Four years would pass from book one to book five, and I decided that the characters would age real-time. When I looked at those time bookends, 1971 and 1975, it seemed logical to aim for one book a year in character time.

EXERCISE

Step 1. How many books in the starter series?

Step 2. How long, in character time, will the series cover?

Step 3. How long will you need to write the series?

Step 4. What is your series arc?

Every series needs an arc. What problems beset the characters? How do they change? Is the underlying situation strong and complex enough to sustain multiple story lines and create multiple changes in fate? Here are some examples of series arcs in long-running series.

- William Monk / Hester Latterly series by Anne Perry: Monk slowly recovers from amnesia and has to come to terms with the differences between the man he was before his accident and the man he wants to be now.

- Benni Harper series by Earlene Fowler: A young widow remarries and gradually accepts that her second marriage is not at all like the first, and is all the sweeter for that.

- Peter Decker and Rina Lazarus series by Faye Kellerman: An Orthodox Jewish woman and a technically Jewish but not especially religious man negotiate a balance between their very different religious and secular worlds.

Step 5. What real life-experience do you have that ties into these books?

This is known as your platform.

Step 6. Put this information together into a series synopsis.

Aim for a series synopsis of fewer than 500 words. Here's an example.

Women of the New West Mystery Series

This is a proposed three-book mystery series set in Tucumcari, New Mexico. The protagonists are independent western women: Ramona Sandoval, a divorced ex-con, who is determined to regain custody of her two teenage daughters; Betty (Whip) Sandoval, her aunt; and Lois Hanna, a rancher turned agricultural teacher. The time frame covered by the series is nine to ten months. I anticipate completing one book every fourteen months.

I am the daughter and wife of ranchers. My mother, like Lois, is a past president of New Mexico CowBelles, the state chapter of American National CattleWomen, Inc. Being around those women has been an education in itself.

Working titles for this series are:

- Mesa Women, *completed, and submitted for your consideration*

- Who Owns the Wind?—*in progress*

- Fire Mesa—*in planning*

In Mesa Women, *Ramona is convinced that her ex-husband is up to no good, but who believes an ex-con? Whip and Lois do. When the ex disappears from a murder scene, leaving Ramona's daughters in trouble with juvenile authorities, Ramona breaks parole and risks going back to jail to find out what's going on.*

Water rights disputes have always been part of the West, but can anyone own the wind? In Who Owns the Wind? *a large corporation brings a lawsuit against Lois, accusing her college of industrial espionage. Can Ramona risk being at the center of a nasty murder investigation just when her daughters' custody petition is going to court?*

Why is Whip sneaking off at night to meet an old man on Tucumcari Mountain? Why does Lois stop speaking to Whip when the old man turns up dead? In Fire Mesa, *there's more than a range fire threatening the mesa and Ramona's daughters. As the characters discover, old secrets are the worst secrets.*

How locked are you into your synopsis? In this example, you've made a general commitment to setting characters and the underlying theme of whether Ramona will get custody of her daughters. You've also made a general commitment to complete a book about every fourteen months. After that you have tons of wiggle room.

If "Is it a series?" is the first question, the last one—discussed ad infinitum—is, "Is the series dead?" The answer is, "Not likely." Go for it!

KATE FLORA

Character Arc Versus Story Arc:
Developing a Successful Series Character

Attorney **KATE FLORA** is the author of seven Thea Kozak mysteries, two Joe Burgess police procedurals, and a stand-alone suspense novel. Her book *Finding Amy: A True Story of Murder in Maine* was a 2007 Edgar nominee. The third Burgess mystery is *Redemption* (2012). Flora is a former president of Sisters in Crime. Until 2011, she was a partner in Level Best Books, which published seven anthologies of crime stories by New England writers. The anthologies included a Fish Award winner and an Edgar nominee.

My advice assumes that the writer who's gotten this far understands the difference between character arc and story arc, but here's a quick refresher: A crime novel involving a recurring character operates with two different arcs—the *story arc* and the *character arc*.

According to the conventions of the genre and to satisfy readers' expectations, the arc of story must be relatively complete within each individual book, with the whodunit and whydunit resolved and justice served. Therefore, when planning the crime novel, a writer needs to have developed a plot in which she knows who the victim is; how, why, and where that person was killed; and what clues and what red herrings* will be planted throughout the book. She needs to know who will populate the story and what their purpose will be. Since conflict

---

*In the mystery world, the origin of this phrase is generally attributed to the practice of dragging a herring across the trail in a fox hunt, to distract the dogs by making them lose the true scent and follow the false trail of herring odor instead, and refers to the practice of complicating the mystery by providing credible alternative suspects, clues, or versions of the story.

moves story, she will need to know what the protagonists' and antagonists' goals will be, where the lies and obfuscations will be, where the dead ends and brick walls will occur, what obstacles will frustrate the sleuths and how those obstacles will be overcome, and what seemingly unimportant information will ultimately prove important.

The arc of a recurring character in a series of crime novels differs from the story arc in the following way: While each individual story is completed within that book, the character's story is not, and thus each book in a series is more like a chapter in the character's life. Put another way, if the mystery must be neatly tied up at the end, the character's story may be full of questions, complications, changes, and loose ends, which will be tied up or further unraveled in subsequent books. The reader expects to learn more about the series character and to see growth or change in the character as a result of the book's events, but not final resolution. Over the course of each book, your character will go on a journey. Ask yourself, what is that journey, and how will my character be transformed?*

Many a writer, a few books down the road in a series, has expressed regrets about some of her initial choices about a series character. Sometimes this is because the character began as a one-off, only to be dubbed a series character by an editor. Sometimes it happens more gradually, when a writer discovers that a pregnancy that seemed romantic in book one results in an endless series of child-care dilemmas in future books. Sometimes the challenge is how to dump a significant other without offending readers who've become attached to him or her. Sometimes the writer herself becomes bored with her character's boyfriend, or faces the challenge (as one might in the real world) of moving the relationship to a new level, or moving on to someone new. Sometimes the writer becomes bored with her own character.

Then there are the strengths and skills you give your character, or failed to give her, that she might need down the road. The weaknesses that she needs to overcome, or that hold her back at all-important mo-

*Note that there are series characters who remain static, such as Sue Grafton's Kinsey Millhone. There are also many mysteries in which deliberate choices are made about the series' time duration and how much the main character will age.

ments. The fears and insecurities that keep her from being all that she can be, or from trusting others and developing mature relationships. And there's the ongoing challenge of your character's job. Will it continue to suit your character or prove to be boring or inflexible?

Whatever the source of those challenges—and they will be legion as your series character moves forward with her life—many of them can be anticipated if you spend some time in advance prepping your leading lady (or man) before she makes her on-page debut, and knowing your character in depth so you can exploit her flaws and blind spots as well as strengths when she sets out to solve mysteries.

EXERCISE

A. GETTING TO KNOW YOUR CHARACTERS

As you fill in the Character Development Checklist, create a character sketch for each of your central characters. Yes, you've heard this before. And perhaps resisted it. But instead of dreading this task like hated homework, think of it as an exercise in discovery by trying the following as preparation for that sketch.

1. Select an item from the checklist and then write a free-association paragraph from your character's point of view about that subject. Observe what your character reveals to you. What her voice is, the language she uses to describe her feelings about this particular subject.

2. Select another item from the checklist and repeat the exercise. Repeat as many times as you wish, and consider returning to this list as you prepare for future books and anticipate the ways your character will grow and change, and how she has been changed by the challenge of facing down bad guys and solving a crime.

CHARACTER DEVELOPMENT CHECKLIST				
Character name	Age	Place of birth	Ethnic background	Job
Nickname (if any, and given by whom/why?)	Hair color	Eye color	Body type	Height

THE DETAILS	
Birth order/siblings	Social or a loner?
Marital/relationship status/ attitude toward marriage/ relationship history	Amount of money in the bank/ attitude toward money
Level of education/parents' level of education	Health problems/issues/ challenges?
Attitude toward job/bosses/ coworkers/authority	How athletic?
Level of ambition	Hobbies and special interests?
Areas of expertise and what this tells us about her	Pets?
Religious background/religious beliefs/superstitions, if any	Favorite music?
What kind of car/truck does she drive, and why?	Most treasured possession?
Relationship to mother/father	What is her handwriting like?
Best friend, and why?	Favorite/least favorite clothing

B. EXPLORING YOUR MAIN CHARACTERS' WORLDVIEW

1. Take your character with you while you're riding in the car, and let her tell you what she is seeing. How does she relate to other drivers? To traffic? To natural features and to geography? Pay attention to what she notices.

2. On the basis of what you've learned from reading the checklists and thinking about how the points apply to your protagonist, write scenes putting your character in situations where she is in conflict with another character. How does she react, and how does she feel when the confrontation is over?

3. As you are plotting your story, consider what situations you will be putting your character in—dangerous situations, romantic situations, frustrating situations, states of pure exhaustion or fear. Then consider how your character will be changed by the experience. This will make the emotions of the situation clearer, first to you as the writer, and consequently to your reader.

DIGGING DEEPER	
Best qualities of personality	Attitude toward body
Greatest fear	Attitude toward death
Greatest flaw	Feels ashamed of?/Is proud of?
Greatest strength	Darkest secrets/Achilles' heels
Greatest blind spot about self	Attitude toward public speaking
What kind of baby was she?	What kind of adolescent?
Biggest problem right now	Biggest change on the horizon
What does her house/ apartment look like?	What's in the fridge? Trash can?

Attitude toward young children/old people	Secret prejudice
Attitude about job/school/daily activities	Earliest memory
Good sleeper?	How will she die, and when?

Remember that it is always part of your job to attach your reader to the characters emotionally. This is how you hold them in the book, and how you make them want to come back for more.

BILL CRIDER

The Importance of a Series Bible

BILL CRIDER is the author of the Sheriff Dan Rhodes series and more than seventy-five other novels. He lives in Alvin, Texas, with his wife, Judy, and their two cats. He spends too much time on the Internet and not enough time writing.

I've written several mystery series, including one featuring Sheriff Dan Rhodes, which is up to nineteen books and counting. So you might think that I know what I'm doing.

You'd be wrong. I do, however, know more about writing a series now than I did when I began, and maybe I can help you avoid some of my mistakes.

For example, when I started writing the first Sheriff Rhodes novel, I had no idea that some writers made outlines. I thought that writing a book was simply storytelling, which I thought meant making things up as you went along. That was my first mistake, but it wasn't my biggest one. That one came later.

When I got a letter of acceptance from Ruth Cavin, at that time the mystery editor at Walker Books, I paid particular attention to the last line: "You are working on a sequel, aren't you?"

Since I had no idea that I'd ever sell a book, I hadn't given much thought to the possibility that someone might want another one about the same characters. Not that I let Ruth Cavin know that. When I wrote her back, I told her that indeed I was working on a sequel, and by that time, I was.

And that's when the trouble started.

As I wrote the first book, I created characters and scenes as I told the story. I created a whole town and put it in a fictional county, and the county had more towns in it. The towns had inhabitants and streets and businesses. The characters had distinguishing traits, like the color of their hair, the sound of their voices, the way they walked and smiled and laughed. And so on.

That's only natural, of course. Not a thing wrong with it, not in the first book, anyway. The problem is the second book, when you realize that you're going to have to make the characters look and sound the way they did in the first one. You can't change their hair color. You can't move the businesses from place to place, either. And it's not a good idea to change the characters' names.

There are people who can remember everything about their characters and their settings. I was one of those people when I wrote the second book about Sheriff Rhodes. I was young, and I'd finished the first book only a couple of months earlier. No big deal.

The second book sold, and so did a third, and then a fourth. After a while, memories begin to dim. Or at least mine did. I found myself thumbing through the earlier books to find out what kind of car a character drove or what kind of house he lived in.

Keep in mind that this was before computers. I worked on an electric typewriter, so I couldn't call up the previous manuscripts and use the search function. It was all done the old-fashioned way. I know at least one writer who claims to having occasionally resorted to calling up a friend who read all her books to ask if he could remember specific points and save her the trouble of doing all that work.

EXERCISE

Why am I telling you all this? To let you know that everyone who's planning to write a series or who even has hopes of developing a series should have a "bible." Not a book of sacred scriptures, but a compendium of facts that will carry over from book to book. These are some things you'll want to include:

1. *Characters.* Whatever you've written about the characters should go here: personality traits, physical descriptions, quirks, habits, past experiences, their relationships, their families, and anything

else you need to remember. Do this for all the characters, even the minor ones, since you can't be sure which ones will turn up in future books. No detail is too small to record, because if you make an unexplained change, some reader is sure to catch it.

2. *Settings.* Everything about the fictional world your characters inhabit: homes, businesses, outlying areas, streets, buildings. For one of my series, having learned my lesson from previous errors, I even drew a map of the town that played a part in the stories. As in point one above, no detail should be overlooked.

3. *Events.* Important things that happen in the characters' lives. For instance, if someone has a special party, that party might be mentioned in a later book. If there's a catastrophe (someone's house burns, someone has a serious car accident), it's likely to be thought of and mentioned again. You'll need to be able to recall the details.

4. *Plots.* You should have a brief description of the plot of each book so you'll know who did what to whom. This doesn't need to be quite as detailed as numbers one and two, but you never know what might come up in a future book. I used an incident from the first Sheriff Rhodes book as the plot springboard for a book I wrote more than fifteen years later.

The best time to update the series bible is when you're revising a manuscript. You can usually spot anything you need to add, and these updates will make the bible as thorough as it needs to be.

Having all the information about your series saved in one document on your computer (and on another disk, too, of course, just in case) will make your series writing life much smoother. It will give you peace of mind, save you from doing a lot of additional hard work, and keep you from annoying your friends. Who could ask for anything more?

CONTRIBUTORS' WEBSITES

Lou Allin louallin.com
Emily Arsenault emilyarsenault.com
Deborah Turrell Atkinson deborahatkinson.com
Frankie Y. Bailey frankieybailey.com
Aileen G. Baron aileengbaron.com
James Scott Bell jamesscottbell.com
Gerard Bianco gerardbianco.com
Juliet Blackwell julietblackwell.net
Jon P. Bloch drjonpbloch.blogspot.com
Rhys Bowen rhysbowen.com
Rachel Brady rachelbrady.com
Simon Brett simonbrett.com
Jan Brogan janbrogan.com
Graham Brown authorgrahambrown.com
Robert Browne robertbrownebooks.com
Andrea Campbell womenincrimeink.blogspot.com
Rebecca Cantrell rebeccacantrell.com
Lorenzo Carcaterra lorenzocarcaterra.com
Thomas B. Cavanagh thomasbcavanagh.com
Henry Chang chinatowntrilogy.com
Philip Cioffari philipcioffari.com
Jane K. Cleland janecleland.net
Reed Farrel Coleman reedcoleman.com
Sheila Connolly sheilaconnolly.com
Deborah Coonts deborahcoonts.com
Douglas Corleone douglascorleone.com
Bill Crider billcrider.com
Bruce DeSilva brucedesilva.com
Matthew Dicks matthewdicks.com
Sean Doolittle seandoolittle.com

Wayne D. Dundee	waynedundee.com
Peggy Ehrhart	peggyehrhart.com
Hallie Ephron	hallieephron.com
Brian Evenson	brianevenson.com
Kate Flora	kateflora.com
Jack Fredrickson	jackfredrickson.com
David Fulmer	davidfulmer.com
Meg Gardiner	meggardiner.com
Kate M. George	kategeorge.com
Kathleen George	kathleengeorgebooks.com
Sophie Hannah	sophiehannah.com
Karen Harper	karenharperauthor.com
Gar Anthony Haywood	garanthonyhaywood.com
Lynne Heitman	lynneheitman.com.
Vicki Hendricks	vickihendricks.com
Reece Hirsch	reecehirsch.com
Roberta Islieb	lucyburdette.com
Peter James	peterjames.com
Chris Knopf	chrisknopfmystery.com
Harley Jane Kozak	harleyjanekozak.com
William Kent Krueger	williamkentkrueger.com
Ken Kuhlken	kenkuhlken.net
Will Lavender	willlavender.com
Robert S. Levinson	robertslevinson.com
Steve Liskow	steveliskow.com
Sophie Littlefield	sophielittlefield.com
John Lutz	johnlutzonline.com
Doc Macomber	docmacomber.com
Tim Maleeny	timmaleeny.com
G. M. Malliet	gmmalliet.com
Christopher G. Moore	cgmoore.com
Jim Napier	deadlydiversions.com
Diana Orgain	dianaorgain.com
Katherine Hall Page	katherine-hall-page.org
Louise Penny	louisepenny.com
Henry Perez	henryperezbooks.com

Twist Phelan	twistphelan.com
M. William Phelps	mwilliamphelps.com
Cathy Pickens	cathypickens.com
Stephen D. Rogers	stephendrogers.com
Stephen Jay Schwartz	stephenjayschwartz.com
Michael Sears	detectivekubu.com
Kelli Stanley	kellistanley.com
Valerie Storey	valeriestorey.com
Andy Straka	andystraka.com
Marcia Talley	marciatalley.com
Jaden Terrell	jadenterrell.com
James Thompson	jamesthompsonauthor.com
Stanley Trollip	detectivekubu.com
Judith Van Gieson	judithvangieson.com
John Westermann	johnwestermann.com
Sharon Wildwind	wildwindauthor.com
Michael Wiley	michaelwileyonline.com
Kenneth Wishnia	kennethwishnia.com
Nancy Means Wright	nancymeanswright.com
Elizabeth Zelvin	elizabethzelvin.com

CREDITS

"Layering the Landscape" by Lou Allin © 2011 by Lou Allin

"Characters and Their Secrets" by Emily Arsenault © 2011 by Emily Arsenault

"Protagonist in Jeopardy" by Deborah Turrell Atkinson © 2011 by Deborah Turrell Atkinson

"Creating Depth through Character Relationships" by Frankie Y. Bailey © 2011 by Frankie Y. Bailey

"Plausibility" by Aileen G. Baron © 2011 by Aileen G. Baron

"Maintaining Suspense" by James Scott Bell © 2011 by James Scott Bell

"Planting a Seed" by Gerard Bianco © 2011 by Gerard Bianco

"Driven 'Round the Bend: What Drives Characters?" by Juliet Blackwell © 2011 by Juliet Blackwell

"Creating Believable Dialogue" by Jon P. Bloch © 2011 by Jon P. Bloch

"The Importance of Setting—Grounding Your Story in Time and Place" by Rhys Bowen © 2011 by Rhys Bowen

"No Sloppy Seconds: Write a Purposeful Supporting Cast" by Rachel Brady © 2011 by Rachel Brady

"Controlling the Flow of Information" by Simon Brett © 2011 by Simon Brett

"Between the Drafts" by Jan Brogan © 2011 by Jan Brogan

"Humanizing the Character Arc" by Graham Brown © 2011 by Graham Brown

"The Parts People Skip" by Robert Browne © 2011 by Robert Browne

"Investigative Techniques" by Andrea Campbell © 2011 by Andrea Campbell

"Murder from the Point of View of the Murderer, Victim, and Detective" by Rebecca Cantrell © 2011 by Rebecca Cantrell

"Ready, Set, Action" by Lorenzo Carcaterra © 2011 by Lorenzo Carcaterra

"Keep the Pages Turning" by Thomas B. Cavanagh © 2011 by Thomas B. Cavanagh

"Setting and Atmosphere: Writing *from* the Element and Writing *in* the Elements" by Henry Chang © 2011 by Henry Chang

"Creating Mood in Crime Fiction" by Philip Cioffari © 2011 by Philip Cioffari

"Avoiding Saggy Middles" by Jane K. Cleland © 2011 by Jane K. Cleland

"Let's Get Engaged" by Reed Farrel Coleman © 2011 by Reed Farrel Coleman

"To Whom Does Your Character Turn When She Needs Help, and What Do They Bring to the Equation?" by Sheila Connolly © 2011 by Sheila Connolly

"The Offbeat Protagonist" by Deborah Coonts © 2011 by Deborah Coonts

"Forensics: The Cutting Edge" by Douglas Corleone © 2011 by Douglas Corleone

"The Importance of a Series Bible" by Bill Crider © 2011 by Bill Crider

"Scene of the Crime" by Bruce DeSilva © 2011 by Bruce DeSilva

"Villains" by Matthew Dicks © 2011 by Matthew Dicks

"Road Trip" by Sean Doolittle © 2011 by Sean Doolittle

"Convincing Threats for Your Protagonist" by Wayne D. Dundee © 2011 by Wayne D. Dundee

"Clues Are All Around You" by Peggy Ehrhart © 2011 by Peggy Ehrhart

"Choosing Details to Reveal Character" by Hallie Ephron © 2011 by Hallie Ephron

"On Revision" by Brian Evenson © 2011 by Brian Evenson

"Character Arc Versus Story Arc: Developing a Successful Series Character" by Kate Flora © 2011 by Kate Flora

CREDITS

"Murder with Giggles: Humorous Voice in Crime Fiction" by Jack Fredrickson © 2011 by Jack Fredrickson

"The Reality Show Called Settings" by David Fulmer © 2011 by David Fulmer

"Ratcheting Up the Suspense" by Meg Gardiner © 2011 by Meg Gardiner

"Using Everyday Activities to Create Conflicting Emotions and Increase Tension" by Kate M. George © 2011 by Kate M. George

"Casting Your Characters" by Kathleen George © 2011 by Kathleen George

"First Lines" by Sophie Hannah © 2011 by Sophie Hannah

"Amateur Sleuths for Professional Authors" by Karen Harper © 2011 by Karen Harper

"You Can't Cheat an Honest Reader" by Gar Anthony Haywood © 2011 by Gar Anthony Haywood

"What Drives Your Character?" by Lynne Heitman © 2011 by Lynne Heitman

"Exposing the Sex Scene" by Vicki Hendricks © 2011 by Vicki Hendricks

"The Most Common Mistakes in Plotting a Thriller (from Someone Who Has Made Them All)" by Reece Hirsch © 2011 by Reece Hirsch

"Characters from the Inside Out" by Roberta Islieb © 2011 by Roberta Islieb

"The Importance of Research" by Peter James © 2011 by Peter James

"What Madison Avenue Can Teach You About Writing Better Dialogue" by Chris Knopf © 2011 by Chris Knopf

"The Telling Detail" by Harley Jane Kozak © 2011 by Harley Jane Kozak

"Setting and a Sense of Place in Mysteries" by William Kent Krueger © 2011 by William Kent Krueger

"Crime Fiction—What For?" by Ken Kuhlken © 2011 by Ken Kuhlken

"The Hook: Killer Beginnings in Mystery Fiction" by Will Lavender © 2011 by Will Lavender

"The Truth Is in the Fiction" by Robert S. Levinson © 2011 by Robert S. Levinson

"Voice and the Private Eye" by Steve Liskow © 2011 by Steve Liskow

"Creating Emotional Depth" by Sophie Littlefield © 2011 by Sophie Littlefield

"Action and Reaction" by John Lutz © 2011 by John Lutz

"Finding the Key Strengths and Weaknesses of Your Detective Character" by Doc Macomber © 2011 by Doc Macomber

"First Lines—An Exercise for Writers" by Tim Maleeny © 2011 by Tim Maleeny

"Stormy Weather" by G. M. Malliet © 2011 by G. M. Malliet

"The Cultural Setting and the Cultural Detective" by Christopher G. Moore © 2011 by Christopher G. Moore

"Putting Your Protagonist in Jeopardy" by Jim Napier © 2011 by Jim Napier

"Putting Yourself in the Characters' Shoes" by Diana Orgain © 2011 by Diana Orgain

"Point of View: An Exercise in Observation" by Katherine Hall Page © 2011 by Katherine Hall Page

"Setting as Character" by Louise Penny © 2011 by Louise Penny

"Conflict! Conflict! Everywhere!" by Henry Perez © 2011 by Henry Perez

"Getting Your Story Off to a Fast Start" by Twist Phelan © 2011 by Twist Phelan

"Hooking Your Reader From Page One" by M. William Phelps © 2011 by M. William Phelps

"Character Motivations" by Cathy Pickens © 2011 by Cathy Pickens

"Tell the Truth and Lie" by Stephen D. Rogers © 2011 by Stephen D. Rogers

"Dontcha Just Hate the Research Part?" by Stephen Jay Schwartz © 2011 by Stephen Jay Schwartz

"A Feeling for Location and Culture" by Michael Sears © 2011 by Michael Sears

"She Can Bring Home the Bacon" by Kelli Stanley © 2011 by Kelli Stanley

"Deep Motivation: Characters Have Feelings, Too" by Valerie Storey © 2011 by Valerie Storey

"Sea of Troubles: The Art of Outlining" by Andy Straka © 2011 by Andy Straka

CREDITS

"Detectives Have Weaknesses, Too" by Marcia Talley © 2011 by Marcia Talley

"Make 'Em Real: Reveal Your Characters Through Relationships" by Jaden Terrell © 2011 by Jaden Terrell

"Conflict and Scene Design" by James Thompson © 2011 by James Thompson

"Writing a Non-English-Speaking Character" by Stanley Trollip © 2011 by Stanley Trollip

"Writing the First Chapter" by Judith Van Gieson © 2011 by Judith Van Gieson

"Build the Cast for Your Police Procedural" by John Westermann © 2011 by John Westermann

"Keeping a Series Going" by Sharon Wildwind © 2011 by Sharon Wildwind

"Writing in Place" by Michael Wiley © 2011 by Michael Wiley

"Getting Out of Your Comfort Zone: Writing from Different Points of View" by Kenneth Wishnia © 2011 by Kenneth Wishnia

"Discover Plot and Character Through the Journey Quest" by Nancy Means Wright © 2011 by Nancy Means Wright

"'Let Me Out!' Helping Characters Find Their Voice" by Elizabeth Zelvin © 2011 by Elizabeth Zelvin

ABOUT THE EDITORS

SHERRY ELLIS was a writer, social worker, writing coach, and the originator of the *Now Write!* series of writing exercise books. She edited *Now Write!* and *Now Write! Nonfiction*, and coedited *Now Write! Screenwriting* with Laurie Lamson, her niece. Her author interviews were published in literary magazines and are anthologized in *Illuminating Fiction*. She passed away during the process of putting together this fourth book in the series. She is greatly missed by authors everywhere.

LAURIE LAMSON is a story and screenwriter with a filmmaking background. She coedited *Now Write! Screenwriting* with Sherry Ellis and edited two other books. She has worked on four feature screenplays for independent movie producers; produced and directed two of her own short scripts; and one of her short stories was published in an anthology, *All in the Game & Other Short Stories*.

LEARN MORE ABOUT ALL OF THE *NOW WRITE!* TITLES AT:
WWW.NOWWRITE.NET.